I Heard Their Cry

God's Hope for the Chortí People of Guatemala

Ray and Virginia Canfield

WESTBOW·
PRESS
A DIVISION OF THOMAS NELSON
& ZONDERVAN

The Scriptures quoted in this book are from the New American Standard Bible Translation, 1978 Edition.

WestBow Press books may be ordered through booksellers or by contacting:

WestBow Press
A Division of Thomas Nelson & Zondervan
1663 Liberty Drive
Bloomington, IN 47403
www.westbowpress.com
1 (866) 928-1240

ISBN: 978-1-4908-2096-5 (sc)
ISBN: 978-1-4908-2098-9 (hc)
ISBN: 978-1-4908-2097-2 (e)

Library of Congress Control Number: 2013923355

Printed in the United States of America.

WestBow Press rev. date: 02/26/2014

Dedicated to our children:

Linda   Tad   Kenneth

Thank you for being with us through the days in El Florido. You brought fun and laughter to our lives while living there. You opened up doors for outreach to our friends, the Chortí. And you always encouraged us to stay and keep helping the Indian people even when you had to leave for school. Thanks.

Contents

Foreword

It was 1964, and my heroes, Ray and Virginia Canfield, were not yet missionaries in Guatemala. But God's call gave them burning hearts, and it was only a matter of time until they arrived. I was a college student, just graduated, on a short-term mission trip to Central and South America. In Jocotán, Guatemala, I saw something firsthand that shocked me— starvation. Men were lying on the ground beside the markets, doing nothing. When I asked missionaries about it, John and Joyce McNichols explained about drought and starvation. Far from lazy, these men were gathering enough energy to work some the next day. It is what Ray and Virginia call "desperate hunger."

Through the next twenty years I heard the reports. The Chortí people lived close to the land, did not trust outsiders, and resisted change. They most often kept quiet, making it difficult for outsiders to penetrate their worldview. When desperately hurting, they would smile or laugh; anything to keep back the tears. Among themselves the starvation and lack of tillable land led to machete fights and family feuds. It all looked so hopeless.

Ray and Virginia were not the first to arrive on the scene. Other faithful missionaries worked among them for twenty years before. Yet it was Homer and Evelyn Sharpless, along with the Canfields, who led the way in the El Florido Relocation Project. It meant persuading more than forty-five families to move to the jungle, learn a new way of life, and harvest bigger and better crops than they ever dreamed possible. But the whole thing might well have collapsed without Ray and Virginia Canfield.

The stories in this book come alive with real people, real conversations, real feelings. There were experiments and failures in teaching agriculture— and a few breakthroughs of success! The challenge of moving to a new land, building rules for a new community, and making the commitment to live among them for ten years was all-absorbing. A new church, a new clinic and a new school were part of the plan. God's hand of provision—finances, land, government approval, Chortí buy-in—is evident everywhere.

It was not always easy. In the hardest times many of the Chorti people wanted to quit and go back to their mountain villages. Internal strife, power struggles and even a murder mark the adventures recounted in these pages.

One astounding fact bears mention here. Virginia, a Registered Nurse (RN), transferred her medical clinic knowledge and skill into an uneducated Chortí man. He became so proficient that later the Guatemalan government certified him. Simply amazing! But that's only one step in this story of struggle, survival, and finally flourishing. Anyone with an interest in the medical profession or tropical medicine will find Virginia's many stories in this book simply fascinating.

Twenty years after my first visit I returned to the Chortí people, both in mountainous Jocotán and lush El Florido. The contrast was astounding. Up in the mountains, life changed little; droughts came and went, and people struggled to survive. Down in the jungle, the Chortí people were thriving in every way imaginable. Their crops were abundant. Their health clinic drew people from villages all around. They planted new churches in the surrounding areas. Their school produced well-educated children who qualified for advanced studies. They governed their own village well. All of this with no missionaries on-site and only occasional visits from the outside.

In later years, Ray became superintendent of the Friends Mission in Guatemala, and I held a similar post in California. We talked often by phone and in person whenever he and Virginia returned to the United States. At about age sixty, he and Virginia left Guatemala and moved to Cambodia. They established a whole new mission field with a new language (Khmer), a new religious background (animistic Buddhism), and new customs and culture. No wonder they are my heroes!

—Chuck Mylander
August 29, 2013

Chuck Mylander served as superintendent of Evangelical Friends Church Southwest for seventeen years and then as director of Evangelical Friends Mission. He and his wife, Nancy, live in Yorba Linda, California. His books include *Blessed Are the Peacemakers*, *The Christ-Centered Marriage*, and *Extreme Church Makeover* (all three with Neil T. Anderson), and *More Energy for Your Day*, *Running the Red Lights*, and *Secrets for Growing Churches*.

Preface

We had to write this story because we are witnesses to an awesome God who has an amazing love for all of us. He wants us to share this truth with as many people as possible who will listen.

The title *I Heard Their Cry* is taken from Exodus 3:7: "The Lord said to Moses, 'I have surely seen the affliction of my people who are in Egypt and have given heed to their cry—for I am aware of their sufferings.'"

Likewise, we knew that the Lord heard the cry of the Chortí people in their sufferings and He sent help. We were among several people who responded to that call: "Therefore, go" (Exodus 3:10).

Upon arrival in Jocotán, we noticed that our Chortí friends never cried visible tears. They responded to injustice, no harvest, starvation, and death with a smile, chuckle, or even a slight laugh. At first we could not understand this response to a terrible situation. Then we remembered, "But the Lord looks at the heart" (1 Samuel 16:7). God heard their deep heart's cry.

As doors opened for our courageous Chortí friends to move to a strange, uninhabited jungle and begin a new life, we noticed they grew in their trust in and love for God.

We were surprised to see that we too had changed. Our faith in God and love for Him had grown deeper than when we began this journey. Material things that used to be important to us were no longer so important. Communion with the Lord became a way of life. Our constant prayer had been, "Help them, Lord, to see Jesus."

Note to Reader: Soon after we began writing, we realized there were two stories - Ray's agricultural work, and Virginia's medical ministry. We decided to combine both into one book. To eliminate confusion each voice is identified as **Ray** or **Virginia**.

Acknowledgments

We want to thank our friends in El Florido who had patience and love for us as we lived together in the village. We had ideas that were strange to them, but they listened and tried. They wanted a complete written record of what God did for them in El Florido.

We want to thank Quaker Men of California Friends Churches who faithfully supported and encouraged the relocation project.

A special recognition goes to Ray's mother, Lydia Canfield, and Virginia's mother, Marjorie Wood, who saved all the letters we wrote and returned them to us. Many details in this manuscript came from those letters.

We want to recognize the faithful prayer groups in many churches in California and Iowa that held us up in prayer for years. Everything is possible when we pray.

A big thanks goes to John and Joyce McNichols who shared their photos and stories of life in Jocotán. David Hamm helped us recall events of the early days of the relocation project because he was there.

Elise LeFeuvre, our granddaughter, patiently arranged things correctly in the computer for us. We thank her.

Bruce and Terri Miller gave us valuable input from their agricultural and medical expertise. Doris NcNatt from my Bible study group read the first draft and gave her input.

Mick Silva, our leader in a Christian Writers Seminar of Orange County, encouraged us to keep on working on this project. Terri Taylor read the final draft and contributed good suggestions.

To Linda LeFeuvre, our daughter, who spent long hours editing and getting the final draft ready for submission, we give our heartfelt thanks.

We are grateful to Westbow Press staff for all their help.

And to World Photo of Brea, California (www.worldphoto.us.com) we extend our thanks for their excellent work in photo restoration.

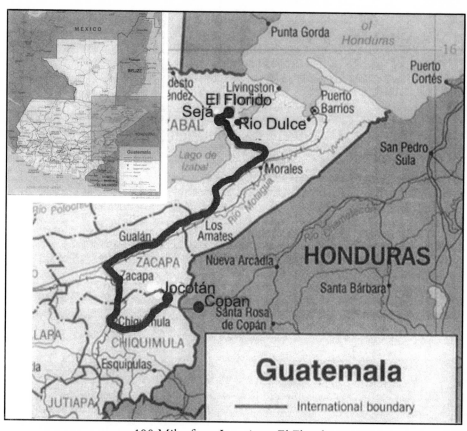

100 Miles from Jocotán to El Florido

1

The Plight

Virginia

One day John McNichols, a fellow missionary who was working on the translation of the Bible into the Chortí language, came to our house. "Virginia, there is a sight I think you might want to see down at the mayor's office. And by the way, bring your camera." He was hesitant to invite me, a new missionary and young mother because he was not sure I was ready for this.

John had caught my nurse's curiosity, so I left our two children with our house helper, Aneliana, and followed him to the mayor's office in the center of town.

We found two crude stretchers on the cement floor in front of the office. On one stretcher lay a man, Juan from Pelillo Negro, from one of our village churches, who had deep cuts across his face, left eyebrow, and hands. His right ear was almost cut off, and his right shoulder had a deep, open gash. The blood was caked on his torn clothes and skin. Nothing had been cleaned or washed since the fight occurred in the village the night before.

He looked at us and said, "Hello, Don Luis" (this was the name John used in Guatemala). He did not complain of pain or discomfort; he was just quiet. In the village, someone had put ashes and hair in the gashes which effectively stopped the bleeding, making the whole scene look even worse.

The other stretcher held his nephew, Julio, who had a deep, open gash across his left cheek and through his lip. He had two deep gashes in his scalp, and his left arm had an open gash to the bone up to his elbow. The blood from the gashes was caked on his torn clothes and on his face. Julio said nothing to us and avoided our greeting, and he also showed no sign of discomfort or pain.

I was horrified and nauseated. *What happened?* I wondered. *How could people do this to members of their own family?*

I started to reach out to touch and comfort them, but the police who were guarding them yelled, "Stop! Don't touch them!"

I obeyed, but I had no idea why we could not touch them. I did not take any photos, as they would not want me to take pictures of them in this traumatic situation. It was just too embarrassing and degrading.

John and I bowed our heads while standing near Juan and Julio's stretchers. We prayed to the Lord for the healing of their injuries and of their hearts. As I slowly returned to our home, I thought, *How awful! What really provoked this fighting?*

Later we learned that the uncle and nephew in the fight were taken by the town police to the Catholic clinic up on the hill where their wounds were sutured and bandaged. Sadly we never saw those two men in our church again. Shame and fear reigned in their hearts.

We learned from others in the village church that there was much contention between them over a plot of land up in their village. Juan and his brother were given a small piece of land that they were to divide between two young families, but the new plots were not large enough to raise food for one family. So the son of Juan's brother, Julio, fought his uncle with a machete for the land.

Often on Sunday afternoons after selling their coffee and beans at the market, the Indian men would spend their earnings on cheap liquor called "chicha." Subsequently, they would drink and fight each other with machetes.

Ray had brought up many poignant questions: What aspects of their ancestry do we need to know in order to understand them better now? Is there any way to help them? Do they want help? Most importantly, what does God want us to do for the Chortí people?

Ray

The Chortí are descendants of the great Mayan civilization. When the empire collapsed, there was a mass migration by the Mayan people away from the major cultural center of Tikal to the northwestern highlands of Guatemala. However, the Chortí remained close to Copán, the southernmost major Mayan cultural center just across the Guatemalan border in Honduras.

It is estimated that at one time there were approximately one hundred fifty thousand in the Chortí tribe. They were concentrated in the department (state) of Chiquimula in eastern Guatemala and in a small area of western Honduras. As we began our ministry, only about forty thousand still spoke the Chortí language. The group of Chortí speakers was concentrated in about twenty-two villages throughout the mountains surrounding the town of Jocotán, their trade center and marketplace.

Why they settled in that area was unclear. Why they stayed there over the centuries was perplexing. The Jocotán area was hot, dry, and rocky. Their land, with a semiarid climate, was on steep mountainsides. None of these factors were conducive to agriculture, the only way of life the Chortí knew.

Guatemala had been primarily an agrarian society. The large landowners produced coffee, bananas, cattle, cotton, and sugar for export. The mid-sized and smaller farmers produced food for the cities, so most of the productive land was in cultivation.

The good land all around the Chortí people was occupied by Ladino farmers (people of mixed races, usually Spanish and Indian). The Chortí, who lived in extended family units, were forced to do subsistence farming on the steep mountainsides that were worn out, eroded, and worthless. As the country progressed around them, the Chortí became a forgotten people. With no more land available and no resources for moving away, they were boxed in on the edge of existence between life and death.

The marginal climate in the Jocotán area was an obvious negative factor in the plight of the Chortí people. There were only two seasons in that area: wet and dry. The early storms that signaled the beginning of the rainy season were hard thunderstorms that caused rapid runoff and heavy erosion of the steep mountainsides. Year after year, topsoil would wash away, exposing more and more rocky subsurface structure.

The second climatic problem was that the rains would often not continue long enough to mature a corn crop. The fear of drought became a reality on the average of one year in five, according to rain records. Then there was the hunger that followed, devastating an already-weakened people living on the edge of existence.

As a result of the impossible land situation, the Chortí society had become violent. Fighting was common between neighbors who were often extended family members. The only weapon the Chortí used was a machete, so many of the men had large scars on their heads and arms, and some were missing fingers, hands, or arms. Often there were reports of killings.

The Chortí demonstrated living hopelessness not seen in other groups in Guatemala. Out of necessity, they worked hard to produce what they could and to protect what they had. They never talked about the future.

"Life is today," they would say. "If I wake up tomorrow, I am blessed with another day. Will I have something to sell? Will I work for pay at least one day this week in order to buy what my family needs?" Beyond that, there was almost no thought of a future. They usually spoke only in the present tense.

One day we made a trip to a village during a severe drought. The sun was beating down, and the air was so hot and dry that the earth and weeds crumbled under our shoes. The acrid smell of the air was almost like burning hot coals. No green vegetation was visible, and no water ran in the small creek bed. The atmosphere seemed lifeless and depressing.

In these desperate times men had to leave their families to find work. There were two areas where they could go—one was the Pacific coastal lowlands to work on the sugarcane and cotton plantations and the other was the mountains to work in the coffee plantations. Both of these areas were a great distance from Jocotán, but there was no alternative. With no harvest, they had to hire themselves out in order to provide food for their families.

On Sunday mornings representatives from these large plantations drove their trucks, with high side-boards for livestock and cargo, into town. The Chortí men lined up, were hired, and then climbed aboard. If they were going to the Pacific coast, they stood on that truck in the sun for about eight hours. The workers were promised a wage and a place to sleep. The work agreement was usually for one or two months. Their food was provided by the employer and discounted from their wages when they left. They were not paid, of course, for the days they could not work. Any medical expenses were also taken out of their wages. On the Pacific coast, malaria was rampant and illnesses were common.

After their work agreement was completed, the trucks brought them back to Jocotán. The net result was that they brought a meager-to-reasonable amount of money back to the family, depending on their medical expenses and days they could not work. This would allow them to survive until they had a harvest or until they could find some other work.

Another hardship that affected most Chortí families was the scarcity of firewood with which to cook their beans and tortillas. Successive generations on that overpopulated land had removed virtually all the wooded areas. Now they had to go long distances to find wood. An alternative was to buy firewood, but it was expensive and beyond their means. A particularly blessed and favorable time was when the rains came and the river rose. The men would be found along the banks with ropes to snag driftwood as it floated by. The women, while at the river washing clothes, would always be on the lookout for sticks and limbs that would wash up among the rocks.

One other source of firewood was the brush that grew on land that had to be rested for a year or two because it had become unproductive. When it was cut down, only the smallest twigs and leaves were left behind. Everything else was taken for firewood. Every time a fire was lit for cooking food, there was a conscious thought of the wood source for the next one.

A huge obstacle to the Chortí people's prosperity was the lack of education in the villages around Jocotán. When we began our ministry with them, there were no adults who had finished first grade. Some knew how to read because missionaries and pastors were instrumental in teaching them how to read the Bible. But beyond reading, there was very little education.

In the mid-sixties the government was graduating many teachers from the universities and establishing village schools in the rural areas. Some of the twenty-two Chortí villages around Jocotán had received a school, but not all of them. The education of the children could in time provide a way out of their severe poverty.

At first, this educational program had little impact on the Chortí people for various reasons. The teachers were raised and educated in the cities and did not understand or appreciate the rural way of life. There were no roads into any of the Chortí villages, so the teachers had to walk the steep trails to get to their schools. There was usually no adequate place for the teachers to live so they stayed in town and walked each day to the village. If the teachers wanted to live in the village, they would be relegated to an inconvenient room with a dirt floor, no electricity, no running water, and no bathroom. And lastly, the appointed teacher would not speak the language of their students. Schools by law were to be taught in Spanish, the official language of the country, but there was no program to bridge the children from their mother language to the Spanish language. These factors were frustrating for the teacher and discouraging for the students.

This unfortunate educational set-up resulted in the following two problems: Students would drop out in large numbers because of the lack of ability to understand the teacher and the assignments; and, even more damaging was the fact that the teachers would lose interest and stop coming. Sometimes teachers opened the school only sporadically to show that the school was functioning.

The net result would be that the children would start first grade two or three times and never finish the grade in order to move on to the next. After a while, the parents would say they were too old for school and were needed to work in the fields or to care for the younger children at home.

Virginia

This lack of education affected the Chortí's understanding of health, hygiene, farming, and marketing, so they would traditionally turn to the local medicine man for help and instruction.

One morning a young Indian mother and her mother came to our house with a beautiful, healthy-looking newborn. After several minutes of discussing family news or the corn planting, the older woman leaned over and said, "This baby will not suck the breast."

I began asking, "Did he ever nurse? How old is he? When did he stop nursing?"

Then the young mother put the seven-day-old infant up to her breast to show me, and the baby wanted to suck but could not. After watching the mother attempt to nurse her baby several minutes, I became alarmed. Ray and I decided we should take the infant with the mother and grandmother to the county public hospital in Chiquimula. It was a forty-minute ride in the cab of our pickup down a winding dusty road, and we took our children with us as well.

We arrived at the hospital, rang a bell at the door, and a Catholic sister finally invited us in. We had another long wait in a hall of the old hospital. Another sister came in and took the infant to examine him; finally we were getting attention. I explained the baby's history. Then the sister brought in a Guatemalan doctor who examined the baby and his umbilical cord.

The sister looked me in the eyes and said, "This is tetanus of the newborn."

"Okay, what can we do about it?" I asked. "Let's get the tetanus antitoxin started."

The sister looked at me and shook her head. "No, we do not have any tetanus antitoxin here."

"Well, then could we get it in Guatemala City?" I asked. "Let's do something!"

The sister slowly turned away and said, "This baby will die; there is nothing we can do."

The young mother kept her eyes glued to my face, trying to read my expressions since she did not understand the Catholic sister's words.

She probably hoped the foreign missionary who knows Jesus could save her baby.

I wanted to give her hope but felt helpless and defeated. I began to feel the hopelessness and sadness the Indians carried with them all the time. I turned to her but I did not want to tell her the truth, so I said, "Come with me outside."

They followed me outside and then I said as gently as I could, "The sister told us there is no help for your baby."

She looked up into my eyes and then looked down to her baby and pulled the worn blanket closer around him. But she did not cry, nor was there any other expression of sadness. She put on the usual expressionless, stoic stare and followed me down the sidewalk.

But I felt shock as I thought, *tetanus of the newborn. I have never seen a case of it before. This is horrible and so unfair for this family.* My thoughts continued. *If only we were in the States, we would have medical help for this baby. But we are in Guatemala with minimal medical help.* Then curiosity replaced my shock and I wondered, *How did this baby get tetanus?*

"God, what do You want me to do?" I prayed. "Please, God, show me what You want me to do." But it seemed as though God was silent. I had no inkling of how He was going to answer that prayer.

Together we sadly returned to Jocotán in the pickup. Seven days later the infant died in his home in the village. His mother wrapped his little body in a woven mat and buried him beside his grandparents in the village cemetery. This little Indian family suffered from a lack of education and from fear.

Ray

Some of the Chortí lived in villages that allowed them to develop cottage industries. One area produced the maguey plant from which fibers were stripped and made into products like rope, hammocks, shoulder bags, and nets for carrying corn and fruit. Another area had a special soil ideal for making clay earthenware such as bowls, large kettles, water jugs and flat dishes on which the tortillas were cooked. The tule reed that grew in a few villages near streams, springs, or seepages of water was used to weave sleeping mats and baskets that were sold in the market on Sundays.

Because these commodities were well known throughout the country, buyers would come in from long distances and load their trucks. The buyer would set the price, and the uneducated Indian would humbly accept it with no argument, sometimes not even receiving the exact price he was quoted. Sadly, the Chortí sellers were fearful because the buyers would offer a price for a quantity and the Chortí could not calculate the right price.

Jocotán, like all municipal towns, has a mayor and a town council; a registrar to record births, deaths, and marriages; a police station; a school; some general stores in the center of town; the large Catholic Church surrounded by a park; and an open plaza where the market was held on Sundays. With a relatively small number of Chortí living in Jocotán, the Ladinos owned the shops and dominated the economy.

Without educational opportunities and with no voice in the government that controlled them, they were often taken advantage of and looked on as second-class citizens. They seemed to have no self-respect, even in their own marketplace.

Superstitions, Animism and Beliefs

The Chortí people had never had opportunities for formal education, but they were descendants of the Mayan civilization, which had been advanced in many ways. After the collapse of the Mayan structure about a thousand years earlier, there was a disbursement of the people into at least thirty groups that now have their own languages and regional habitats, mostly in Guatemala.

At the time of the Spanish conquest and later colonization of the area, the Mayan people, although Christianized in the Roman Catholic tradition, continued to practice their animistic religion. Animism is a belief that every object has a spirit.

Because of the Chortí Indians' animistic worldview, spirits were a predominant factor in determining their actions. They believed illnesses were caused by evil spirits, so they appeased the spirits to prevent or get rid of illnesses. Certain colors were considered to have power. For example, to protect a newborn child or animal from the spirits that bring diseases, they tied a red string or ribbon around the neck or arm to ward off evil spirits. Anytime a person became sick, something red would appear somewhere on their body.

Even plant diseases were thought to be caused by angry spirits. In these cases the color white was the strong color. It was not unusual to see whitewashed rocks in fields of tomatoes, corn, beans, or squash with the hopes that they would ward off a plague. When I observed these examples, it reinforced my opinion that the Chortí Indians continued the animistic belief systems handed down from their Mayan ancestors.

Virginia

We faced serious challenges in the medical work in which I was becoming involved. I was a newcomer who did not know the Chortí language or their customs yet, so it was difficult for me to understand their medical practices. Witch doctors had power in the villages. They sometimes were able to call on demons to do harm to another person and to make them sick. Sometimes they made incantations over sick people hoping the evil spirits would leave. And sometimes those spirits obeyed.

People talked about the "ojo," the evil eye, which was a power some people had over others. It functioned like a "hex" that certain people could put on others or their children by simply looking at them. The witch doctor was able to undo the power of the "ojo."

Here is a case in point. Our experience with an epidemic of amoebic dysentery taught us how extensive the control of spiritism was on the Chortí. It was late one night when Ray and I and our children were getting back to Jocotán after visiting a church in another village. We received a message to go to the clinic because the nurse needed our help. A four-year-old child with dysentery was taken to a doctor in Chiquimula at our suggestion. The doctor had sent the child back to our clinic with medications and an IV fluid to be administered because of dehydration. The clinic nurse could not get the IV needle into the child's small, thin veins. I was also unsuccessful, so we decided we must give the fluid subcutaneously (under the skin). The child was so sick that he hardly complained of the pain of the needle. The child's father, Ernesto, sat with his son, trying to comfort him.

At 1:00 a.m. the sick child was resting easier as his little body received the much-needed fluids.

"Do you think he will live?" Ernesto asked.

"I'm not sure, only God knows," I slowly replied. "Let's pray right now and ask the Lord to save him."

"Hhhmm," he responded. "You see, I'm not a believing Christian now."

"Does that mean that at one time you did believe in Jesus?" I asked.

"Yes," he replied, "but now I don't believe the Bible is true, and I don't think there is a God. I'm not sure God answers prayer."

"The Bible is God's wonderful message to us of help and hope," I said as I was praying quietly for the Holy Spirit to be with us and guide me. "God tells us that if we ask Him, and look for Him, He will help us. He is the only one true God; there is no other. Can I pray for your little child and for you?"

"Oh, okay," Ernesto replied.

"Lord, please be with us now. We thank you for Your power and for Your love," I prayed. "Please heal Ernesto and his little boy. I give You all the honor and glory. Amen."

By 3:30 a.m. half the fluid was given and the child was sleeping peacefully. We decided to let him rest and continue treatment in the morning. A couple hours later the child was much better, and they left the clinic for their home, since we did not have room for inpatients.

I visited the family the next day and found the child worse again. The family reported that when they gave him the medicine the doctor ordered he grew worse. This superstition was common. We pleaded with the family to bring the child back to the clinic so we could give more IV fluid.

"No!" Ernesto and his wife replied. "And we are not going to give any of the prescribed medicine that the doctor gave us."

Instead of following our instructions, they burned incense under the child's cot and brewed a drink for him made of leaves. They were waiting for the witch doctor to visit later in the day and sprinkle chicken blood over the child and the bed with incantations.

On the fourth day after we had given the IV fluid, Ernesto brought the child back to us, and in desperation he stated, "The witch doctor sprinkled the blood, but it did not heal him. Could you please help our little boy?"

We took the child back to the doctor in Chiquimula, who we hoped could administer IV fluids, but it was too late. He died that night.

I learned that witch doctors have powerful influence over villagers' lives. People went to them for advice on almost all the decisions they had to make. Often I felt that the villagers saw me in the same category as a witch doctor. The only difference they saw was that the witch doctor was very expensive while the mission nurse in the clinic cost only twenty-five cents each visit.

I felt helpless and frustrated in cases like this because we needed to fight ignorance and superstition in addition to physical illness. We had to practice spiritual warfare as we confronted people like Ernesto. Often ignorance, superstition, and spiritual darkness were the deadliest enemies to the Chortí Indian families.

2

Bringing Hope to the Hopeless

Virginia

G od heard their cry and He had a plan that began many years earlier. It was Sunday morning in Jocotán, Guatemala, and we were new missionaries who had just arrived at our appointed ministry among the Chortí Indians who would work alongside Homer and Evelyn Sharpless. We were attending the Sunday morning worship service in the Jocotán Friends Church. Pastor Chon Vargas read an invitation to a wedding: "Saturday morning at nine there will be a wedding of Nicolas and Juana at the Chortí Friends Church. All of you are invited."

We gladly accepted the invitation and wondered how this ceremony was carried out in the Chortí Indian church. The groom's family and the bride's family were members of the church. We wondered what gift was expected from us and what was appropriate from us as missionaries. We arrived right on time at nine, the announced time of the ceremony, but there were only ten people in the church. *Well,* I thought, *this is going to be a very small wedding.*

As we waited, however, the women entered little by little and took their places with their children on the left side of the church. The Indian men sat on the benches on the right side, where Homer and Ray sat also. An aisle went down the center of the church to the front altar. The back- half of the church floor was hard-packed dirt, and there was a rough adobe brick floor around the front altar and for two rows of benches near the front. The front altar was a platform built six inches from the floor of the church.

John McNichols, a fellow missionary, played familiar hymns on the small pump organ while we waited. I loved to hear the familiar melodies of the hymns we sang as we were growing up in the church in the United States. John grew up in the Bell Friends Church in Bell, California. He received his Master's of Divinity from Fuller Seminary. Joyce, his wife, finished her work at Pacific Nazarene College. They married and answered God's call to serve in Jocotán alongside Helen Oakley.

"Joyce, who is Miss Inez?" I asked, taking advantage of the wait, since I had heard our Indian friends talking about a "Miss Inez."

"They're talking about Helen Oakley, who served here from 1947 to 1962," she said. "There were two other Friends missionaries in Chiquimula (the Friends Mission headquarters at that time) with the name Helen, so she gave the Indian people her middle name, Inez, to eliminate confusion. But she left Jocotán five years ago for retirement." And I reflected, *they are still talking about her as if she left just yesterday. She still has a profound influence here. Amazing!*

At 10:00 a.m., the bride entered the church with her family. She wore a new simple blue dress and had ribbons in her long braided hair. The groom wore long dark pants and a new white shirt. They were a very attractive young couple. There was no wedding march, no flowers, no long white dress, and no ring. The couple sat on the rustic front bench with their families.

Pastor Chon, the pastor who studied the Christian Workers' Course in Berea Bible Institute, gave a regular Bible message, and the congregation of about fifty people sang a hymn. Then the pastor invited the couple to come to the altar. The young man and woman never looked at each other, nor did they touch. The pastor asked if they would accept each other as husband and wife. They whispered yes. Pastor Chon prayed over them and then pronounced them husband and wife. All during the ceremony the bride never looked up at the groom or at the pastor.

After the benediction, the couple was not sure what to do, so Pastor Chon told them to go to the patio of the church where there were tamales for them and everyone else in attendance. Doña Tomasa, Chon's wife, helped make the tamales for the visitors and guided the proceedings.

As I sat observing this wedding celebration, I thought, *this service has just the basics—the promise, the commitment, the prayer for God's blessing, the pronouncement, the celebration—the important points of a wedding. Maybe this wedding was closer to God's plan than our own, that are encumbered with all the lavish decorations and costly attire.*

Later we learned that formal weddings and marriage ceremonies were not traditionally held among the Chortí. The marriages were arranged between the two sets of parents, with the approval of the young people, like common-law marriages. The brides were usually fourteen to sixteen years old, and the grooms were usually two to four years older. The agreement involved the groom's family paying a dowry of sacks of corn or beans to the bride's family. After the arrangements and agreements between the families were finalized, the couple began living together in her parents' house. He also usually worked for the bride's father for many years. The bride worked in the kitchen alongside her mother and learned the "work of a wife" from her. Children were raised in the residence of their grandparents. When the grandparents were old, the children and grandchildren cared for them.

Pastor Chon carefully discipled the Chortí Christians to put their "lives in order" and sign legal marriage contracts. This was a stabilizing commitment to their spouses, to children, and to God. Sometimes this entailed a wedding ceremony in the church like we had just observed. We always appreciated Pastor Chon and his sincere commitment to help the Chortí people.

Twenty years earlier, Manuel Colindres, a Berea Bible Institute student, had visited Jocotán and began a Spanish-speaking church there. He realized the Chortí needed to hear about Jesus, but Manuel had no opportunity to learn their language. So he encouraged two Chortí men, Atenacio and Calixto, who had accepted Jesus as their Savior to record one message about Jesus on a phonograph record in their language. This was used to evangelize the Chortí villages. Soon a group of fifty or more Chortí met to hear the Bible verses read by Atenacio.

Helen Oakley had heard Manuel's concern for evangelizing the Chortí while Manuel was giving his testimony in the Berea Bible Institute. Helen said, "I will go to the Chortí." She moved to the town of Jocotán to study the language and translate the New Testament into that unwritten language. This was a daunting task because she had to organize the grammar, develop an alphabet, and set up a dictionary. Later she moved up the mountain to live in a thatched hut to work on the translation of the Scriptures in the village of Pelillo Negro. She walked one mile to a stream to bathe, wash clothes, and carry water in a clay jar back up to her hut. Some months later she moved back to Jocotán.

As the Bible was translated into the Chortí language, eight or ten Indian people gained courage to attend the Spanish services in the Ladino church in Jocotán. That number soon grew to twenty.

John and Joyce McNichols learned the Chortí language and translated books of the New Testament into Chortí while Helen evangelized and ministered to the Indians in Jocotán. John and Joyce, who raised three daughters in Jocotán, gained the trust and love of hundreds of Chortí, as did Helen.

From 1955 to 1957 there was a severe drought. Helen Oakley wrote, "We need wisdom in how to help relieve the hunger situation in these difficult months. The Indian people need one pound of corn per person each day to make their tortillas. So three pounds of corn in one day is not adequate for a family of six people. Suddenly we have found ourselves facing the fact that the people, whom we know and love, are facing starvation with no money, corn, or other food. We have had seven nearly rainless years."

James 2:15–16 says, "If a brother or sister is without clothing and in need of daily food, and one of you says to them, 'Go in peace, be warm and be filled,' and yet you do not give them what is necessary for their body, what use is that?"

Helen and John and Joyce agreed that it does not do much good to evangelize a man whose family needs food and medicine; nor can a young man learn to read the Bible when he is very hungry. So they supplied powdered milk for the children, they gave the farmers improved corn seed to plant after the rains began, and they provided medicine for the sick.

Helen and the McNichols prayed together, and they prayed with the Chortí; they wanted to help the Chortí people help themselves. The missionaries did not want the Chortí to be dependent on them, nor did the Chortí people want that. The missionaries could not give them more land, but they were trying to help them get more harvest from the land they did have. And the task of helping these hungry people survive became daunting. Facing the stare of so many sick and starving children was depressing.

There were also other missionaries who played a key role in the development of the Chortí people. John and Diane Lubeck, Wycliff Bible translators, went to Jocotán to continue the translation of the Bible into the Chortí Language. Their work resulted in the Chortí New Testament being published. Dorothy Andersen also contributed by compiling a Chortí dictionary and by teaching them to read their language.

In 1962, Homer and Evelyn Sharpless, citrus ranchers and prominent leaders in the Friends Churches in California, heard God's call to help the farmers of Central America. Homer had served on the Friends mission board and visited the field once previously to help drill a water well. He had seen the plight of the Chortí people and was convicted that he must return and help the Indian farmers improve their lives by producing more and better crops.

Homer and Evelyn sold their citrus ranch and served as managers of the Friends Youth Camp, Quaker Meadow, for a summer before they moved to Guatemala. It was at this particular camp where Ray was working as the assistant manager, and I was camp nurse, that Homer gave his testimony around a campfire. He asked if anyone felt God's call to serve Him on the mission field. God did speak to me that night so I quietly bowed my head and told the Lord I wanted to obey Him.

When Ray and I married we committed our lives to serve Him together on the mission field. Inter-Varsity Christian Fellowship recommended that young missionary candidates should serve in a local church in the U.S. for a couple years before beginning service in a foreign land. So Ray accepted a position with Bank of America in Imperial Valley, California, as an agricultural loans officer. We attended the North Holtville Friends Church and served in that church. At that time our little daughter, Linda, was six months old.

One day while playing with my delightful daughter, I looked up and began bargaining with the Lord, "Lord, I know missionary kids are sent to boarding schools for their education. I don't ever want to send Linda away! So, You knew, Lord, that I was willing to go, because we have made all these preparations. Now you can call someone else instead of us to go as agricultural missionaries to Central America and we will stay here. Maybe You had just wanted to test us to see if our hearts were willing to serve You."

As I quietly bowed my head, I heard the Lord ask, "Do you trust me?"

I fell to my knees and cried, "Oh yes, Lord, I do trust You! Forgive my doubt and desire to turn away from obeying You." I remained on my knees crying and praying until my baby began to whimper to let me know she was hungry. It was settled. We would obey the Lord's direction in our lives wherever He would lead us because we loved Him more than everything else.

In 1966, at the end of our second year in Imperial Valley, we applied to the Friends Church Mission board to work as agricultural missionaries in Central America with Homer and Evelyn Sharpless. We were accepted and immediately began planning our move to the mission field. Our son, Tad, was born four weeks before we left the United States.

For the year of 1967 we were sent to San Jose, Costa Rica, to study Spanish. We learned missionary strategies from many influential mission leaders who spoke at our chapel services. Our Spanish language teachers taught about culture as well as language.

This year was like a bridge taking us from our culture into a completely foreign culture and language where God wanted to use us. We had experiences of being robbed, having problems with our house helper, feeling lonely, being sick and speaking as a child speaks in a new language. Even those troubling experiences prepared us for our ministry ahead.

After our last class in December 1967, we flew to Guatemala City. Homer and Evelyn met us at the airport, and they began the paperwork to get our six barrels, that served to store and ship all our worldly belongings, out of customs. Then Homer and Evelyn picked up our family in their Chevrolet pickup and drove the four-hour trip down through the mountains toward Chiquimula in eastern Guatemala. We were excited to at last get to our home and ministry.

We stopped at the Friends Mission Headquarters in Chiquimula to greet the resident missionaries. Then Homer hurried us on the hour ride up the mountains on a winding, narrow, steep gravel road to Jocotán. It was almost dark when we arrived.

We were ushered into our new home, which had twelve-inch thick adobe walls, a red tile roof, and doors and wooden windows. There were only two rooms, one large and one smaller. The back door to the porch had a wooden plank to be placed on the inside so it could not be pushed in by a thief. The front door also had a wooden plank for security. The floor was red tile, and the back porch had only a screen wall. There was a bathroom with a flush toilet and shower with running water. The kitchen was an add-on building that was only screened.

I gradually began to realize we were going to live with Homer and Evelyn in this small adobe house that was located in the central plaza of Jocotán. *How is this going to work?* I wondered.

"They are grandparents, and our very active children are younger than three, and one child does not sleep all night," I grumbled. "The mission knew we were coming for more than a year, and now there is no place for our family?" I asked as I started to feel sorry for myself. "Lord, please calm my spirit," I prayed as the temptations to be angry and resentful came over me.

Two weeks later I prayed, *"Thank you, Lord, for letting us live with Homer and Evelyn so we could learn from them how to do missionary work."* They taught us how to love and relate to the Indians, and they always spoke of the Chortí Indians with respect and dignity. They taught us how to appreciate fellow missionaries who do missionary work differently from how we think it should be done. They taught us how to filter and boil all our drinking water. They taught us how to laugh and have fun. They taught us how to walk through difficult situations and see the bright side of things, which was especially helpful when living among a desperately hungry people.

Once a month, the Friends missionaries that were serving in Guatemala and Honduras met together to hold a "mission council meeting" in the Bethel headquarters in Chiquimula. We were informed that we, as new missionaries, were an important part of this meeting. We would ride with Homer and Evelyn to Chiquimula in their pickup truck, and it was always good to see the other missionaries. Our two children looked forward to playing with another missionary child, Jackie, daughter of Jack and Waynel Wing, missionaries in Zacapa, Guatemala.

John and Esther Astleford were the administrators of the mission work in Central America. At our first mission council meeting, John came to me. "How are things going for you?" he asked. "Just tell me what you need, and I'll tell you how we get along without it."

"Oh...," I did not know how to answer him. Then, as I thought about what he had just told me, I did not like it. *No,* I thought, *I'll do something about it.* I felt offended by his response to just "accept the living situation" in which we found ourselves.

We entered the Mission parlor for the prayer meeting, which was led by one of the missionaries. Everyone got down on their knees and knelt at their chairs or at the sofa.

Come on, I thought, *I can pray just as well sitting as kneeling; the position is not that important.* But I reluctantly followed their lead and knelt. Then I learned it became easier for me to humble my attitude before God and to honor Him on my knees because this reminded me of my place before Him.

"The harvest is plentiful, but the workers are few, therefore, beseech the Lord of the harvest to send out workers into His harvest" (Matthew 9:37–38) was the benediction that was prayed at the close of every prayer meeting. These prayer meetings lasted one to four hours depending on the concerns around us.

Slowly I began to realize the privilege and honor that was mine to work and pray with a group of saints who knew how to serve our Living Lord and how to live sacrificially among Central American people. I realized I had a great deal to learn about walking with Him before He could use me effectively.

In Jocotán one evening I met Homer with his Bible and hymnbook in hand. I asked, "Where are you going?"

"I'm going to the church prayer vigil," he replied.

"Oh, but this is not the regular prayer meeting service night," I said.

"No, this is an all-night prayer vigil."

All night? I thought, *How could a person pray all night?*

Later I thought more about the prayer vigil. *Here I am a missionary bringing the Good News of Jesus to people, and they are teaching me how to pray. Yes, Lord, I have a lot to learn.*

The church had a prayer vigil the following month, and I decided to attend. Ray agreed to stay with the children after I fed them and got them in bed.

There were at least fifty or sixty people attending, and the only light came from a pressurized Coleman kerosene lantern that needed to be pumped every hour. Songs were sung, some in Spanish and some in Chortí, and Scripture was read out loud by two different people. Then the Indian people knelt around the altar or at their benches to pray. They talked softly to the Lord, some in the Chortí language and some in Spanish. I noticed when sleep would almost overcome them; they stood up or walked quietly in the back of the church to wake themselves up.

At 1:30 a.m. I too almost fell asleep. So I got up and walked back and forth to stay awake in order to keep praying. About every thirty minutes someone would lead in a couple songs and another Scripture. At the front of the church behind the pulpit was a rustic blackboard that had a list of seven prayer requests that we prayed about together. Periodically individuals would go to the front and give their testimonies about what God had done for them.

During one of these all-night vigils, don Inéz, a former maintenance worker in the large Basilica of the Black Christ in Esquipulas, Guatemala, told the story of his salvation. His job included cleaning the statues of the saints inside that church. He told us his reflections, "These are only wooden. I have to clean their wooden bodies with glass eyes and wash their hair. They can do nothing for themselves." He continued, "Why do I pray to these lifeless statues to help me?"

Don Inéz said, "At Easter I was told to crawl on my hands and knees over a rocky trail for a mile to the entrance to the basilica as penance for my sins. At the door, with my hands and knees bloody, I crawled another three hundred feet to the altar. But last month John McNichols, a missionary, told me Jesus Christ died on the cross and was raised up and lives. I knew this was the truth," he said.

"I asked Jesus to forgive my sins, and He did," he exclaimed. "My burden of sin is gone and I am forgiven! Those people in that church of the Black Christ did not tell me the truth."

From don Inéz's testimony that night, I received new insight and vision about God's plan to change the plight of the Chortí Indians. I thought, *It is truly amazing to think that a simple man who has never completed even the first grade could hear and quickly understand God's Word. He quickly trusted the truth and it dramatically changed his life. THIS is why we are in Guatemala—to help men and women find Jesus Christ and to be part of God's response to their cry for help.*

3

Family Life in Jocotán

Virginia

In those early years, much of my time was spent caring for our children, going to market, preparing meals and building friendships with our neighbors and friends in the church. On one particular day, Tad, our two-year-old son, stood beside me watching me make bread, when all of a sudden he grabbed the bowl of flour and tipped it up as if he was going to drink from it. All of the flour flowed over his head to his toes, and all I saw were two big eyes peeking out from a white mask of flour. I could not stop my giggle when I saw his funny face. Then I stifled my laughter because he thought I was laughing at him and he began to cry. I reassured him that the flour just made him look funny, and I cleaned up the mess.

Once in a while homesickness would sneak up on me as I focused too much on the inconveniences. I learned to look for the things for which I could praise the Lord with a genuinely grateful heart and to focus on all of His blessings around us. This quickly removed homesickness for life and family back in the United States. I learned that the grateful heart brought contentment.

Our young children easily adapted to their new surroundings. They were happy in our new home in Jocotán, with Homer and Evelyn being our patient substitute grandparents. Linda quickly made friends with the little girls who lived next door. She liked to carry small clay jars or baskets on her head just like the women in the market. Her best playmate was her little brother, and they played "house" on our back patio when Tad would cooperate.

One day I was sitting out in our back patio watching six neighborhood children, ages one to nine, playing with our two "pale faces." Most of the conversation among the kids was some sort of Spanish/Indian street language, of which I understood very little. Linda and Tad, however, had learned many of these words. It amused me to see my children coughing and spitting, just like their Indian friends.

Our Indian friends liked to watch our white children play or interact with their children. Often the women would reach out and pinch Linda's arm or cheek and comment, "Oh, how fat she is!" Linda didn't appreciate this, and I appreciated it even less, but I tried not to show this.

We quickly realized the Chortí loved children and our children were a bridge for us to them. Our kids learned to speak Spanish to their friends outside the home, and inside the home we only spoke English as a family. We were advised to do this to ensure our children did not lose their mother tongue.

Black beans and tortillas were on our menu daily with vegetables from our own garden and beef or chicken that I purchased in the open meat market. Evelyn advised me to buy our meat before daylight to get a good piece before the flies arrived. Then I would cook the tough grass-fed beef in the pressure cooker on our kerosene stove so we could chew it. Linda and Tad enjoyed the beans and tortillas and fruit. We bought powdered milk in five-pound cans imported from Europe, and reconstituted it with boiled water for our children.

Jocotán had a city water delivery system that piped water into our kitchen. Often the water that came out of the faucet was brownish in color, and leaves and sticks came along with it. So we first had to filter it through a large cement filter, and then we boiled it for twenty minutes like most of the people did in town. We stored it in large aluminum kettles to cool.

The large town generator provided us with electricity from 4:30 p.m. to 9:30 p.m. only, and then it was turned off. We quickly adjusted to that situation and learned to always keep a flashlight under our pillow to use at night when we got up with the children. We used kerosene lamps when the generators failed.

One afternoon I wanted to let the Mission headquarters in Chiquimula know that our family would be in Chiquimula the following day and would need a room and meals. Evelyn suggested I send a telegram. I thought that was too slow and "old fashioned." The telegraph office that also had the only telephone in town, was two doors down the street from our house.

"I want to make a call to Esther Astleford, a missionary at the Friends Mission in Chiquimula," I explained as I filled out the information on a slip of paper in the telegraph/telephone office.

"Fine. I will send a message by telegram to the telegraph office in Chiquimula, and ask a runner to go to the Mission and advise Mrs.

Astleford to come to the telephone office in Chiquimula, because a Virginia Canfield wants to talk to her on the phone," he explained with a strange look on his face.

Is he laughing at me? I wondered.

Meanwhile I waited at home three hours. Finally the Jocotán operator came to our house to advise me that Esther was in the Chiquimula telephone office. I was excited that I was actually going to talk to someone on the phone. The telephone/telegraph operator led me to the back of the rustic office where there was a wooden stall with no door. A large, black, old-fashioned dial telephone hung on the wall inside the stall. He picked up the receiver and handed it to me.

"Hello, hello, Esther? Hello?" I yelled the last word, thinking maybe the communication would improve if I yelled louder. Her voice was so faint I could only hear every other word or less, and she could hardly hear me at all. So in those circumstances, one naturally starts yelling louder and louder to get the message across. It was so frustrating.

When I got back to our house, Evelyn quietly stated, "I could hear you yelling in the telephone clear over here at our house." She didn't laugh at me and discreetly kept her thoughts to herself.

"I think I'd better stick with the accepted form of communication—the telegraph—and forget about it being 'old fashioned,'" I told myself.

The telegram rate was fifteen cents for five words or fewer and then five cents for each additional word. We worked at conveying our messages in the fewest words possible. Most of the time, our messages arrived in two to four hours. And we received return messages in about that much time.

Kenneth's Arrival

Kenneth, our third child, arrived in June 1968 in Guatemala City. He was the most content baby of our three, and he would wake up to be breastfed and then go right back to sleep without a whimper. He looked a little like Linda. He immediately fit right into our family, and Linda and Tad adored their new brother.

We had a nice surprise on our return to Jocotán from Guatemala City when we learned that Homer and Evelyn had moved out of their/ our house in Jocotán and into an apartment in Chiquimula. We had a whole house to ourselves, and all five of us were thankful and happy. Most of our things were still in the metal barrels that had been shipped to Guatemala for us. We had to immediately move our things from the barrels into our home.

My parents, Oscar and Marjorie Wood, flew to Guatemala City on Christmas Eve to visit us. Ray met them that night in our white pickup truck and drove them the four-and-half-hour trip down through the mountains.

I stayed in Jocotán with the kids and waited for their arrival. They arrived at 9:30 p.m that night, and we hurried them to the Chortí Indian church for the Christmas program. There were almost seventy-five different songs, poems, and skits that were presented by small groups of men and women. The children were bursting with excitement and a joyful feeling was in the air.

Mother sat on the left side of the church on one of the rustic wooden benches with Joyce McNichols, me, our children, and approximately one hundred Indian women and children. The church had a hard-packed dirt floor, and if a baby had to urinate, the mother would hold the baby in front of her legs so the urine fell on the floor and was quickly absorbed by the dirt. Even though I had already lived in Jocotán a year, I was still surprised by this. It was simply a practical solution to a situation where there were no diapers.

Dad sat on the opposite side of the church with Ray and all the men, as was their custom. The church was packed to overflowing with humanity and all the smells and sights you can imagine from a primitive people. On top of it all, my folks did not understand a word that was being said!

Oh, it is so good to see my mother, I thought, *and she is smiling so brightly here at 11:00 p.m. It's amazing!* She could not take her eyes off her three grandchildren, who really did not know her.

"Okay, you've had enough for one day," I told my parents. "And my kids are almost asleep, so let's go home." The program was not over, but we politely excused ourselves.

Mother and Dad were tired, and they quickly climbed into bed at our house. Our children were more than ready for bed.

Suddenly at midnight, the whole town erupted into a roar of firecrackers, and for ten minutes there was a constant sound of fireworks and small bombs. I had forgotten to warn my parents of the custom of setting off firecrackers at midnight on Christmas Eve all over town. They were sure a revolution had broken out to top off their day.

After this visit, Mother and Dad had a new understanding and appreciation for the missionary work we were doing in Guatemala. They became very supportive in prayer and promotion of the missionary effort. They encouraged all of us missionaries and never once suggested we leave the work.

Sunday Market Days

On Sunday mornings Jocotán was transformed into a busy street market. Most Chortí families had left their villages in the early hours of the morning and arrived at the market by 6:00 a.m. to sell the produce they had brought from their villages. They carried heavy sacks of grain on their backs, held in place with a leather strap across their forehead. Several men and women sat on the curb just outside of our front door to sell their ropes, bags and hammocks. They used the money received for their produce to buy supplies such as a machete, a hat, salt, and materials to make new clothes to take back to their villages.

The women wore colorful blouses and skirts, and the men wore white, loose pajama-type shirts and trousers. All wore sandals that were cut from old tire treads for a sole and strapped on their feet with rough leather straps, or they were barefoot. All the women from one village had the same colorful design in their blouses, and that design distinguished them from women of other villages.

Our new culture contained the beautiful and the repulsive. Smells of freshly home-roasted coffee, dried cowhide leather, dried fish, tamales wrapped in banana leaves, fresh corn tortillas, and smoke from small open fires wafted to our nostrils as we walked through the market. We saw small children with runny noses, infected eyes, and bare feet clinging to their mothers who were usually pregnant with another child. Some of the children had protruding stomachs and very thin legs. Seldom if ever were the parents able to buy a toy or candy for a child. When they went home to their villages, they still had no money and a new week would begin.

This is ridiculous, I thought one morning as I was getting ready for church. Our three small children squirmed, crawled under the church benches, and begged to go home during the two-hour church service. My command of the language was still limited to "slow" Spanish, and I understood only about half of the preacher's message. So *why go to the church service?* I complained to myself.

After some thought, I realized we were witnesses for others to see that worship in church was important for us missionaries also. I felt that maybe the more I struggled to understand the message each Sunday morning; the more Spanish I would learn. Sure enough, after one year, it dawned on me that I understood all the words spoken on Sunday mornings.

Clemencia Melara was the nurse in charge of the Jocotán Friends medical clinic. Helen Oakley had met Clemencia, who grew up in the El Molino village, while she was a student in the Friends Elementary School.

Helen noticed Clemencia was a very bright student and they became immediate friends. Clemencia's mother was living, but Helen informally adopted and educated her from the time she was in her early teens. Helen sent her to nurses training in Honduras for three years, and then the missionaries invited Clemencia to serve in the Jocotán clinic. I was always glad to help her whenever she asked me.

One week she asked me to fill in for her at the clinic while she traveled to work in Olopa. On one of those days, Pedro and his wife Victoria, a young couple, carried their one-and-a-half-year-old son on a two-hour trip from the village of Guareruche to our clinic. The child was dying from severe malnourishment and dysentery.

Helen Oakely had led Pedro to believe in Jesus four years earlier. Then Pedro helped Helen and John McNichols with the translation of the Bible into the Chortí language. A close relationship developed between Pedro and the missionaries. Pedro and Victoria were caretakers of the Mission Indian Center in Jocotán for two years before they moved back up to their village.

They had previously taken their baby to the Catholic dispensary and clinic where they could hospitalize and care for such cases. But the hospital and doctor refused to receive the child because they preferred the child die peacefully in his own home rather than in the clinic.

"They said he is dying and they couldn't help him," young Pedro told me.

"Bring him in here, and we will try to do something to help him," I said as I carefully placed the baby on the exam table. The baby was terribly dehydrated and almost unconscious. I began giving the child droppers of Coca Cola in the mouth every ten minutes. I had learned from a Guatemalan pediatrician that Coca Cola had the right ingredients to replace lost electrolytes in infants. I taught the mother how to administer the liquid.

"The baby has not improved," I told Ray five hours later. "We must take him down to the Chiquimula Hospital and see if they can help."

"I agree," Ray said. So we put the young family, along with ours, in the cab of our pickup truck.

"Yes, we can help the child recover, but we will need to keep him here in the hospital and give him IV liquids for about a week. Is that ok?" the doctors at the hospital explained. He knew, as we did, that hospitals were scary places for the Indians, who often did not trust the hospital's procedures.

"Yes, we will let our child stay," Pedro replied. "Can we stay with him?"

"Yes," the doctor replied. "He will be happier when he sees you."

One week later, the young family returned to our house on their way home from the hospital, with their smiling little baby.

"Thank you for all your help," Pedro exclaimed. "We buried our four-year-old son three weeks ago with the same condition. But this son is going to live."

"And we praise the Lord for answering our prayers for little Mario," Victoria added.

"Oh yes," I replied as my own heart sang with praise to God for helping this young, faithful family.

Later in the month, Clemencia was called to a home where the mother was having difficulty giving birth to twins. The mother and relatives were calling out to the Catholic saints for help.

"Stop this!" Clemencia called to the people who were chanting. "Only the Lord God can help you now in this circumstance." Finally she succeeded in getting the family quiet.

"Now let's pray to the Living God who answers prayer," she instructed. And she led them in prayer to God for protection and healing for the mother and children.

After the prayer, Clemencia helped deliver the two babies alive and well. The next weekend the father of the family came in to the Jocotán Friends Church and prayed to accept Christ as his Savior.

"I have seen the power of Christ work in my own home," he explained. "I know He is alive."

One day a member of one of our village churches came to our door, and I invited her to come in and sit in our house. But she was troubled and in a hurry.

"My husband died in the night," she stoically explained. "I need money to buy a straw mat to bury him in, and I need money to buy corn to make tortillas to feed the men who are digging the grave."

She is asking for financial help, I thought. *And we try to not encourage so much dependence on us. But my heart breaks for her and her suffering. She has so little and I have so much,* I told myself. *Yes, I will share $30 with her out of our grocery money.* So I took the money out of my purse and gave it to her.

"Muchas gracias," she sincerely said. "I also want you and don Mundo (the name the Indian people gave Ray) to go back to my village with me," she requested. "I want you to participate in the funeral service." Often a Christian funeral service is an evangelistic meeting where family and friends are invited to accept Jesus as Lord.

All the other missionaries were out of town that day, and Ray was up in a village visiting one of the farmers. I was the only one at home and could not leave our children.

"I'm sorry, but I cannot leave our children and go with you," I sadly explained.

"That's all right," she said as she turned and quickly left.

"Lord, please go with her and help her through this sad, discouraging day," I prayed. "Please put some capable person in my place to minister to the people."

I had never faced desperate hunger before. What do you do when very poor people ask for monetary help? At least once a day a Chortí Indian friend came to our door asking for money, food, or medicines.

"Of course we will help you," was our first natural response. We remembered Matthew 5:42: "Give to him who asks of you and do not turn away him who wants to borrow from you." Paul quoted Jesus in Acts 20:35: "Jesus said, it is more blessed to give than to receive."

Our first response on hearing their sad stories of death and suffering was to feel compassion. We wanted to relieve the suffering, so we handed them money. But as we reflected on this, we realized our gift of money was only a stop-gap, a short-term help. We did not have enough money to help everyone.

We also felt guilty that we had adequate money, clothes, food and even a mission vehicle. Often they resented us and our comparative wealth, and they were humiliated that they had to ask us for help. They had ragged clothes, they often walked barefoot, and they had only enough corn for one to two tortillas apiece per day and no money. So we wanted to show them our genuine love and concern. On the other hand, we realized how quickly they could become dependent on us missionaries and our resources instead of God and His resources. This was a heavy responsibility and concern for us.

We wanted to be Christ-like in every way so they might find hope in Jesus and His salvation. But everyone in the tribe was suffering starvation and hopelessness. People in the churches in the United States sent us money to buy food for the Chortí, but it was never enough. We spent hours in prayer with the other missionaries, and we asked people at home to pray for God's help for us to discern His plan.

The next day another woman, Maria, whose twelve-day-old infant had died of starvation because she had no breast milk, came to the house. Death seemed to be staring us in the face every day; it was hot and rainy and there was very little food because the last crop was lost in the drought, and the new planting season was just beginning.

"Could you please give me some money to pay for the burial?" she sadly asked.

"Yes, we will give you a donation for the baby's funeral," I answered when I gave her $15.

This time we decided we would accompany Maria back to her home in the mountainous village for the funeral. We found the rest of the family less concerned about the death of the infant. This woman had five children younger than thirteen in the home, and three of them were suffering from dysentery and fever. I learned that the rain that drained off the patios contained feces, which washed into the streams and rivers, and the children drank that water without boiling it. Dysentery was rampant.

I sent one of the family members back to Jocotán with a note I had written to Clemencia in the clinic asking her to send medicine for the children in this family. She sent a man to bring us the medication, and we treated the children before we left.

Working in the Jocotán clinic became a trial for me because I was working under the direction of a Guatemalan nurse who treated symptoms differently from my point of view. She often did not have the time or understanding to explain to me the "whys" behind the treatments. She knew a lot more about the culture and belief systems than I did, but scientifically I knew more about the causes of disease and the effect of treatment on body systems.

Here is an example: in one month, the nurse gave 303 vitamin injections for weaknesses and debility. I needed to know the cause of the debility. Was it intestinal parasites, tuberculosis, or malnourishment due to the lack of food? I did not know how to ask without offending her, so I was frustrated.

One thing I did learn was that the country people had misguided beliefs regarding healthcare. For example they believed an injection was always better than oral medication. They also thought feeding a baby with a bottle was much better than breast milk, no matter what might be in the baby bottle, whether coffee or starch mixed in unboiled water. We felt this incorrect information was promoted publicly by a large company that produces baby formula. But the Indian families were unable to purchase the expensive formula, so they just purchased the baby bottle.

Raising Our Children in Jocotán

These days had been hectic and a difficult with three little children while adapting to this foreign culture. One particular day I was overwhelmed. Linda had a common infection in her eyes that I was treating. Tad slipped and fell on the sidewalk and cut a small gash on his head. Kenny was crying to be fed. Then Tad stepped in a tub of water with both shoes on, Linda ran off to the neighbor's house, we ran out of gas for the washing machine so I had to go get a can of gas.

On top of all this, I remembered at 11:30 a.m. that it was Tuesday, the only day of the week that beef is on sale at the open market, where it is displayed on hooks in the sellers' booths. I knew the flies had plenty of time to enjoy it, so I planned to pressure cook my piece a little longer than usual.

Breast-feeding babies was a common sight and custom among the women at church or in the market. They would have the fronts of their dresses unbuttoned and were breastfeeding their babies most of the time. Even the grandmothers pacified the babies.

We found that Linda was adapting most easily to the culture. She often balanced a basket of rocks or a clay jug of water on her head. She actually got quite proficient at this. This was a common sight, but the women had fruit in their baskets. Linda liked to pat out tortillas using the corn dough and she could make some pretty nice tortillas.

Tad, our eighteen-month-old son, loved to pick up the almendra fruit, (a species of almonds that grows in the tropics) from the ground and chew on the tough skin. Sometimes he would pick up a mango seed from the street in the market and start chewing on it. He got a stern scolding for doing that and later had other consequences in the form of intestinal parasites. One day Ray and I noticed him lugging an empty suitcase up the hall in our house and we laughed. He knew we packed our suitcases often and went somewhere. I wished we had the Kodak Instamatic Camera that was stolen out of our barrels while they were in customs, to take photos of the kids.

Later I wrote, "Mother, as long as I keep Kenny fed, he is a content baby. He sits up by himself and grabs at anything he can reach.

"Tad, now two years old, and Linda, now four, have intestinal worms again, so they both are taking medication to treat that. They are healthy and strong and the size of six- and seven-year-old kids here, so they are not suffering. I am thankful that I am able to catch their symptoms of parasites early," I related.

Homer and Evelyn invited me to accompany them to Guatemala City to purchase a washing machine and refrigerator that would be for our use in Jocotán. Ray encouraged me to make the trip with Kenny for a rest. He kept Linda and Tad with him at home.

It was so quiet in my guesthouse room. I had time to think, pray, and rest, which I had not had for months. I realized my family was a heaping handful! Raising three small children in the town of Jocotán was a constant challenge. I thanked the Lord many times for my nursing education and the assurance that I knew how to care for our children. But I also felt frustration as an idealistic young missionary nurse wanting to "do more for the Lord," while at the same time my little children needed my full attention. There was also a subtle undercurrent of criticism by other missionaries toward young missionary mothers as to whether we were doing our share of the ministry.

Then I remembered that one day back in our home in Jocotán Joyce had visited me.

"Hi, Joyce," I had called as she stopped by to bring some fruit from the market. I was rocking in the chair with baby Kenny on my left arm and Tad on my right.

"I thought I would stop by and see how you are," Joyce replied cheerfully.

"Joyce, all I can do is rock these little boys," I replied as tears came to my eyes. "I feel like I am useless as a missionary. I can only take care of my own children."

"Listen, Virginia, you are taking care of these little children for the Lord. That is your important ministry now," she counseled. "Later you will have more time to serve Him as missionary nurse to others." Her words, coming from an excellent veteran missionary, were more precious than gold to me that day. God gave me a new peace about caring for my family and fulfilling my responsibilities as a missionary nurse.

As I had time to reflect there in my room in Guatemala City, I realized I was feeling stronger and the culture shock around us seemed less. However, I was struggling with how to protect my children from diseases and yet love and minister to the Spanish and Indian people and not isolate ourselves from them. God reminded me in John 17:15–17 that we are to live *in* this world but not to be *of* this world. Likewise, Jesus has sent us to live in Jocotán but not to take on their beliefs and culture. He wanted me to just slow down, live one day at a time, and trust Him with all my heart.

Back home in Jocotán, the evenings were special times for our family when Ray came in from the villages. The kids loved to play with him, and he loved to play with them on the floor. I could fix the evening meal without too many interruptions. My heart was thankful to the Lord for our wonderful family.

Kenny was one year old and too little to defend himself, so he got pretty rough treatment sometimes from his big brother and sister. He became an expert at emptying waste baskets, drawers, and pulling stuff off the table to the floor such as cake batter.

One day I was trying to make two lemon meringue pies because visitors were coming. As I was stirring the pudding part, I heard Kenny gasp. I looked around to see that he had poured six egg whites down his front and on to the floor! I was so upset that I forgot to put the lemon in the pudding and the pies were terrible without lemon and without meringue.

On another day, Tad ran a fever of 103.8 degrees F. and had diarrhea. I examined him and diagnosed part of the situation as a bronchial infection and gave him medications for fever and diarrhea. I slept with him all night, but neither of us actually slept. The next morning his fever was almost normal and the diarrhea had stopped.

When all three kids and Ray and I had head lice, I scrubbed all of our heads with detergent and warm water. I refused to use kerosene on our scalps as the local "home remedies" suggested. I kept checking all of our heads. Apparently the detergent was effective because I did not see any more nits. Head lice were quite common among the children who probably got it from dogs, cats and chickens.

A couple months prior Kenny had dumped a waste paper basket on the floor and I had scolded him. He turned and went out the kitchen door, and he was so mad at me for scolding him that he stomped on the cat. A few hours later the mother cat delivered seven kittens in our closet. I was the one who had to give the kittens away after the mother weaned them. What a chain of events! And this was a glimpse into our daily lives the first two years in Jocotán.

4

New Lessons Learned

Virginia

Asmall village outside Chiquimula invited Ray to teach agriculture classes to the men and me to teach health and hygiene classes to the women. We gladly accepted the invitation. We took our three children with us and hired a village girl to watch Kenny while we taught these classes.

During my class I glanced up and saw Tad on the roof of the church. There was a tall ladder leaned up against the church roof and he loved to climb, so there he was. I stopped my class and sternly told him, "Tad, you get down right now!"

"Okay, Mommy," he replied.

Meanwhile, the women in my class gasped and gave many different suggestions on how to get him down.

"No," I replied, "he got up there, and he is a strong boy. He knows how to climb down the ladder by himself." But all of us watched as he carefully climbed down the ladder.

"Never do that again," I told him as I met him at the foot of the ladder. He hung his head, and I knew he heard me.

The class on health and hygiene resumed. After the class one of the families from the church invited us to eat supper with them. We felt it was important to build friendships with the people in the village churches, so we appreciated an invitation like this.

It was evening when our hostess told us the meal was ready, and on our way to the dining area I noticed a man sitting on the steps bent over, holding his stomach. He barely spoke to us and I wondered why. Later our hostess apologized that there were several in the household who were ill.

The meal of black beans, tortillas, white cheese, and cool coffee was tasty. All of us ate their gracious meal except for Kenny, who wanted to play with their cat instead of eating. I knew I had a bottle of milk for him in the truck, so I did not worry about him.

Exactly six weeks later Ray became sick. I took one look at his yellow skin and I knew he had hepatitis. Then four days later Tad and I had all the symptoms of hepatitis too. So John and Joyce drove Ray, Tad, and me to the Centro Medico Hospital in Guatemala City. Linda and Kenny stayed with our missionary friends Jack and Waynel Wing.

Then two days later, Linda walked into our hospital room. "Hi, Mommy and Daddy!" she gleefully called to us. Evelyn held on to her hand and led her into our room. Linda now also had hepatitis. She was happy to be with us, and we were so glad to see her. Now, all four of us were together in the same isolation room in the hospital.

While we were in the hospital, Ray's mother, Lydia Canfield flew to Guatemala to care for her grandson, Kenny, whom she had never met. He, too, was not sure who she was. She took care of him in the mission headquarters in Chiquimula. After eighteen days in the hospital, we were discharged to the Wycliff guest house in Guatemala City. We had a joyous reunion with Kenny, who had almost forgotten us. We recuperated there for two weeks and then returned to our home in Jocotán. It took us a couple months to completely get our strength back.

With our youthful zeal to reach out to the country people, we had disregarded the caution extended to us from the older more experienced missionaries. They had warned us about the risks of eating away from our own kitchens, but we wanted to communicate love and friendship to our friends in the village churches. We had decided that instead of isolating ourselves we would eat with them when invited.

Hepatitis brought to the forefront our dilemma between taking risks for the sake of fostering relationships, and protecting our health. On the one hand, as ambassadors representing the churches in the U.S., we needed to be good stewards of their trust. On the other hand, we realized that sometimes there is an economic and physical toll in missionary work. We were greatly encouraged by 2nd Corinthians 4:8,10 which reads, "...we are afflicted in every way, but not crushed; perplexed, but not despairing... that the life of Jesus also may be manifested in our body."

Linda's Injury

Clemencia Melara, the nurse in the Jocotán clinic, was taking four days off and asked me if I would work in the clinic in the afternoons for her. I jumped at the chance.

I carried Kenny in his infant seat. Tad, who was two, and Linda, who was almost four years old, walked with me to the clinic. We opened the clinic door, and three patients were waiting for attention. I sat Kenny's infant seat on the counter, and Tad and Linda ran out to play in the back patio.

Suddenly I heard Tad cry, "Mommy, Mommy come quick!"

I ran to the backyard. Linda and Tad had pushed a picket fence over, and a rusty nail had gone into Linda's knee under the knee cap. She was trying to get up and walk. I ran to her and grabbed the picket fence with the nail in her knee and pulled out the two-inch nail. I felt a sickening fear for her.

"And now how am I going to get all three kids home by myself?" I asked.

I quickly closed up the clinic, picked up Kenny with one arm, and told Linda to hang on to my neck and shoulder as I carried her. Tad hung on to my skirt as we trudged home the five blocks of rocky street.

When I arrived home, I explained the situation to Ray. We agreed to take her in our pickup to the Catholic clinic up on the hill where we heard a North American doctor was working.

I explained to the doctor from New York about the nail and he replied, "Oh, I'm sure you don't have anything to worry about, but I will give her an oral antibiotic if you insist." And he did.

We returned the one-and-a-half miles back home. That night she developed a fever and she began crying in pain. I gave her aspirin. The next day we returned to the Catholic clinic. Now Linda's fever was higher and she was in more pain.

"Oh my, she does have an infection," exclaimed the American doctor. "I'll just give her an injection of penicillin and that should take care of it." I was quickly losing trust in that doctor and began to wonder what was going to happen.

We took Linda back home, and she had so much pain that her lower leg was doubled back at the knee and her fever kept rising.

We told the pastor of the Jocotán Church, don Chon Vargas, "Linda is very sick with an infection in her knee."

"Have you prayed about this?" he asked us.

"Yes," I replied. "Ray and I have prayed."

"No," he said, "I mean let's have a prayer meeting here! I'm calling the elders of the church to come and pray now." And that is exactly what he did.

Within an hour, twenty-one Indian men and women and four children filed into our house to the bedroom and knelt around Linda's bed. They began to quietly call on the Lord: "Oh Lord God, hear our cry and help us. Please heal little Linda's knee."

It was such a comfort to hear them praying for Linda. At the same time I felt embarrassed that I, the missionary, needed to learn how to pray from humble brothers and sisters who knew how to sincerely call on the Lord.

Early the next morning, we packed all three kids in the truck and began the five-hour drive up the mountains to Guatemala City, to visit the emergency room in Centro Medico Hospital. During the trip Linda had a fever of 102 degrees, and her swollen leg was drawn up under her. We continued to pray.

Upon arrival to the medical center emergency room, the doctors examined her, took a thorough history, and consulted with specialists. They immediately began IV medications and admitted her to the pediatric department. Dr. Von Ahm explained they would give antibiotics intravenously around the clock and put her leg in traction to straighten it. He added, "I hope her body responds to the treatment so that amputation won't be necessary."

We decided that Ray would return to Jocotán with baby Kenny, and Tad and I would stay in the hospital with Linda. A couple of hours later while I was standing at Linda's bedside, a young MD resident came in to check on her.

"How did this happen?" he asked me. "Why didn't you get help sooner?" I explained the whole story.

"Well, listen to me, a puncture wound here in Central America is always an emergency!" he admonished. "Tetanus antitoxin is always given along with large doses of antibiotics."

I took his wise advice to heart. I realized contrary to my nursing education that taught me to always follow doctor's orders, I should have trusted my own medical judgment in this case. This was a turning point in my nursing practice. I needed to follow the good education I had been taught and apply the plan of treatment that it gave me. I had to have the courage to work alone when necessary. Later on, I realized that God wanted me to exercise leadership as a missionary nurse.

I stood by Linda's bed praying and crying out to the Lord, "*Why has this happened to us, Lord?*" Immediately I sensed a presence around me like someone was very close. At first I thought maybe Ray had come back, so I turned to look—no one was there.

But the presence continued and I prayed, *"Lord, why did this happen? Please heal Linda."*

Then I heard a voice—not audible, but a definite voice—say, "I will go with you through this." And then it was gone. God knew exactly what I needed at that moment. I needed His assurance and presence. My heart was strengthened with a deep peace because I knew He was right there with me and He would help me. The deep sadness was lifted and I praised Him. He did not promise to heal her, but His presence and assurance was sufficient for me.

Two days later Linda's temperature began to slowly come down, and little by little the swelling diminished. After eight days of hospitalization, she and I were discharged. We returned to Jocotán, and four weeks later Linda walked again. Through all of this the Lord had many lessons for me to learn and remember, and I thanked Him for them.

Ray

Since the Chortí were deprived of classroom education, nature had become their teacher. At first, a Westerner like me looked with skepticism at the "signs" of nature that the Indians followed in making decisions. I looked at them as nothing more than unfounded superstitions practiced because their ancestors had believed in them.

But I asked myself, *were not a lot of our own understandings (beliefs) based on observations that repeated themselves over time, long before "science" confirmed them to be true?* So why should we dispute the Chortí when he says the time to plant corn is three days after the new moon? Interestingly enough, after years of keeping rain records (a controlled study) we affirmed that there is more rain during the phase of the new moon than at any other time. They also believed they must cut down a tree for lumber only on the waning of the moon or it would be attacked by wood weevils or rot. This also was found to be true.

A wide variety of plants had been recognized to have medicinal qualities and used in ancient cultures for treating a multitude of sicknesses and diseases. Now today many of our modern medicines are synthesized from those plants. Therefore, rather than totally discounting or being skeptical of their beliefs, we tried to learn from these people who had looked to nature for guidance for thousands of years.

We know the Creator God is a God of order, so it should not be a surprise that these people had found direction from God's creation. Many of their practices, however, were only as reliable as the variances in natural cycles. But most of them were consistent enough over time that they had something to go by when there was nothing else.

But I had a hard time giving credence to some of their beliefs. For example, they believed the way the mango tree bloomed in February told them whether it would be a good growing season or not, still four months away.

One of the oddest beliefs was what they called the *cabañuelas*, a practice used to predict the weather for the whole year. Each of the first twelve days of the year, January 1 through 12, represented a month—January 1 for January, January 2 for February, etc. On each day they would go out early in the morning and take note of the sky, the horizon, and the wind. All day long until sunset they would make those observations, especially noting the cloud formations and the temperature. Each day they would do this and then make a prediction at the end of the twelfth day what the year's weather would be.

Another Machete Fight

Virginia

The Chortí population was increasing, which meant there were always more mouths to feed from the same amount of land. The result being that the Chortí had succumbed to quarrelling, stealing, fighting, and even murdering to secure and protect what they had in order to survive.

It was Friday morning, and Ray had just left home to take visitors back to Chiquimula in the pickup truck, when a little boy came to our door.

"Hello, doña Virginia," he greeted me. "Could you take my dad to the hospital in Chiuquimula?"

"What happened to him?" I asked.

"He fought with his brother," the boy replied.

So I accompanied the boy to the mayor's office to see the situation.

Oh my goodness, I thought. *I have never seen in my life a human being cut up so badly, bleeding and in shock, yet he is talking.* His skull was just about cracked open from the top down, his arm was about severed in two places, both shoulders were slit, and a thumb was almost amputated. Ashes and hair were in all the wounds to control the hemorrhaging.

The story was that this man fought with his brother after drinking in a local tavern. At 6:00 p.m., the family carried this severely injured man up the mountain to his home in the village of Pelillo Negro so he could die at home. At 10:00 p.m. seeing that he was still alive, the neighbors decided to carry him back down the mountain to Jocotan on a crude stretcher for medical help. They arrived in Jocotán at 4:00 a.m. The other fighter was able to walk with them. Soon John drove the two men, along with a policeman, to the hospital in Chiquimula for sutures and treatment.

These people faced anger and desperation daily. *"Lord, what do You want us to do about all of this?"* I prayed.

Ray

Once again, we braced ourselves to face yet one more drought. Homer remembered the conversation he had had earlier with the agricultural attaché at the United States embassy in Guatemala City. He had explained the plight of the Chortí Indians and what he was trying to do to help them. The attaché's response was, "Those people should be moved out of that God-forsaken place into the coastal planes where land is cheap and rains are plentiful."

So we gathered the Chortí men together after one church service and asked them if they were willing to move to the coastal low lands. *No* was the answer. That was too much for them to consider. They were Indians and the Jocotán villages had been their homes for generations. To go to a land they knew nothing about was too much for them to fathom. Also because of stories they had heard, they were deathly afraid of tigers, snakes and diseases that would kill them in that unknown land.

What could be done to help them? We offered a compromise: If we could find land to rent for one season on the coast, would they be willing to go and plant a corn crop to get them through the drought? Finally out of desperation twenty-five men agreed to go.

Homer made a quick trip to the coastal area of the department of Izabal, and through our church contacts there, he located a man who was farming land across the Motagua River. The United Fruit Company had abandoned this land some years earlier because of the Panama Disease that wiped out the banana plantings. This was very fertile land. Our friend agreed to let the Chortí plant as much land as they needed with the understanding that they would clear the land and leave it after they harvested their corn.

The timing was perfect. The fall weather on the coast was ideal for planting corn. The twenty-five men quickly joined together to plan and gather their supplies. They enlisted the help of three women to accompany them to cook the meals. They all piled into a bus for the one-hundred-mile trip to the village of Dartmouth.

When they arrived, they were confronted by a daunting obstacle. They had to cross the wide Motagua River in dugout canoes. None of these people had ever crossed a body of water on a boat before. Great fear set in as they contemplated the crossing. There was some legitimate reason for concern because the river was about three hundred feet across and had a moderate current. Dugout canoes were made from hollowed out tree trunks that range from twenty to thirty feet long and two and a half to three feet wide. Because they were long, narrow and had a rounded bottom, they were very unstable and tipped easily. The boat operator, while standing in the boat, would use a long pole to push against the bottom of the river. He moved the dugout across the river in this way, while keeping the bow faced into the current.

After that first crossing, they were more at ease about being on water. On the other side they walked about one third of a mile to where they set up camp and would be working. The work took several weeks. Homer did not stay with them once they were established and the work was organized, but he visited them regularly.

The men were planting their corn fields in an area where guerilla rebels were in a conflict with the government soldiers. The Chortí farmers were inadvertently in harm's way. One day, while they were working, the army came into their camp and arrested all the men. The three women were terrified, thinking they would be raped, beaten, or killed. Everyone was praying for protection. The next day the men were released and returned to the camp, finding that God had answered their prayers and nothing had happened to the women. The corn crop had matured enough so they could all leave and go back to Jocotán to avoid more conflicts.

After a period of time a report came to Jocotán that the corn had done very well and was ready for harvest. So the entire group of farmers boarded a bus and traveled back to Dartmouth, this time with much more confidence and a feeling of hope. They were going to harvest corn at a time when there was no corn in their villages and the next harvest was still eight months away. They crossed the Motagua River again and hiked out to their crops with a sense of expectation.

The harvest took longer than any of the men had ever expected. The plants were tall and the ears large and full. The unhusked corn was packed into twine nets with a draw string. A full net would weigh between 125 and 150 pounds. Each had to be carried the one-third mile back to the river on a man's back. Considering that an average Chortí man weighed about 110 pounds, it was astounding the strength these men had. Dugout canoes moved the corn and men across the river. Then the corn was loaded on a large truck for the trip back to Jocotán. The truck was full, even over the six-foot sides. When it entered the town and pulled up beside the mission, there was an excitement that had not been experienced in a long, long time. In the midst of the famine in the area, there was now a new hope.

After the corn harvest at Dartmouth, we asked the Chortí farmers again if they would be willing to move permanently to land like they saw there. Again they refused. The rains had begun in Jocotán and the drought was over. They did not have the courage to move away from what was familiar.

However, this was not a futile experience. God used it to teach new lessons, not only for us missionaries but also for the Chortí people. The significance of this project was multifaceted. First and foremost, it provided food for twenty-five families plus extended family members, and they had corn to sell at a time when they had run out of options. Secondly, the men were exposed to a land that was productive beyond anything they had ever imagined. Thirdly, their fears of tigers, snakes, diseases and even the fear of riding in boats on the water had been overcome, because they had all returned safely. And fourthly, it had opened their eyes to a fertile land that would provide an abundance of food for their families.

But they were unable to think of permanently moving from their ancestral land. They would let life go on as usual. The reality was that we were living and working with a people that existed in constant poverty and desperately needed help.

5

Corn, Chickens and Soybeans

Ray

I n our hearts we knew there was little we could do on a large enough scale to help the Chortí people out of poverty. But Homer and I were willing to pour ourselves into doing as much as we possibly could.

Our resources were limited. Our thoughts turned to how we could best reach as many people as possible. There were probably two or three hundred Chortí chrisitans scattered out in many of the villages. Our decision was to work with the believers and encourage them to take the new teachings back to the wider communities where they lived.

In order to help the Chortí Indian people where they lived, we had to come to grips with certain realities. Any agricultural help had to be applicable to the land that was already being farmed. No more land was available to them for expansion.

It was clear these people had not changed their ways of farming for perhaps hundreds of years. We knew they would not change easily, or at all, just because some foreigners came and told them there were better ways of farming. Therefore any new ideas that we presented would have to be demonstrated, and the demonstrations would have to succeed for them to even consider trying something new.

After considerable time evaluating the situation, we agreed on the following five areas that we could work on to hopefully improve the lives of the Chortí people:

- Increase the productivity of the land they had.
- Introduce new agricultural crops that were not land intensive.
- Improve the quality of their yard animals and introduce new ones.
- Train the men in non-farming skills.
- Again try to move the people off their land to a more productive area.

Our biggest concern was to increase corn production. These were Mayan Indians, "men of corn." If they had not eaten corn tortillas with a meal, they felt like they had not eaten at all! If there was nothing else to eat, they would survive with a few tortillas and maybe a little salt. But they had to have their tortillas.

Increasing corn production on the steep hillsides and worn out, heavily-eroded rocky land was a big challenge. We would dedicate much time and effort to corn.

There was a piece of land for sale along the river that ran past Jocotán. It was about four acres, with a gentle slope and would suit our purposes fine for teaching new farming methods and crops. So it was purchased. A pump and irrigation system was installed and work began.

This was an important economical help for these families during difficult times. We set up a schedule where the villagers alternated work time, each working just one week. Every morning before work began there was a devotional time of reading the Bible and prayer. The initial work consisted of clearing the overgrown land.

After the clearing of the land was finished, the work continued as the men, under our supervision, planted and cared for the crops. After a few weeks of not working, the men would cycle back in for another week of work. They could then see the changes and the results of using new methods as well as learn about new crops.

Hybrid seed corn was now available in Guatemala City, and we acquired some for our trials. Using fresh, new seed and fertilizer, we also incorporated different planting techniques as a part of the teaching.

Alongside our hybrid plots we planted a section using their seed and had them plant it their way. Their method was to take a stick that had been cut with a tapered end, make a small hole in the ground, drop in three to five seeds, knock a little soil over them, take one step (about three feet) and repeat the process. At the end of the field they would take one step over and come back. Therefore, the corn was planted on three-foot centers in rows and between rows. This system is called hill planting.

There were multiple problems with this method of planting. First, there were too many seeds in a small space which was a waste of seed. Secondly, crowding resulted in root systems that could not develop well and competed for the water and nutrients that were available. Thirdly, the corn stalks could be easily broken and blown over. Fourthly, not all plants that grew would produce an ear of corn, and all the ears were small.

Several plots of hybrid corn were planted as trials using different methods. The men planted one using their technique for planting but with hybrid seed. This was going to bring some improved yield, but our goal was to show how to get more corn on the same land by using different techniques. We also planted on the contour, a technique of planting across a slope of the hillside, to demonstrate how to prevent soil erosion.

The number of seeds and the spacing were going to be the main emphasis in our teaching. Using the same sharpened stick to make the hole, they dropped in only two seeds. The next hole was only *one foot* away. In one plot the rows were three feet apart, like their plantings. In another we used two-and-a-half feet between rows. All the trials were irrigated the same, and all the hybrid trials were fertilized with chemical fertilizer.

The results were magnificent. We made sure that as many men from the villages as possible participated and learned as we explained the demonstrations and the results. The trial that did the best was the one that had rows two-and-a-half feet apart. Corn planted their customary way, but using hybrid seed, produced more corn. But in no way did it compare with the new planting method.

We were very pleased with our work and the results. Then a shocking reality check came. When asked how many of them would like to buy hybrid seed corn for their next planting, *no one* responded. We continued to encourage them, but to no avail.

Finally one of the church men explained, "Thank you for showing us what can be done, but look," he said, "you are gringos [foreigners]. You have deep, rich river bottom land. Our own land is soil that is worn out and rocky. You can afford gasoline for a pump to irrigate your land. You have money to buy fertilizer and new seed every year. We do not. We are Indians. It will not work for us on our land."

They were right. What we were able to demonstrate with great success was not reproducible by them in any way. What we had was a very successful failure. We would no longer talk about hybrid seed corn.

Meanwhile, the purchased land continued to provide the men with work, instruction, inspiration and fellowship. New crops to that area were introduced, such as different vegetables, peanuts, tomatoes, onions, and cantaloupe. Cantaloupe and the large tomatoes were especially successful.

Insect pests and plant diseases were big problems in that climate. The identification of the pests, and the use of appropriate pesticides and in the correct dosage were important parts of our teaching. But here again we were introducing concepts that, for a people living virtually outside of the economy, were not feasible. They did not have the money to purchase insecticides and fungicides. However, we were planting seeds in their minds of better ways, and perhaps in some future time their lives would improve.

Demonstration Plots in Villages

After our apparent failure in promoting hybrid corn, we went in another direction using open-pollinated corn. The Ministry of Agriculture of the Guatemalan government had been developing new open-pollinated varieties of corn. Kernels from these varieties could be selected and replanted with predictable results for several years. Open pollenated corn had been used for centuries before hybridization became popular. The problem for the Chortí was that their seed had not been replaced for generations. Gradually it had degenerated, resulting in weak plants and small ears. Purchasing the government's new seed, we set out on a different approach.

The demonstration plots would be transferred to the villages and carried out on their land. In as many villages as possible we looked for at least one farmer who had land along a main path that led into and out of their village. These men had to be willing to plant the new corn seed that we provided and plant it the way we instructed. Those who agreed to do this would get to keep the harvest.

One of the villages where we wanted to plant a corn demonstration plot was Matazano. Leandro, a faithful believer and good friend, lived there, and he was well respected in his village. Although Leandro had very little land, he did have a piece along the main trail leading from Jocotán into Matazano and beyond to the next small village.

We had not seen Leandro at church so I decided to pay him a visit. Planting time was approaching. I needed to know if he was willing to dedicate that small plot of land by the trail for our trial.

The April weather was atrociously hot, so I left early in the morning. Winding my way out of town to the Jocotán River, I gingerly walked across the hammock bridge, also known as a swinging bridge. Both terms are very descriptive of the action one encounters while walking the 150 feet to the other side on a bouncing bridge while the water rushes beneath you.

The village of Matazano was not very far from Jocotán, only about a forty-minute walk, but it was a very steep climb. The village which was situated on a narrow mountainous shelf of land, had only about twelve or fifteen homes, all of them with thatch roofs, stick walls and dirt floors.

Leandro's first wife had died. He married Calixtra, and they had two lovely daughters. When I arrived at the house, Calixtra greeted me warmly with her ever-present smile.

"We missed you at church on Sunday," I said. "I need to talk to Leandro. I assume he is in the fields preparing the land for planting. Where can I find him?"

"Sorry we didn't get to town last Sunday," Calixtra said. "We were not well. Leandro is here, back behind the house in the lean-to shed. Go on back."

Leandro was lying in a hammock in the shade under the palm roof of the shed. "Hello," he said, greeting me warmly in his quiet manner. "Welcome to Matazano. It is good to see you. What brings you to our village?"

I was perplexed and could not really grasp what was going on. It was mid-morning and much too early to have finished the day's work. The rains would come soon. Everyone was preparing land for planting. This was a busy time of year. Still, here was Leandro lying in the hammock.

"Are you sick?" I asked cautiously, picking up on what Calixtra had said about not being in town last Sunday.

"No, not really," Leandro replied with a typical smile, the only real expression of emotion most Chortí demonstrate, especially in awkward situations.

I paused and thought a minute and then moved on to explain the purpose of my visit. Leandro was more than willing to be part of our village demonstration project. It helped that he would receive the improved variety of corn seed and the fertilizer free. When I explained that he would get to keep the harvest as well, he was excited.

Before I left, I engaged in general talk about farming and life in the village. "So, Leandro, it looks like you have finished preparing your land before the rains."

"No. I have a lot to do still. I'm not sure I will be ready," he said with the characteristic smile but looking away.

Not sure how to proceed, I said, with an encouraging tone, "It's early; maybe you could still get some more work done today."

"No, not today," he said. "You see, we don't have much to eat. I worked yesterday. Today I will rest and eat a few tortillas and whatever Calixtra can find. The Lord willing I will have enough energy to be able to work tomorrow."

I did not know how to go forward with the conversation. I felt deep shock and sadness because I had never faced hunger this severe. It was hard for me to comprehend the idea of working one day, and then resting and eating a little bit to have energy to work the next.

"Well, I need to be getting back to town," I murmured. "But first let me pray for you, that God will provide the energy you need to get the land ready to plant."

We said, "Good-bye," but he never got up from his hammock.

I met up with Homer a little farther down the trail. As we started down the mountainside there was a long silence. When the conversation picked up we were both thinking the same thoughts. There was little we could do to permanently help people like Leandro and Calixtra and their beautiful girls.

We were praying that there would be adequate rains. The people desperately needed a good harvest. Also, our demonstration plots would fail without the rains. If they failed, the farmers would lose trust in us, and the progress we were making would be set back.

This effort was going to take a lot of supervision. We wanted to be present for the planting and the follow-up. Our instruction to the participants was to plant on the contour. They were to plant two seeds per hole, one foot apart in the rows, and there would be thirty inches between the rows.

God answered our prayers, and the rains came on time and continued through the growing season. When the plants were six- to eight-inches tall, we took fertilizer to the plots and had the owner apply it as we instructed.

By this time there was quite a buzz in the villages because the new planting method was obviously successful. Once the fertilizer took effect, the contrast was undeniable. On one side of the path a thick patch of tall, deep-green corn stood where the farmer planted it using our methods. And on the other side, where they used their traditional methods, stood sparsely planted corn with a yellow color and short, thin stalks. By harvest time most people were inquiring about the new corn. The following planting season we had plenty of seed available, which we sold at a reduced price, and a lot of people wanted it.

In contrast to the hybrid trials, on the river bottom, this one was a success! It was successful for a variety or reasons. We used a new and improved open-pollinated corn variety (not hybrid) that they could save seed from for next year's planting. We had the Chortí farmers plant it on their own land. They used a new planting technique that was easy to learn and resulted in more productive plants per unit of land. It demonstrated the positive effects fertilizer had on their land. And by planting these demonstrations along the main trails and having it succeed, it inspired many others to want to have that seed the next planting season.

The bad news was that new and improved varieties generally need good soil in order to produce up to their expectations. With the shallow, poor, rocky soil of the Chortí land, it was the fertilizer that produced good results on the poor land. But fertilizer was expensive, and this was the limiting factor in a virtually moneyless society. While animal manure was an option, the Chortí had only a few small animals that could not supply adequate fertilizer for their corn fields.

Corn Yield Contest

After the success of the demonstration plots along the trails in the villages we went one step further. A "corn yield contest" was sponsored to encourage the Chortí men to put into practice, on their own, the changes we were recommending to increase corn production.

The contest took place in the villages on the individuals' land. People from the villages of Pelillo Negro, Guareruche, and Matazano signed up to participate. The amount of land used for the contest would be one "tarea." A tarea in the Jocotán area is an officially recognized unit of land measuring twelve arm lengths squared. If a man worked for wages, a tarea is the amount of land he had to cover in a day.

The new corn production factors that had been introduced were reviewed for the contestants, such as using the best seed, planting on the contour, spacing of seeds in the row, spacing between rows, and using fertilizer. However, each contestant was on his own to produce as much corn on his tarea as possible. He had to make his own decisions and do the work himself.

At harvest time the picking of the corn was supervised so only corn from the designated land was included in the contest. Then all the corn was shelled and weighed. Not too many men participated in the contest, but there was considerable interest in the results.

The overwhelming winner was a young man, Gonzalo, from the village of Gareruche. He was the son of Ismael, one of the early Chortí believers. Gonzalo was an active member of the youth group in the Jocotán Church. Gonzalo obviously had some money to spend on this adventure. He not only used the new variety of seed and planted according our guidelines, he also applied an abundance of fertilizer.

Prizes were handed out at a special ceremony in the church. The first prize was a pair of pants and a shirt. The second prize was a pair of pants. The third prize was a shirt.

There was a significant difference between the corn yield contest and the demonstration plots along the village trails. In the demonstration plots the missionaries gave instruction and provided the seed and fertilizer. In the corn yield contest, the missionary had no participation; all the decisions were made by the Chortí.

The results of the corn yield contest successfully met our expectations. It showed that they could produce more corn on their land by changing the ways they farmed.

Rats and Weevils

In the villages, the unhusked corn was piled in a corner of their huts and shelled out daily for making tortillas. Unfortunately, there were two enemies of the stored corn: rats and weevils. The farmers were able to do battle against the rats with their machetes but could never eradicate them. They had no recourse against the weevils. The loss of their small, precious corn supply year after year because of the weevils was devastating to an already severely impoverished people.

We felt there was a solution. We contacted a sheet metal worker in town and together designed a round grain storage container. Each had a six-inch opening at the top for filling and a four-inch opening at the bottom for taking the corn out. These two openings were covered with almost airtight caps.

These containers became popular and were sold to the men for a nominal price, which they could pay off over time. Since they were made from tin, they were not heavy, but they were bulky. For transporting these bins up to the villages, the men would put a strap around it, back up to it, loop the strap over their forehead, tilt it against their back, and take off. It was quite a sight to see the five-foot tall Chortí man carrying this eight foot metal container through town and up the trail to his house.

All of the corn that was stacked in the house was shelled and put in their new containers. Immediately the rats were out of luck. However, the weevils and their eggs were already in the corn kernels, so the corn once in the container, had to be treated. There was a safe pill available for treating stored grain pests, and this had to be put in with the grain in order to kill the weevils. The families using the grain storage units now had their limited harvests protected.

Burning

Probably their most devastating practice was cutting back the old corn stalks and weeds and burning them. This was a practice not only of the Indians but of the Ladino farmers. The first storms of the season brought heavy rains with wind, lightning, and thunder. The obvious danger was erosion of the soil off the steep hillsides that had been burned clean of any plant material.

When we inquired as to the reasons for this practice of burning their land, we received a variety of answers:

- Corn needed clean land to grow on.
- The worms that ate the center of the corn stalks were killed by burning them.
- It sent smoke up to the sky making clouds that would then bring rain.
- It was what they had always done!

Keeping these beliefs in mind, we began a campaign to educate the people to not burn off the old stocks and weeds before planting. I used their list of reasons as a launching pad to encourage them to discontinue the practice of burning. The training involved considering the following observations:

- Where does soil come from? It comes from the dead plants that over time break down and become new soil. By eliminating the dead plant matter, you are preventing the creation of new soil.
- With no organic matter on top of the soil, it is exposed to the rain and washed away. It ends up on your neighbors' land and eventually in the river and is lost forever. That captured their attention because they were not interested in giving any soil to their neighbors.
- If the worms were in the corn stalks and you burned the stalks to kill them, why did you still have worms the next year? Teaching this lesson after the harvest and before burning, we would go out to their dry corn stalks and look for worms. They would never find any. I explained a beetle's life cycle: When the corn dried, the worm would eat its way out of the stalk and fall to the ground. It would burrow underground about four to six inches and when the field was burned, it was protected. When the corn started growing the next spring, they would emerge.

51

- If smoke made rain and you burned your land every year, why are there so many years when it does not rain? The process of explaining the making of clouds and rain was long and complicated and difficult for the men to grasp. Our only objective was to teach them that smoke does not make rain, but decaying plant matter does make soil.

- By doing it the way you always have, is your life getting better by doing it that way? Their answer was always that their crops were not getting better; in fact, they were getting worse.

So what were the results of all this teaching? Actually, in the short run very few men changed their ways and stopped burning. Tradition, old beliefs, and their fatalistic nature of defeat was more than most could overcome. However, some years later the government took steps to curb burning by educating the farmers using some of these same teachings.

The Introduction of New Crops

Because land was a limited resource, we needed to keep in mind that anything we introduced related to land use would be taking the place of their essential corn. That was going to be a formidable task, as corn was first and last in the minds of the Chortí.

There were two crops we introduced that had great potential. The first was grain sorghum, also known as milo maize. Sorghum had some distinct advantages. It could be planted with the corn toward the end of the first rainy season, getting established before the next dry period. Its biggest advantage was that it is quite drought tolerant. It would finish maturing during the fall rains even when they were very limited. The taste of sorghum was accepted and liked by the people as a corn substitute and held together well in the making of tortillas.

This would have become a very important crop except for one thing: the birds. The grain head of sorghum is exposed on the end of the stalk and has no covering like an ear of corn. The birds would harvest the crop! When the grain head was present, someone had to be in the field from dawn to sundown. Often it was a losing battle as it seemed like the birds were as hungry as the people and would not be easily dissuaded. However, the advantages were strong, and grain sorghum became, to some degree, an established crop.

The second new crop was soybeans. Soybeans were available in Guatemala but not on a large scale. It was mostly planted by the Asian population for making soy sauce. It is very high in protein, something the Chortí diet lacked. We planted some on our river bottom land to see if it grew well in our area, and if it did, we would have seed for trial plantings in the villages. Soybeans did grow very well, so we made some tortillas from it to see if the people liked it. Pure soybean tortillas were not palatable. The taste was too different. After trying several mixtures we found one that the people really liked. Tortillas with a combination of one-third soybeans and two-thirds corn were liked by everyone who tried them. Men who ate tortillas made with the soybean mix testified that they had more energy and could work longer than usual.

One of the blessings of making tortillas with soybeans was that nothing new or complicated had to be learned. This was an important hurdle because these people were resistant to adapting to new practices. The dry corn and soybeans were mixed together, and then all of the steps of making tortillas were the same as before.

So up to the villages we went with soy seed. This variety was a compact plant that could be spaced close together so not much of their corn land had to be sacrificed, which helped in the acceptance of this new crop. Soon we discovered that like anything in that area, there were problems. The worn-out rocky condition of the soil was always the most formidable. They would have to use fertilizer in order to have any kind of a decent harvest, and that expense would seriously limit the planting of soybeans. And while insects continued to be a problem, something appeared that we had not had to deal with before. The wild rabbits decided soybean plants were the best thing they had ever tasted!

For the most part the soybean project was a losing battle as the farmers did not have the resources necessary to catch or kill the rabbits. This wonderful new source of protein was in jeopardy of being lost, and very few families continued planting soybeans. Trapping the rabbits was something that could be developed, and we determined to get back to the project.

Our experiment with soybeans, however, attracted quite a bit of attention. I do not know how word spread so far, but one day a reporter and photographer from the second largest newspaper in Guatemala, *El Imparcial*, came to Jocotán to interview us about the high protein "wonder bean" that can be used in tortillas to greatly improve the health of the poor people. A few days later a feature article appeared complete with pictures and quotes. Of course we did not mention anything about the very healthy rabbits that were now living in the villages!

The Chortí diet was seriously lacking vitamins, so we turned to vegetable gardening as a possible improvement in their nutrition. We requested assistance from a U.S. relief organization for our vegetable garden project. They happily provided several dozen boxes of basic hand tools (shovels, hoes, cultivators, etc.) and a very large quantity of seeds.

The seeds were of every imaginable kind of vegetable and some flowers. Many were not applicable to the Jocotán climate and/or to the Chortí diet but many were. We gave them instructions in Spanish and as many tips as possible on preparing the soil and growing vegetables.

Gardens could be planted close to the house where they could be easily tended. Any excess water that was brought into the house (which was very little) could be put on the garden plants. In addition to the rabbits, the pigs, turkeys and chickens also became a problem to the garden project. For that reason, people in town were more likely to have success with vegetable gardens than in the villages.

Improving the Yard Animals

Most of the Chortí families had a few small animals such as chickens, one or two pigs and a turkey in their yards. The pigs had to be cared for carefully and often they were more trouble than they were worth. None of the animals were fenced in or caged, and pigs would wander extensively. They would root up anything planted in their roaming area, which often included the neighbor's crops. This resulted in serious fighting between families. We put pigs on a low priority at this time.

Turkeys and chickens did not pose the extent of problems that pigs did, but they were scrawny and certainly not very meaty. They would scratch and eat bugs, and when the corn water was thrown out they would get a few nuggets. The moldy or otherwise undesirable corn was thrown on the ground in the yard for them to eat, and that was the extent of their food. Because of these very harsh conditions, the animals that survived were a very hardy species.

Homer and Evelyn had an idea that would improve the quality of their turkeys. Making a trip to the U.S., they shared their idea with a turkey farmer. The farmer donated two dozen fertile turkey eggs, which the Sharplesses carried on their laps on the flight during their return to Guatemala.

As soon as possible, the eggs were distributed to Chortí families that had turkeys. Thankfully, some of these eggs hatched and as the chicks grew and developed, the people were pleased to see a bigger, stronger bird. Nutrition was going to be the key factor as to whether this improved strain of meaty turkeys would survive the stark existence in a Chortí family compound. However, like improved strains of anything, this would take special treatment. Would the families be willing to sacrifice a little more corn or find other supplements to nurture these birds to market size?

Well, God showed favor on the turkey project, and some grew into fine big birds. The next step was to breed some of the imported turkeys together to maintain the pure strain, and breed some with their native turkeys to improve that very resistant breed of birds. This project worked well and helped several families. It was unfortunate that they were limited in space and feed and could only raise three or four birds at a time.

Chickens that had survived in the villages were also by definition a tough breed. While their egg production was not very high, they did provide a healthy food source for the family if they were eaten rather than sold. Only the old, tough hens that stopped laying eggs were eaten or sold at the market.

Putting to work our Western minds, we came up with the idea of caged laying hens. That would allow them to raise many more chickens in their small yards. Baby chicks of the very high-producing white leghorn chickens were available in the capital. We were sure we could safely transport them the 120 miles to Jocotán. Because of the high cost of this project, we were only going to offer it to two or three families as a business, and we would subsidize it out of our operating budget. This included preparing a place in Jocotán to raise the chicks from two-day-olds to the pullet stage when they were ready to start laying eggs. We also needed to purchase and assemble the metal cages at the site where the hens would be housed.

The main project was in the village of Guararuche, about a two-hour walk from Jocotán. Ismael, one of our trusted church leaders in the village, wanted to do this project. He was an older man and the father of sixteen-year-old Gonzalo. He began with two hundred hens. The feed had to be special ordered and carried up to the village each week.

When the first eggs were produced and taken to the market, wouldn't you know it? Nobody wanted to buy them! "White eggs? Who wants white eggs? Eggs are supposed to be brown," they said.

When word got out that there were no roosters with the caged hens, the fate of the caged hen project was almost finished. In the eyes of the people, the only good eggs were the brown "eggs of love" from hens running loose with roosters.

So we looked for a market for white eggs, which we found in our own mission system. The Friends Christian School and the Friends Bible School in Chiquimula each had a kitchen, and they agreed to buy the eggs weekly. The logistics of getting eggs from the village to the schools were daunting.

Gonzalo made the two-hour walk down the mountain with a twenty-dozen crate of eggs on his back. He put the crate on top of a bus for a twenty-mile ride on a gravel road to the bus depot in Chiquimula. Then he carried them again across town to the schools. Miraculously, very few would break. On the way back to the village he would carry a hundred-pound bag of feed. Next week he did the same thing.

This was a profitable business for Gonzalo and Ismael, but the labor was hard. Then when the school year was over and the schools closed, they had no big market for the eggs until three months later when the schools opened again. The only thing they could do was sell the hens and then start again with new ones.

Another successful project that we introduced to the villagers was beehives. There was a market for honey and some families already had bees, usually in hollowed-out logs. With wooden hives and foundation comb, production was higher and easier to control and harvest.

The Dyer family, beekeepers from California, donated four queen bees, which were carried on a plane to Guatemala by another missionary. These queen bees were successfully introduced to four hives in Guareruche, and honey production increased even more.

This idea was popular with some of the people and it provided an economic help. The honey-extraction method used by the people was crude and wasteful, so we looked for a honey extractor.

In Guatemala City we contacted a German buyer and seller of honey who also sold equipment. He was interested in who we were and why we wanted an extractor. We described our ministry with the Friends Mission in Eastern Guatemala and how we were helping an impoverished Indian group.

He asked us again who we worked with, so we explained a little about the Friends Church and our history from the Quakers of England. He sat in silence for some time, and then said, "In Germany, after the war, we had nothing. Our home and our town were destroyed, there was no work, and we were starving. The first people who came to our aid with food and clothing were the Quakers. They literally saved our lives. You will have your honey extractor, and it will cost you nothing."

We recognized this as a divinely-appointed moment. Our German friend had an opportunity to repay an old debt and say thank you. For us it was another sign that God was using many different ways and means to help the Chortí people survive and have a better life. The unit we were given was a large, hand-cranked, four-frame extractor. It served for many years being carried from house to house and village to village among the Chortí people.

Skill Training

Our next step was contacting some tradesmen in town who would be willing to teach their skills to some Chortí men. These were Ladino men, which was a breakthrough in itself as they would normally not reach out to help the Indians, especially if it meant competing with them for sales. The favorable response was probably due to the fact that our Mission had been present in Jocotán for more than twenty years, and the missionaries and the believers had an excellent reputation among the townspeople.

Three or four Chortí men started as apprentices with a tailor and a couple of men started to work with a carpenter. The mission lent money to the tailors for treadle sewing machines and to the carpenters for their wood-working tools. Because of the famine these men were willing to move to town to learn a useful skill. Over time they paid their loans and indeed were able to provide for their families in a meaningful way.

When the agricultural ministry among the Chortí was going well, and there were two of us missionaries, we were able to visit other villages and towns when invited by interested believers. We were able to give classes in the Ladino communities and still follow through on the projects in the Jocotán area.

It is worthwhile to note here that the political climate in Guatemala had changed drastically. By the late 1960's the military had subdued the Communist guerilla movement in eastern Guatemala. The guerillas that survived went into hiding. The decade of the 1970's was to be a time of peace and relative prosperity for the people of Guatemala. The emergence of a middle class, that until now was nominal, began to grow rapidly. This peaceful time certainly made our ministry easier as we could move through the region without worry.

The U.S. government played a pivotal role in bringing peace through a program of "pacification." The philosophy of this program was to build trust in the government in order to turn the people away from supporting the guerilla movement. Interestingly enough, a big part of their program was to improve the farming in rural areas through a program that was known as the Mobile Agriculture School. It was operated by the Guatemalan government and taught by agricultural specialists.

The Mobile School classes had been publicized in eastern Guatemala for a period of time when we met one of the top leaders of the program in Chiquimula. He was frustrated because the farmers would not attend the classes. When he heard that we had been having success with classes in the area he asked for our help, especially in the municipal centers. The program was solid and we could see how it would benefit the rural farmers greatly, so we agreed to help.

When we went to our church people in those towns, they informed us that they were not interested because it was a government program. They had never trusted anything from the government or any of its representatives. However, if we recommended the classes, they would be willing to attend and encourage others in the towns and villages to attend. From then on the Mobile Agriculture School had no more trouble organizing classes in eastern Guatemala where there were Friends Churches. We also made sure the Chortí Indians would be included in these courses. The officials were more than happy to comply with whatever we asked because without the Friends Mission support, their program would have had very limited success.

The Option of Moving the People

While some of the relief projects that were introduced brought moderate success, they still did not accomplish the over-arching success that we had hoped for in bringing about lasting improvement to the quality of life of the Chortí people. We once again turned to our final remaining option for helping these Indian people. That option was to move them off the land where they had no hope and no future. Obviously this would be a huge undertaking, and we needed to be sure it was the right thing to do. God would have to give us great wisdom and energy.

Jocotán, Guatemala

A Home on the steep mountains of Pelillo Negro Village

Cultivating corn in a rocky cornfield

A Chortí family in their home in the village of Guareruche

Helen Oakley serving Christmas breakfast at the Friends mission

Pedro Ramirez helping John McNichols in Bible translation

Listening to a Bible story in their own language

Carrying a sack of corn on his back.

Chorti boys from the Pelillo Negro village

Carrying an empty grain bin up to the village

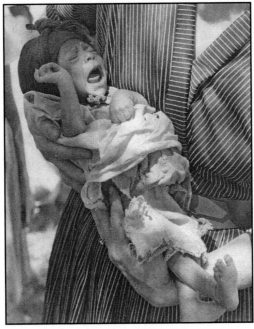

A starving baby

6

Looking for Land

Ray

The trips to look for land actually began two months after we arrived in Guatemala and before our third child born. They were made periodically while we continued the agricultural and clinical ministries in Jocotán. We felt like Abraham in the Bible when God told him to just go, and He would show the way. We were confident that God was leading us down a path that would ultimately bring hope to His Chortí people.

We made one of our first trips to look for land by horseback with two Ladino guides who used us as a source of entertainment all day. To start with, when I attempted to get on my horse, I put my foot in the stirrup, swung my leg up, the saddle slipped down under the horse's belly, and I was on my back. The guides were polite enough not to laugh too hard, but it seemed to me this incident might have been planned.

The farther we went, the denser the jungle became until finally they told us to tie the horses and we would walk. It also seemed that we were just going in a wide circle. Then even walking became difficult and none of us had a machete. Fortunately, Homer and I were in good physical condition. When we came to a small stream, they said we would walk in the water rather than in the thick brush. They enjoyed watching us walk in our leather boots down that stream. Finally we got back to the horses and back to the starting point, making us glad to be on our way home. As we reflected on that day, we concluded that we had not found the land we were looking for or they did not want us to consider buying it.

One of our first priorities was to do research and get as much information as we could about relocation projects that had been attempted around the world. A relief organization called Agricultural Missions sent us Dr. Richard Milk, a wise Christian with experience in third-world agricultural assistance.

Dr. Milk spent two-and-a-half weeks with us visiting the Chortí villages and listening to the plight of the Chortí people. His conclusions confirmed ours, that these people should be moved to a more productive and secure area. From his experiences and studies, he prepared an extensive report with suggestions for our project, many of which we put into practice as we moved forward.

We received helpful input from Dr. Lester Zook, who worked with colonization projects in Mexico. Drawing from his expertise, he strongly recommended that in our kind of project, the participants should be chosen from among one religious group and from one cultural group. Such a homogeneous community would have greater unity and many of the larger problems between people would be minimized. We had been told that the Kibbutz colonies of Israel used this very model with great success.

We were encouraged by the change in the political climate in Guatemala. As I mentioned earlier, the military had won major battles over the Communist guerrillas in the coastal area where we anticipated locating land for the relocation project. This region now was experiencing new political peace and it appeared that God was opening the door.

The counsel of these experienced advisors seemed wise. We would choose Chortí Indian families only (one culture) with a clear Christian testimony (one religion). The Jocotán Friends Church, which was virtually all Chortí, had grown to at least two hundred believers. We invited families from this congregation and Chortí believers from two other municipalities to apply and commit themselves to move to a new more productive land.

With the information we had gathered and the affirmation we felt from the Lord, we were ready to go back to the Chortí people and ask again if they would be willing to move. To our surprise, this time a significant number said *yes*. Most of those interested were the young married men who had no hope if they remained where they were. With much prayer we sought wisdom and direction from the Lord. This would truly be an enormous and daring undertaking.

We missionaries met with the interested men to discuss the relocation proposal. The mission was to take the leadership role, but it was our intent to involve the Chortí people in each step as the development of the project moved forward. It was for them and their families' future. Since the Chortí had never felt they had a future to plan, they were initially uncertain about helping in the planning of their relocation. However, as the project developed they became more comfortable with the decisions and responsibilities we were giving them that would ultimately bring them a new life.

About fifty families originally applied. We asked this group to name a committee of five to work directly with us. This committee of five men came from different villages, including Francisco Garcia from Pelillo Negro; Pedro Ramirez from Guareruche; Leandro Succhite from Matasano; Vicente Mendez from Encuentro; and Lucio Perez from Guayabo. These men were faithful members of the Jocotán Friends Church.

There was a discussion with the committee about what their new village would look like and what would be expected of the families living there. "How would you like to live?" we asked them. "Would you like to be on your own land like you do now in your villages, or in a village with streets and blocks like the town of Jocotán?"

"We want to live together in a town with streets and blocks," was their overwhelming response. We were not sure if this decision was due to their desire to live like the Ladino people or due to their fear of the wild animals and snakes. It was probably both. The idea of living in a formal town setting was the biggest cultural change that they would be making. They did not have close neighbors in their villages in Jocotán other than extended family units. When we met with the families, we made sure they clearly understood that they were to pay for the land. Each family would receive a total of sixteen acres for $500. They could work on their first eight acres upon arrival and when those eight acres were paid off, the remaining eight acres were granted.

The committee established a set of bylaws that we had developed together in meetings. The participants would sign this formal document which had to be clear and fairly firm.

An applicant must:

1. Present a request to be a member of the relocation project in writing.
2. Be a Christian for at least six months.
3. Be married.
4. Have a latrine for household members to us.
5. Fence all yard animals to protect to minimize problems with neighbors.
6. Receive a house lot and sixteen acres of land to farm.
7. Sign a contract-to-buy stipulated by the project committee.

8. Work voluntarily one day per month for each member of their household toward community improvements, such as running water, road, boundaries, and other services.

9. Cooperate with the other members and the project committee and work to preserve the peace and well-being of the group, or he may be expelled by the committee.

10. Agree to the following procedures if asked to leave the project,
    A. He will lose all rights to his house lot and parcel of land.
    B. A refund of money he has paid toward the parcel of land be given.
    C. H will not be reimbursed for his work on the land.
    D. All current accounts owed to the project must be canceled upon leaving.

11. Agree to all the rules of number 10 above, even though he leaves voluntarily.

Because of the peoples' anxieties and fears and their reliance on the missionaries, we had decided that one of us would move to the project land and live with them. In part, this came about as a result of our research into successes and failures of colonization around the world. In places where technical assistance was provided by hands-on administrators, land development programs tended to have much better success. Where people were moved onto a land and left alone with no technical assistance, they often failed.

However, while dialogues and meetings were going on, our primary concern was to find adequate land at a reasonable price. The Friends Mission Board in California was asked to approve and fund the relocation project. The project was approved, but the Board declined to budget money for it. They gave us their blessing and authorization to raise the money any way we could. That was not a win/win situation, but for the moment it was all we needed. Since Homer was well known in the churches in California, he contacted several influential friends asking for financial help for the project.

The Caribbean coastal area drew our attention, especially because of the successful corn harvest in that area during the severe drought that Jocotán had experienced two years earlier. After getting word out that we were looking for a large parcel of land, leads began coming in. We would assess these leads and decide whether they were worth a follow-up.

Because the objective was to include the Chortí men in every aspect of the project, members of the project committee were sent out to look at the leads we selected. They were given an orientation as to what characteristics to look for: topography, soil appearance, cleared land or jungle growth, accessibility, and proximity to larger towns or villages. When they returned with their report, we would use that information to decide whether it was worth considering. If so, Homer or I and sometimes both of us, would make the trip and check it out. Meanwhile, we continued working in the Chortí villages around Jocotán.

Virginia

As Ray and Homer were making preparations for an upcoming trip, Homer asked Evelyn and me, "Would you like to go along with us and stay at the San Felipe Fort Resort?"

"Yes," I excitedly answered, jumping at the chance to visit the coastal area and get out of Jocotán for a while. "We'll take Tad and Linda with us; they'll enjoy the trip," I continued. Tad was one-and-a-half years old, Linda was three, and I was seven months pregnant.

Homer told us about this resort with cabins and a restaurant at the San Felipe Fort. Evelyn and I would be comfortable there while the men looked for land to purchase.

I was happy to be nearer to Ray as he made his trek into the jungle. We packed the kids' suitcases with clothes for the five days. We would take the fold-up playpen for Tad for his bed. We purchased sleeping nets to protect us from the malaria-laden mosquitoes and brought plastic jugs of water.

The men had their usual equipment of soil-testing augers, insect repellent, hats, machetes and boots. They carried bags made of rope that contained their note pads, pencils and sharpening stones for their machetes.

All four of the adults and two children climbed into the cab of Homer's truck. Being the protective mother of small children, I asked, "What about food? Shouldn't we take some food with us?"

Homer, the senior missionary, looked at me and said, "Oh all right, I'll get some fruit." I'm sure he was exasperated with a young missionary worrying about such incidentals.

He walked to the marketplace in the center of town and came back with a third of a gunny sack of granadillas (passion fruit). This fruit was orange/green in color, the size of a small hand grenade filled with juice sacks surrounding seeds. The fruit had to be pulled open, the slimy seeds sucked out and chewed up like grape nuts. The fruit was disgusting to Ray and me, but our kids loved them. I was satisfied now that we had some food with us.

We had the usual pleasant ride down the mountains toward the Atlantic coast. Then we turned off the Atlantic Coast Highway and drove toward Mariscos, a town on the edge of the large Lake Izabal. We arrived at the boat dock and climbed out of the truck. Homer began bargaining with a man about the price he would charge to take us in his dugout canoe across the lake to San Felipe.

Slowly I began to get the picture. That dugout canoe with the ten horsepower motor and with no covering over the top, would be taking us across this thirty-five mile wide lake. Fear and panic began to build in my chest. I quietly thought to myself, *"I am not a swimmer, and I am very pregnant. My little son, Tad, is hyperactive, and how am I going to keep him still for the three-hour ride in the dugout canoe? And there are no life vests anywhere. I cannot believe we were going to do this!"*

I pleaded, "Ray, isn't there a land route we could take to get to San Felipe?"

"No," he replied. "The road to Rio Dulce is not built yet; this is the only way to the San Felipe Fort."

I was so frightened, but I was ashamed to let Homer and Evelyn see how scared I was. Bowing my head, I begged God to protect us and help me have courage to get through this. And then we climbed into the dugout. The playpen was tied on the front of the boat, and our suitcases and sack of fruit were in the back along with cans of gas and oil for the outboard motor. There were three boards for seats and two of us sat on each board. If anyone moved, the whole boat tipped.

Lake Izabal is like a huge inland sea. One cannot see the shoreline on the other side. I looked for other boats, but there was not a single one during our whole trip. It felt as though we were a tiny boat bobbing in the middle of an immense sea, surrounded by a huge sky and bright sun.

The monotonous rhythm of the motor and gently rolling waves calmed my nerves and I relaxed. Tad fell asleep at the bow of the boat. After an hour he woke up and was restless. He looked around and then grabbed his little shoe and threw it overboard. Shoes for our children were hard to come by and were purchased in Guatemala City. His little shoe floated on the water right-side up. He was fascinated and giggled as it floated along.

"Oh no!" I yelled. "His shoe!"

Our watchful pilot throttled down the motor and then carefully circled closer and closer to the little shoe, and Ray picked it out of the water. We happily continued on our way.

Finally, three hours later, we could see the shoreline ahead of us. Then a few minutes later we heard Homer gasp, "Uh oh!"

"What happened, Homer? What's wrong?" I asked.

"Look—the restaurant is gone! It must have burned down," he exclaimed.

I immediately I remembered the sack of slimy fruit that Homer had brought. *Well, at least we have that fruit with us,* I thought.

San Felipe is a peninsula of land at the mouth of Lake Izabal where Rio Dulce flows out of the lake. It is lush, tropical lowland with flowering hibiscus bushes and towering palm trees.

In the 1600's a Spanish fort was built on the tip of that peninsula to guard the entrance into Lake Izabal from English intruders. The fort was intact with canons, turrets, living quarters, a dungeon, and a chapel. *Wow, our kids will enjoy playing in that fort,* I thought.

When our pilot docked our canoe, it was so good to finally be on solid ground. We unloaded our suitcases, bags, and the playpen. The resort owner, who greeted our boat, explained that they had had a fire and the restaurant was destroyed, but he thought we could find someone in the village who would like to cook meals for us. We made arrangements with the Barrientos family to prepare breakfast and supper for us. We would eat the "fruit" for lunch. *Well,* I thought, *I'm going to like the passion fruit by the time this week is over.*

The guest facilities were about a block inland from the castle. We were assigned rooms that had single cots and a common bathroom between the two rooms. A single light bulb hung in the middle of each room. The climate was very tropical—hot and humid—so there were only screen windows all around the room. Our mosquito nets were hung over our cots from nails in the walls. We hung one net over the playpen for Tad.

The Barrientos family happily prepared cooked oatmeal for breakfast and black beans, tortillas, and white cheese for us for the evening meal, and we gratefully paid them. The whole family was jovial and friendly. Linda and Tad enjoyed their food, while being entertained by the dogs, cats, and chickens that were under our table waiting for the scraps to fall. But when the family's pig rubbed against my legs under the table, I cringed.

Ray

Early the next morning, Homer and I took off down river to meet our guide, Mateo, a Kekchi Indian. We informed our wives we would be back in two days. Each of us carried a gallon of water and a lunch our wives had packed. We also carried the ever-present machete, soil auger, and notebook. Mateo was a fine Christian man, and we soon became good friends. He knew the area well and how to get to the land we had heard about, a place called Baranco Blanco (White Bluff). Leaving Mateo's house at the edge of the river we hiked through the dense jungle, sometimes on a trail, sometimes not. The canopy of the jungle was very tight allowing virtually no sun to reach the ground. That made walking easy most of the time as relatively few plants grew with so little sunlight. In the middle of the day we stopped for lunch, sitting on a fallen tree. We ate a sandwich and some fruit and kept walking. The shade was comforting as the sun was blazing above the treetops. Because it rains almost every day, the humidity made us feel like we were in a sauna all day.

It was not until about five in the afternoon that we arrived at our destination of Baranco Blanco. We had trudged through the jungle for eight hours and we were exhausted and hungry. There was a settlement of Kekchi Indians across the Cienega River, a small river that wandered through the jungle on its way to the big Rio Dulce. We waded across, and Mateo, who spoke Kekchi, went to ask if we could buy some food and spend the night there. He informed us that they would let us stay the night under a thatch roof at the river's edge where they had two small dugout canoes, but they had no food for us. *No food?* I thought. *But we had just watched a man upriver butcher a pig! But for us there was no food.* Fortunately we had saved a sandwich from lunch, so we did not spend the night on completely empty stomachs.

We were supposed to sleep in the bottom of the dugouts, which is rounded and hard with no way to turn over. The nightly thunderstorm came through on schedule, but at least the thatched roof kept us dry. All in all, neither of us slept.

It was barely dawn and we were on our feet. That felt good! Mateo went up to the huts and after a while came back with some fried pork rinds. That was all they would give us. We had taken a few soil samples and observed the lay of the land, but we did not stay long. We were not going to be interested in land that had people living on it, and this parcel was much too isolated for our relocation project. It was a grueling eight hour hike back to Mateo's house with hardly anything to eat, and our water had run out. We were back at his house by about 3:00 p.m., and his wife fixed us some food while Mateo climbed a coconut tree to pick some young coconuts. I had never had fresh coconut juice that tasted so delicious!

Before we left, Mateo told us why the people at Baranco Blanco had treated us so badly. On another land where they had been living, some white men came one day and burned their houses and ran them off because they wanted the land. These Kekchí people thought we were going to do the same. We praised God that Mateo was with us because he had told them that we were helping Indian families find land. God goes before and leads better than we know or imagine!

An hour after leaving Mateo at his home, we were back at the hotel where Evelyn, Virginia and the kids were waiting. We were dehydrated, extremely tired and achy, but we slept well that night. In the morning we returned across the lake Izabal by dugout and then back home.

Another trip to look for land took us back to Mariscos at Lake Izabal. There was no road or a known trail to this land; travel was only by boat. The trip in the dugout canoe was about two hours to the head of the lake in the Polochíc area. The boat ride itself would eliminate this site because the Chortí, especially the women, would be afraid to travel that far by water. Much of the area was swampy and the mosquito population was unlike anything I had ever seen. In fact, the mosquitos had a feeding frenzy while we spent a sleepless night in hammocks. Leaving the next morning, we knew this was not going to be our land.

Now we were at a crossroads. It had been almost a year since we had signed up the people and began looking for land. They were beginning to doubt us. We were becoming frustrated. What was God trying to tell us? Had the door we thought God was opening now closed? None of the land we had looked at fell within the parameters of what we wanted for the families. The properties were either too big or too small (we needed between 1,000 and 1,500 acres); too mountainous or swampy; there were people already living on the land; or was only accessible by water. And besides all that, we were unable to find financial backing for the project.

So far, nothing seemed right, but we felt sure that God was still leading us down this path. We decided to give it a little more time and keep looking. There were still some pieces of land we needed to see. In a meeting of the families that were waiting, we explained the dilemma so they would not get their hopes up too high.

We did find a piece of land that sounded promising, so we sent the committee men out to look one more time. Homer and I privately agreed that if this was not what we could use, we would cancel the project. We were very discouraged.

Two Chortí men from the project committee, Francisco Garcia and Pedro Ramirez, made the trip to the Rio Dulce area and, together with the overseer, looked the land over and gave us their favorable report upon returning.

A few days later Homer and I visited the land. It was situated near a road project that would be completed within a couple years. It was gently rolling land (which meant no swamps) with a small river running through it. The soil structure was adequate, and there were no people living there. The size of the parcel of land was 1,200 acres! Homer and I looked at each other and agreed that this piece of land met all of our criteria and would be a good place for the Chortí relocation project.

Only one obstacle remained. There was no money to buy the land. The people could not be told we had found the land if we were unable to buy it.

Our drive back to Jocotán was a quiet one. When we pulled up in front of the house, Virginia and Evelyn rushed out to meet us. Evelyn was holding an air-gram letter. "Look at what came in the mail today," she said. "It is a letter from Cliff Marshburn, a prominent farmer in one of our churches in California, saying that if we could find land for the relocation project, he would guarantee the money."

We stared at them and said, "We have found the land!" It was one of those rare moments when we knew we were standing in the presence of the Lord. We immediately went to prayer, thanking God for faithfully encouraging us to go forward until we found the place He had reserved for His Chortí people.

7

Stepping into the Unknown

Ray

Exhaustion after our last search for land and exhilaration from news of financial sponsors hit us all at once. Where do we begin?

"Lord, thank you for answering our prayers," Homer prayed. "Please guide us." It was just past the "siesta hour" in the hot afternoon sun, and no one was in sight on the street as he led the four of us into the house in Jocotán.

"Let's meet tomorrow morning and plan how we will move forward," he said as he walked to his bedroom to rest. Now we were reminded of Moses in the Bible and how he led his people in the Exodus.

Homer wrote a letter to the California Friends Church Board of Missions to inform them that we had found the land for the project. He told them the price for the one thousand two hundred acre property was $15,000. We estimated the cost of the survey and title transfer would be another $3,000.

I sent a telegram to Mr. Mancia, the overseer of the land, to inform him that we would like to discuss the purchase of his property. And it was suggested we meet in the office of our lawyer, Mr. Hugo Morales, a renowned Christian lawyer who helped missionary organizations and churches in Guatemala. He had helped our Friends Mission in legal matters several times over the years.

Mr. Mancia replied by telegram that he would meet us in the Guatemala City office of our lawyer, on June first. I knew I would already be there because Virginia's due date for the birth of our third child was around that time.

Before we left, we called together the Chortí people who had signed up to move on to the project, to inform them that we were going to be able to secure the land. We asked if they were still committed to moving and being part of the project. All affirmed their desire to move. While some would later decide to not to go, others were coming forward who took their place.

I met our lawyer and Mr. Mancia in Mr. Morales' office. After the customary small talk, we got down to the purpose of the visit, which was the sale and purchase of the piece of property.

Mr. Morales had drawn up the legal papers for the sale. Mr. Mancia signed and then I signed them. I handed the lawyer $6,000 as the first payment. It was a quiet, solemn moment as I heard the scratch of the pen on the paper and the flip of the one hundred dollar bills on the desk. The burden of this transaction felt heavy on my shoulders because of the effect this would have on so many people's lives. I wondered what lay ahead.

Mr. Mancia, a Guatemalan civil engineer, had purchased this twelve hundred acre piece of land north of Rio Dulce from a landowner in the United States, with the purpose of selling it to Chiquimula Friends Mission. He also wanted to be the official surveyor of the property to establish the exact boundaries. I left the remaining money for the land purchase with Mr. Morales to pay the Mr. Mancia when he delivered the reports of his survey.

After the purchase of this property, we learned that none of the land north of Rio Dulce had been surveyed for at least sixty years. This land was thick jungle with no roads. When these lands were originally deeded, the owners had only one thing in mind, and that was to find all the mahogany trees, cut them down, float the logs down the rivers to the ocean, and export them. When that was done, they had no more use for the land. A generation or two later, the descendants of those original landowners had deeds to what they considered worthless, inaccessible land with no idea of where it was.

As his benchmark, our surveyor, Mr. Mancia, used an old fence post near the large Rio Dulce about three miles from our property. He claimed it was the corner of a property bordering ours. From that point he surveyed a line to our property, and following the measurements on our deed, he surveyed our land. To our consternation, this survey brought our property line right through the village of Sejá, a new settlement of road construction workers and their families.

While we started marking our village boundaries and house lots, the technical logistics of the land purchase was time consuming. The survey took more than three weeks to complete. Then we put the registration and transfer of title in the hands of our lawyer, who gave us no assurance of expediency.

Now we were ready to begin moving families to their new homes on the relocation property. It had to be done in stages, however. First, we took Pedro, Francisco, Vicente and Leandro from the Chortí project committee, down to build two provisional huts in Sejá.

We consulted our friend Mateo, who had been our guide when we looked for land. We hired him to show the Chortí men how to select materials from the jungle that were durable, and how to construct dwellings that would hold up well in that very rainy climate.

When the provisional huts were completed, the plan was to move the first two families to the project. They would occupy the huts while they cleared their assigned lots in the village and then moved into their new homes. Once this move was completed, the next two families moved into the provisional huts and they could follow the same process.

Suddenly, just before we took the first families to the project, we received a notice that affected this whole process. Homer and David Hamm, a short-term volunteer from Berkley, California, drove down to the project to visit and encourage the four Chortí men who were building the two provisional huts. Francisco Garcia and Pedro Ramirez ran out to meet Homer.

"A surveyor from the neighboring San Humberto property has crossed our survey line to measure his land," they exclaimed excitedly. Homer's heart sank. He and David knew trouble may be brewing.

The San Humberto property was owned by a retired army colonel who had sent a crew out to survey his land, and they had just crossed our boundary on an angle. Their surveyor came to visit Homer and David the next day with his maps of the area.

By comparing the maps, Homer and David quickly saw that someone was wrong about the location of the properties. The colonel's surveyor used a cave as a benchmark for his measurements, while our engineer had used a rotted post. Our engineer's work did not look good.

The whole relocation project was in jeopardy if our land had been surveyed in the wrong place. We needed God's reassurance that He had led us into this ministry for the Chortí people, and He does not make mistakes. We had to trust Him to lead us through this crisis. Our prayer was for wisdom.

The San Humberto land had ten thousand acres, and the colonel was wealthy and well connected with the government. We were foreign missionaries working with limited funds and trying to acquire only one thousand, two hundred acres. We wanted to help a group of poor Indians who were disenfranchised, uneducated, and had no knowledge of legal solutions for disputed property boundaries.

If the San Humberto survey was accepted, the calculation was that about one-third of our land, as surveyed, really belonged to the colonel. And we were about to lose it. Our lawyer was unable to contact our surveyor to get him involved in helping us resolve this situation. Mr. Mancia had conveniently disappeared. We were not interested in a court battle, so we had to look for other ways to secure our land and go forward with the relocation project.

A decision had to be made quickly. We needed help from the Lord. The mission in Chiquimula was notified, and we asked everyone to pray. After much prayer and waiting on the Lord, two things became very clear. One, our survey was wrong. Two, it was necessary to acknowledge and accept the San Humberto's measurements as correct, which we did. At that point we had only about two-thirds of the amount of land our deed said we had bought.

The maps showed our property joined the San Humberto on two sides. We decided to encourage the colonel to go ahead and finish his survey and register the San Humberto in the government land office (which would be the first officially recognized new survey in the whole vast territory in the northern part of the department of Izabal). And then we would re-survey our land using a recognized corner marker of the San Humberto as a starting point and then register it with the land office.

Mr. Morales had to stop the registration process that he had begun with the erroneous measurement. Even though he finally made contact with the surveyor, Mr. Mancia refused to acknowledge that his measurement was wrong or refund any of the money we had paid him.

The colonel was a very nice elderly gentleman. Over the years he would visit us at the relocation project. He was always accompanied by several armed body guards, a way of life among the upper class in Guatemala. As he developed his land into a cattle ranch, we had good relations with his administrator and workers. On several occasions we were able to help each other.

As the land title situation worked its way through all the legal processes, we went forward with the relocation project. Although we had to wait to do our new survey until the San Humberto land was officially registered, part of our land was not in dispute. So we began internal measurements again to establish a new village site and then the farm parcels. Actually, the probable new location of our land was much more appropriate for our Chortí community than the first survey, which had included the settlement of Sejá.

A new site for the project village was surveyed about two kilometers (a mile and a quarter) east of the road and the Sejá village. A trail had to be cleared through the jungle, crossing a river to get to the new village site. We began again to bring down crews of three or four Chortí men to work on the surveying with David Hamm.

The First Families Moved

Ray

It was September of 1968 when Francisco with his wife, Juana, and two children arrived in Jocotán from Pelillo Negro in the very early morning, carrying everything they owned. Homer put them and all their belongings into his half-ton pickup. Then Pedro with his wife, Victoria, and their three children arrived from Guareruche. I put this family and all their belongings in my pickup truck.

They both took their stone for grinding corn, a clay pot for cooking beans, and a large *comal,* (a clay disc for cooking their tortillas) and a clay water jar. Juana had a couple of turkeys and three chickens. Victoria had three hens with chicks. One small cardboard box each contained the extra items of their clothing. They each took a sack of corn and a few pounds of dry black beans for food to eat.

It was sobering for us when we again realized how little material possessions our friends had. Sometimes on later trips two families at a time with their children and all their earthly belongings easily fit into the back of one of our pickups.

The trip began early in the morning because it would be a long and tiring day for the Indian families. For them, this trip to the new land was to be an adventure of a lifetime, full of uncertainty, anxiety, and an enormous trust in the missionaries were offering them a future with hope. They were willing to walk away from where their families had lived for generations and from the land where life had spiraled downward into extreme poverty and violence. It was inspiring for us to watch them step into the unknown with such courage.

Our destination was about one hundred miles away, from the dry climate of Jocotán at about one thousand, five hundred feet above sea level to the tropical, humid coastal lowlands at maybe two hundred feet elevation and eighteen miles inland from the Caribbean Sea. Juana and

Victoria suffered car sickness since they had never ridden in a vehicle before.

The men in the backs of our pickups had to battle the dust that would swirl in from the open backs of the camper shells. As the day progressed and the sun grew hot, the ride was extremely challenging. We stopped twice to rest, stretch, and go to the "bushes," but when we did, we had difficulty getting Victoria back into the truck. I'm sure she was thinking, *If I had known I would be this sick, I would not have signed up!*

After the first hour and a half we were headed east on the Atlantic highway that ran from Guatemala City to Port Barrios on the Caribbean coast. Another hour and a half we were at the turnoff that would take us north to the large Rio Dulce. The climate had changed from dry-hot to humid-hot, making the packed pickup even more miserable. It was another twenty miles of gravel road, but the road was new and in good condition, straight and relatively level. Because of the evening storms the road was dust free in the mornings, but by midday the intense sun dried everything out and the dust was back.

At the Rio Dulce, the road ended and a new adventure began. There was a settlement of construction workers, a store, and a small eating place on the bank of the river. Men in their dugout canoes, which were the taxis of the area, were waiting to take people up, down, or across the river for a fee. If we thought the women were frightened in their first truck ride, you can imagine what they were thinking when they viewed the nearly six hundred-foot-wide river and a narrow, hollowed-out log that would take them across. Riding on water was another first for them.

Francisco and Pedro carefully placed their belongings in the dugouts. Then Juana climbed in carrying a baby and holding on to her small child. She sat on one of the small boards that spanned the width of the dugout. Victoria, holding on to her three children, sat on another one of the board seats. Once they were seated, fear set in as the long narrow boat tipped easily from side to side with the slightest movement.

On the other side it was another balancing act for everyone to get out of the boats. The settlement here had a store and a couple of houses. Our destination was still four miles to the village of Sejá where the provisional huts were awaiting the Indian families. The jungle had been cleared in anticipation of the road construction, but there were no vehicles on that side of the river to take us there. So we picked up everything we brought and began the walk to Sejá during the afternoon, when the temperature was the hottest.

Walking and carrying heavy loads was not a problem for these people. Fortunately, I was in good shape and was able to keep up and carry my part of the load. It took us about two-and-a-half hours to walk to the village of Sejá and the provisional huts. By the time we showed them to the huts they would occupy, they were exhausted. When the sun went down, about six thirty in the evening, they were in bed. Since there was no place for me to sleep, I returned back to Jocotán that same night.

We knew one of us needed to move with these people and live on the relocation project in order to assure success. We agreed that Homer and Evelyn would move to the project as the advisors and administrators, and Virginia and I would stay in Jocotán, coordinating the moving of the families.

The Sharplesses moved into a third provisional hut that was built outside the Sejá community. Their hut was just like the other two that the families used—stick sides, palm thatch roof, and a dirt floor—with the exception that one side of the roof had corrugated tin to catch the rainwater for drinking and household use. They took their bed, a few wooden straight chairs, and a table with them. Evelyn cooked on a clay mud stove. Rolando and Maria Lopez, pastors from Chiquimula, accompanied them and helped them set up their new home so they could be fairly comfortable in these very primitive circumstances.

While the Sharplesses lived there, Virginia and I and our three children took food, medicines, and another Chortí family in our truck the one hundred miles to the relocation project once or twice a month. We tried to help the Sharplesses with whatever they needed. Since there was no place for our family to sleep, we always returned on the same day.

As soon as they could, Homer walked the new settlers the two kilometer trek through the jungle to the village site. Machetes had been used to cut away the undergrowth, but the larger logs of fallen trees that crossed the path had to be climbed over. About halfway to the site, the River Sejá, which was about thirty feet wide, had to be crossed.

As requested, the village site was marked out with streets and blocks that seemed almost comical considering the dense jungle where it was located. It was decided that each family would be shown two or three lots from which to select their house site so they felt they had a choice about their property. At this point each man needed to buy a machete, an axe and a file, so we extended credit to them and they could pay it back when they sold their first crops.

The families that we moved were able to find all the building materials for their houses in the jungle close to the settlement. Of particular importance were the corner posts that would be sunk into the ground about two feet. Two kinds of wood that were most resistant to rotting were called *rosúl* and *tamarindo*. One that was excellent for beams, if kept dry, was *irayol*. Once cured, a nail could not be driven through it and it would last almost forever.

The roofs were thatched with palm fronds, which were abundant in the jungle, but gathering the fronds took a lot of time. Roofing the house was usually done by at least four people working together and it became a social event for friends and neighbors. A roof would last about four years if you could keep the rats out, two years if you could not. However, the thatch roofs wore out quickly because of the heavy and abundant rains.

When a family had finished their house in the village, serious work began on clearing their parcel of land for planting. Stories from surrounding communities abounded of men being killed by trees that fell on them. So, again, we found our friend Mateo, who gave wise instruction to the Chortí farmers. He told them that a tree they cut will not necessarily fall but may become lodged in another tree or be held up by vines. The situation was dangerous. The men learned to spend time observing and evaluating the area they were clearing and make careful calculations. They soon discovered how to clear a path on which to retreat when trees began to fall.

The roots of the big trees flared out about eight to ten feet up the trunk, so a platform was built at that point to stand on while using the axe to chop the tree down. The planned getaway had to include getting down off the platform. It was not unusual for the second and even the third cut tree to lodge into each other and not fall. Eventually that cluster of trees would begin falling, prompting the men to escape quickly.

One technique the men used when cutting a tree that was going to bring other trees with it when it fell was to cut only until you heard the first crack and then simply go home. The winds that came with the evening thunderstorms would usually bring the cut trees down. The next day the danger would be over. As work progressed, it became easier as the next trees cut would fall into the clearings.

One of my most unforgettable memories is that of Santiago, standing next to one of the enormous trees on the land that he was going to farm. As he looked up at that huge tree and out through the dark, dense jungle, he folded his arms across his chest and just stood there. This is a gesture that the Chortí often used to show inadequacy and defeat. Not a word was spoken, but with that gesture he was saying, "I can't do this. This is beyond my ability. I don't have a clue as to where to begin."

I could not help but smile because I had a pretty good idea of what was ahead for this man and the others. I was thinking, *God is offering hope for you. You have all the support you need. We will be here with you and help you through this. You have an axe, a machete, and a file. You clear that land, you plant and harvest your crops, and you will become a new man, from the inside out. You will feel good about yourself. You will be cultivating a feeling of self-worth and dignity because you have done this work and prospered and raised yourself up. You will pay for your land and will have the title that no one can take away. Yes, you will still be a Chortí Indian but you will be a new person with dignity and self-respect. And there will be no more arms crossed against your chest.*

Land conservation by not burning off the organic matter was emphasized, and cash incentives were offered if the farmers followed this teaching. However, an exception was made for the first cutting of the jungle, as it lay so deep that no one could walk through it let alone plant the land. The burning was successful, with most of the land being exposed so the corn and rice could be planted between the stumps, logs and larger limbs that did not burn. After the initial burning, there was very little need for further burning.

However, each family would have no food from the time of their arrival until harvest time. Having anticipated this problem beforehand, we offered work-for-pay two or three days a week and then they would work the remaining days on their land until their first harvest. We also made it clear that we expected no one to work on Sunday.

One of the first work-for-pay projects was to clear land around the trail near the village to plant demonstration plots of new unfamiliar crops that did well in the tropical lowlands of the coast. Since they were doing the work, they learned how to care for and appreciate each new crop.

The first new crop we wanted to introduce was rice, because it was anticipated that rice would be the principle cash crop that would allow them to pay for their land. There are varieties of rice called upland rice that will do well planted directly in the soil by seed rather than in paddies of water. Our gently rolling land was ideal for upland rice, and we were assured the rains were more than adequate in that area to produce rice.

Other demonstration plantings included bananas (both cooking and eating varieties), pineapple, citrus, a red dye called *acheote*, cocoa for chocolate, and sweet potatoes. The banana bulbs and the pineapple shoots had to be carried in from Sejá. There was plenty of work, and the men were learning a new way of farming.

The trail to the village had to be cleared of logs, widened and turned into a road. It was a blessing for the men that everything could not be brought in by vehicle because they were depending on this work to feed their families while they were bringing their land into production.

Lucio was a young farmer from Guayabo who moved his family with three small children to the relocation project in 1969. He lived and farmed with his father-in-law, Inéz. His mother was estranged from him, and he never talked about his own father. He had served on the relocation project committee from the Jocotán Friends Church. And now he clearly understood the vision and philosophy for helping his people through the relocation project.

Lucio loved the Lord and desired to serve Him. He had taken classes in reading from the McNichols in the mission in Jocotán, and he had studied simple math with Evelyn. He had a quiet, winsome way and a bright smile. He was a Chortí who spoke only Spanish. He had not finished one year of grade school due to problems with the educational system. He wanted to read the Bible, so he practiced and practiced reading it until he could read it well.

Then an accident struck. Lucio was clearing his parcel of land to prepare it to plant his crops of corn, rice, and beans. He used his machete for this labor. The men who were unaccustomed to this climate failed to realize the danger of moisture from sweat or rain on the grip of the machete handle. On this particular day, Lucio was cutting the vines away from a large tree. His machete swung out of his right hand and his automatic reaction was to protect his face. His machete came back and cut through his right arm just above the wrist. His face was not injured.

Homer was nearby and he wrapped Lucio's arm in a towel and drove him four hours to the public hospital in Port Barrios. Lucio stayed in the hospital for three weeks. The doctors were able to save the hand from amputation, but he never regained full use of it. He could not use the axe or the machete after his accident because of the pain. He farmed with his left hand and with the assistance of his son and father-in-law.

In December of 1968, Homer purchased an old Willis Jeep pickup truck that had been converted to a flat-bed truck. It was ferried across the Rio Dulce on a barge that was there for transporting road construction equipment. Our red Willis truck was the first private vehicle on that side of the river and soon became known as the "Colorado," the red truck. This truck was a God-send that greatly facilitated the movement of families and supplies the four miles to the Sejá village. However, it would still be some time before the trail was widened and leveled enough to bring the truck the last two kilometers into the village.

Virginia

During one of the early trips moving families, Evelyn asked if I would accompany Ray to the relocation project and treat the medical needs of the people. Guatemala had endured heavy rains and flooding a few days before this trip, so we were not sure what was ahead of us.

On this particular moving day, our trek began with our family of five accompanied by Bonifacio's wife and young child in the cab. The other family with their children and Bonifacio rode in the back of the pickup with all their earthly possessions. Bonifacio, from Pelillo Negro, had lost his arm in a machete fight, but he did not let this hinder his enthusiasm for the farming opportunity and to be a part of the project.

We turned off the Atlantic highway and drove on the gravel road toward Rio Dulce. Recent flooding was apparent on both sides of the road. As we approached the San Marcos River, we noticed a line of cars parked and the bridge gone. A swinging bridge had been built across the river for foot traffic. As we stood there, we watched with horror as a small Jeep drove across the bridge.

"No, please, don't even think about that!" I pleaded as I noticed Ray sizing up the ropes. "Our truck is bigger than that Jeep."

"Very well, I won't try to drive our pickup across," Ray reluctantly said to me.

The Indians piled out of the back of the truck with all their belongings, and we got out of the cab. Ray parked the truck along the side of the road. Then he got a ride five miles to the Rio Dulce crossing where Homer parked his pickup in storage. Ray found the hidden spare key and drove it back to us waiting at the swinging bridge. We walked across the bridge carrying all of our children and belongings. Then we boarded Homer's pickup and rode to Rio Dulce.

Ray made a deal with two dugout-canoe drivers to take us across the Rio Dulce. Catalina, Bonifacio's wife, shared my fear of traveling across deep water in a tippy dugout canoe. But, gaining confidence when she watched me climb in with my three small children, she followed.

The empty red Jeep was parked on the other side of the river. Now the families did not have to walk the four miles to Sejá. We adults with our children and all our cargo piled on the Jeep bed and drove on to Sejá.

Bonifacio and his family stayed in one of the provisional huts. The rest of us began the trek by foot to the relocation village. The trail was narrow and muddy, but we walked together. Linda and Tad liked to walk in their rubber boots, and Kenny was carried in one of the Indian women's arms. The trail went through very dark, dense jungle and across a small creek. We had to crawl over five huge logs that had fallen across the trail. The jungle was so dark and dense that we could not take a photo of it. The trip was long and had several difficulties, but the adventure and challenge was exhilarating for Ray and me.

Project Dedication

Ray

In January 1969, with ten families present, we had a village dedication celebration service that focused on God and His mercy and provision. Several missionaries from Chiquimula as well as some leaders from the Guatemala Friends churches were present. They were all transported in from Rio Dulce in the bed of the "Colorado." The service was held in the yard of one of the new houses with only wet, freshly cut logs on which to sit, so we stood most of the time.

We sang hymns, many gave testimonies, others prayed, and messages were given by John Astleford and Mario Rolando Lopez. In every way it was a praise and worship to our Lord from whom everything comes. He had heard their cry and was graciously responding to the needs of these Chortí Christians. After this service, the guests returned to Chiquimula the same day.

When a new settler finished his house, he was shown his land. The parcels were distributed in order starting close to the village and working their way out. We walked with the new settler around the four corners of his eight acres, following the narrow clearing the survey team had made. At the end of the first year, there were twenty-five new settlers.

It was going to be quite a while before we would have our new survey and all our land secure again, so everything was being done on the undisputed part. Although this was beginning to limit us in moving more families, the village was beginning to take shape and come to life. Soon we would need to register the new village in the municipality of Livingston. But it had no name.

El Florido

All the families that were living there were called together to choose a name for their village. We missionaries stayed out of the debate. After many suggestions and considerable discussion, the name "El Florido" which means "The Flowering Place," was chosen. We had envisioned the relocation project being a place where the Chortí people would blossom, grow, and honor God.

The Chortí people who had lived near the Honduras border spoke only Spanish. Unfortunately, but in keeping with the way the Guatemalan society had evolved, they thought of themselves as somewhat superior to the Chortí speakers. This group made up about one-third of the settlers. This was a social factor in the project but did not cause any overwhelming problems, and soon it was understood and agreed that Spanish would be the language used in the village. It was interesting to note that the Chortí language speakers were quick to embrace the Spanish language because of the stigma attached to being an Indian. They wanted to speak the language of the Ladinos, the official language of Guatemala.

Since our village now had a name, it was time to register it for official recognition at the county government office in Livingston, twenty miles from El Florido. Twenty miles to a county seat is not far, unless there is no road to it. There were, however, two options for getting to Livingston. One was to drive our vehicle out to the Atlantic highway at Morales and then down to Port Barrios, a trip of between three and four hours. At Port Barrios there was a small, open ocean-going ferry that went to Livingston twice a day. The boat ride across the ocean lasted one-and-a-half hours. This trip took a total of two days.

The other option, which was the one we preferred, was to rent a dugout canoe and driver at the Rio Dulce crossing and take the river to Livingston. The ten-horsepower outboard motor on the dugout did not offer a fast ride, but it was scenic! There was no covering over the boat and only a plank to sit on with no back rest. The trip on the river took two-and-a-half to three hours under a hot sun.

Shortly after leaving the Rio Dulce town in the dugout, we entered a long, narrow, shallow lake called El Golfete that had a reputation of becoming very turbulent in the afternoons when the winds came up. After traveling on the lake for about an hour, El Golfete flowed back into Rio Dulce, again winding through a beautiful jungle with vine-covered cliffs. We spotted only four dwellings along the entire trip. After traveling most of an hour in this spectacular canyon, it suddenly opened up into the ocean. There, nestled on the north shore, was the port town of Livingston.

Livingston was not much of a port and not much of a town in the 1960's and '70's. It had a population of maybe one thousand people, the majority of which were Garifunda and Carob blacks. Livingston flourished in the 1930's and '40's when German settlers began buying bananas along the shores of Rio Dulce and Lake Izabal and shipping them to Europe and North America. However, by the mid-1950's, the banana industry had been completely shut down by a fungus called the Panama Disease and remained that way until a resistant variety was introduced in the 1960's.

After arriving in Livingston, our next hurdle was to get business taken care of before noon. From noon to 2:00 the afternoon, everything, including all government offices, closed down for the traditional siesta. Our dugout operator had warned us that we must start back by 1:00 p.m. or run the risk of a very rough ride through El Golfete because of the afternoon winds.

The people in the government offices were not concerned about doing the paperwork, including the mandatory official signatures, before siesta time. We were kindly told to come back after 2:00 p.m.

This first trip was a learning experience. We did not know that every village must have an auxiliary mayor and three assistants, elected by the village residents. We had not done that. The auxiliary mayor of the village was responsible for officially registering all births and deaths.

In addition, each village was supposed to have two military commissioners, named by the village residents. We had not done that either. The military commissioners are the law enforcers of the villages and are ultimately responsible to the commander of the nearest army base, where they report disturbances of any kind such as fights, arguments, thefts, unrest, etc.

So as these organizational issues were completed, El Florido would begin to appear on the map as a village in the municipality of Livingston, department of Izabal, Guatemala. This was perhaps the first major event that allowed these Chortí families to feel that they were at the beginning of exercising some important rights that had been denied them in Jocotán. For the first time, they now had direct representation in the civil establishment of their country.

Virginia

In April 1969, Ray made a trip to Honduras to teach agriculture and Bible classes. Evelyn invited me to hold medical clinics for them in El Florido for a week. The new house was not finished, but they were living in it.

The road into El Florido was not built yet, but Evelyn had three women from the village meet us at Sejá. The women took our bags and boxes of medicines and put them on their heads just like they carry everything else. Linda and Tad walked in their rubber boots. Homer carried Kenny on his shoulders.

While I was with the Sharplesses, I was busy from early morning until night every day giving hygiene classes and treating the sick. The women were very enthusiastic about the classes.

One afternoon, Catalina brought her little four-year-old son, Ephraim, to Evelyn's kitchen. He had fallen into the fire that was maintained on the dirt floor of their home, where his mother was cooking. He had burned his right hand and arm up to his elbow four days earlier. It was badly infected, and he had a fever of 103 degrees. I gave him some baby Tylenol and injections of antibiotics. I had a set of instruments that were sterilized in my pressure cooker.

"Doña Catalina, I need to cut away all this dead skin on his fingers, so it will heal," I carefully explained, knowing she understood very little Spanish.

"Oh, no," she replied with a look of doubt and horror.

"Yes," I slowly repeated, "This skin needs to be cut away. It will be done very carefully and it will not hurt him," I said, as I tried to reassure her.

She looked down at her sick little boy and then she looked up at me and then back at her boy. I waited.

"Okay," she finally replied quietly. It was a struggle for her to decide whether she would trust me to do that.

"Ephraim, this skin will be cut away very carefully to help you feel better," I slowly explained to him with all the assurance I could muster.

At first he cried loudly and pulled his infected arm away. I waited, and he could see I was not going to force him to do anything. His mother consoled him in their Chortí language. I waited and prayed quietly, "Lord, please help me help this little boy, please give me strength and wisdom to do this procedure. And Lord, please heal his arm and hand."

"Okay," Catalina said. "He wants you to help him."

Efraim calmed down and held his arm out to me, still sobbing quietly.

Slowly and carefully I began to cut away the burned, infected skin and tissue with the sterilized instruments. The dead skin had to be cut away from each of the small fingers, the hand, and finally up to the elbow. This is something I have only seen done in a hospital in sterile conditions. While I was working on his fingers, I looked up and noticed he was sound asleep. His mother was holding his arm steady. It looked like he needed a skin graft, but that was out of the question here.

Women from the Friends Church Missionary Societies had sent me many rolls of bandages made out of used bed sheets. Several rolls of those bandages were sterilized in the pressure cooker. One side of the bandage was covered with antibiotic cream. Each little finger was wrapped separately with the bandage. Then the hand and arm were wrapped.

"You must bring Efraim back to me tomorrow so I can change the dressings," I explained.

"Yes, Doña Virginia, I will," she promised.

The next day Catalina returned with her little boy, who was not crying as loudly as he did the day before. The dressings were changed.

After four days of dressing changes the tissue looked healthy and there was minimal infection. We did the dressing changes now to every other day, and little by little the skin was filling in. Thankfully, a child's skin grows quickly.

Evelyn kept up the dressing changes when I returned to Jocotán. Two weeks later Evelyn telegraphed me that Efraim was almost healed and off the antibiotics. We praised the Lord for answering our prayers for him and for using me to communicate His love and care.

8

Village Development in the Jungle

Virginia

The sun was setting behind the jungle trees and the gentle cool breeze came, bringing a welcome evening reprieve from the hot day. Homer had been working with the Chortí men measuring their new home sites in the village, and he had walked through the dense jungle trail back to their hut in Sejá, where Evelyn was waiting for him.

"I'm so thirsty," he mumbled to himself as he gulped the tepid water. "I must not have drunk enough water today." Evelyn boiled all their drinking water but had no way to cool it down.

Evelyn had prepared their evening meal of black beans and tortillas on the clay stove that Homer had built in their rustic hut. David Hamm, who was helping Homer and Evelyn and living with them, joined them for their evening meal. Wood smoke curled out from the thatched roofs of the huts. They listened to the sounds of the children and adults of the two new Chortí families, living in the provisional huts nearby, talking around their fires.

New Missionary House

The call of the evening jungle birds settling in for the night in the nearby trees was a soothing sound. "David, I want you to design a suitable permanent missionary residence for the jungle village," Homer directed.

David, a recent graduate from University of California Berkley in civil engineering, jumped at the chance to try out his expertise. He quickly began a design for an elaborate house. A couple days later he showed his plans to Homer.

"No, David, the new residence must be simple, inexpensive and easy to construct," Homer replied, a little irritated.

Downcast, David went back to his drawings and developed plans for a simple L-shaped wooden house with a kitchen, bathroom and two bedrooms to be built in the first phase. Another bedroom and a living room would be added later. Homer approved of these plans.

Homer began collecting the needed materials. He bought the creosote-treated pilings on which the house would be built from a wood treatment plant near Morales. These creosote pilings were sunk into holes in the ground that were lined with concrete. He selected trees from the nearby jungle to cut the horizontal six-by-eight beams that would support the house.

The site for this house in the Indian village had a gentle slope to it, so the floor at the front of the house was eighteen inches off the ground, and the back of the house was close to five feet high. This design allowed good air circulation that kept the house dry and cool.

A small sawmill operator began sawing lumber in Sejá. He ordered the wood for framing the walls and tresses for the roof. This operator seemed to have been assigned by God to be there to do this particular work for El Florido because soon thereafter he moved his sawmill out of the area.

The building materials that had to be purchased in other areas were delivered to Rio Dulce and from there they were transported to Sejá by the Colorado Jeep. Then the paid labor crews carried the flooring, siding, plumbing, screening, and roofing materials on their backs to the building site in El Florido. They were earning money to feed their families while helping the missionaries at the same time.

Harvey Flinkinger and Oman Kunkal, two building contractors from Ramona, California, came to build the mission house. They lived in the Sharpless's hut in Sejá. Their bedroom was a loft above Homer's bed. They walked to the village each morning, worked on the house, and returned each evening to the hut. Evelyn served them breakfast and supper and they took a lunch with them.

"It's like working in a perpetual sauna bath," one of them explained when asked to describe the weather.

At the end of their two-month stay, the structure was completed, and even the cabinets and plumbing were in place. The outside walls were four feet high all around, and the other four feet was screening. This design provided the necessary ventilation but the downside was that there was little privacy in the house.

The Sharplesses moved from the packed-dirt-floor hut in Sejá to the new house in the village. This allowed them to finally live among the Chortí settlers and they did not have to walk the long trek twice a day to the village. Now they could bring more of their belongings from Chiquimula to their new home.

Even though the mission house in El Florido was finished enough for occupancy, the bathroom was still inoperable because the septic tank had not yet been constructed. After David Hamm built an outhouse, he proceeded with the daunting task of building the septic tank. It was to have cement sides about eight feet into the ground. Digging the hole by hand and working in the hole was an enormous task because of the tropical heat, humidity and lack of air movement that exhausted David daily. However, he persevered with a servant's heart and finished the project. Then the house was completely finished with a working shower and flush toilet!

Ray

When it was time for the first planting on the project land in the spring of 1969, each of the farmers had cleared as much as half of his land, or about four acres. Because these were new beginnings on new land, we wanted to start with new seed. We purchased a new variety of open-pollinated corn seed that had been developed in Guatemala for this particular zone, as well as certified rice seed. No one was allowed to plant corn that they had brought from their village in Jocotán, which would cross-pollinate and degenerate the new corn. By keeping the corn pure and saving the best for seed, they could have excellent crops for many years without having to buy new seed.

The men were encouraged to plant only as much land in corn as they needed for consumption and to plant the rest in rice. The rice crop brought in the needed cash to pay for their land and other expenses. It was hard to convince them not to plant all their land in corn, because for generations they struggled to have enough to eat, and corn was their basic food staple. However, they cooperated very well and were on their way to being more than subsistence farmers in a barter system like they had been in their villages around Jocotán.

It would be about three months after planting before the corn was ready for harvest, and four months for the rice harvest. They had time to work for pay, which kept food on the table for their families while waiting for the harvests.

The path from Sejá into El Florido had been cleared of trees, logs, and brush. By widening and leveling it, we were able to start using it as a rustic road. The Colorado Jeep was still our work horse, hauling all kinds of supplies from Rio Dulce, where everything still had to be ferried across in dugouts or barges. But at least these loads now could be hauled all the way into El Florido.

Before long, however, our "road" was proving to be difficult to maintain. The road constantly had ruts and mud holes. The Colorado would usually have to be helped into the village with its cargo. Some of the men always showed up to push when they heard the engine roaring and the Colorado not showing up in the village.

Although the Sejá River did provide the needed gravel to fix the roads, it also posed the big problem of frequently flooding. It often rained two or more inches, causing the river to swell four to six feet deep. Fortunately, the flood levels quickly receded, and within four to six hours after the nightly rains it would resume to its normal size.

A hammock foot bridge had been built over the river and during an exceptionally hard rain the hammock bridge was washed away. We still did not comprehend just how powerful that river could become. So we tried again. A large tree of about two feet in diameter on one bank of the river was felled across and anchored by large trunks sunk into the banks on the downriver side of the log to hold it in place. About four inches were sliced off the topside to make it easier to walk across. A cable was strung on one side about three feet higher than the log to hang on to. This worked for quite a while but was still a challenge to cross because it was usually wet and slippery. The water running swiftly underneath easily caused vertigo.

All this time Virginia and I were living in Jocotán and moving families from Jocotán to the relocation project about every two weeks. In between moving families, other trips were made to take supplies. Sometimes Virginia and the kids would join me. When the mission house was finished, we could spend one to two nights and Virginia would take care of the medical needs of the settlers.

Co-op

While we were not at El Florido, my ministry was still mainly with the Chortí in their villages around Jocotán, following up on various assistance programs. The Agriculture Mobile School program sponsored by the government continued expanding.

The Chortí leaders along with the missionaries began the application process for a legal buying and selling cooperative in El Florido. Upon completion, the Guatemalan government officially recognized this as the

"Emaus" Cooperative. The village members took turns going to Morales with Homer once a week to purchase supplies for this store.

The Co-op was only moderately successful. There were records to be kept, money to be managed, purchases to be accounted for and hours of volunteer labor to be coordinated. After a couple of years, one of the men decided to open his own store in his home and soon the Co-op was disbanded. However, the experience was valuable in helping the families learn to work together with people outside their own family, something new for the Chortí culture.

In August the corn was ready to pick. "Look how tall my corn grows!" Pedro exclaimed. "I have never seen corn this tall. Look at the size of these ears! And many stalks have two ears!"

"The nets of harvested ears are much heavier than our nets were in Jocotán," Santiago added, amazed and exhausted after a day's work. "We have so much corn that I have to make more than one trip a day to carry it all to my house."

Corn harvest took place in August, when it rained less. I discovered that their traditional way of harvesting corn was effective. It would start with finding the center of the field. They would pick a circle of ears, knock down the stalks, and start a pile. Then starting from the center, they picked in a circle, tossing ears into the pile until they were at the edge of the field. Then another spot was chosen and the process began all over.

Picking would begin at mid-morning in order to allow the ears to dry out. They would stop by early afternoon, allowing time to haul the corn on their backs to their house. The unhusked ears were gathered into rope nets that had a drawstring that could be pulled together when the net was full. The size of the net was calculated to hold approximately what a man could carry. A twelve-inch-long piece of leather that had rope tied to one end was brought around the net and tied to the other end of the piece of leather. The man would back up to the net, which was usually propped up on a log, bring the piece of leather over his forehead, and lift the net full of corn onto his back and walk to his house.

The women husked and shelled the corn they needed for that day's tortillas. Corn that was going to be sold was shelled by the women and carried out to Sejá by the men after work.

The process of harvesting rice was new for everyone. For that work they needed three things: a sickle, a canvas tarp and burlap bags. These were purchased for each of the men and added to their accounts. The women sewed the canvas tarps from unbleached muslin, which was purchased for them in bolts.

After cutting rice with the sickle for two or three hours, the farmers would spread out the tarp with one edge draped over a limb or small log. A piece of board was laid against the log and onto the tarp. Then the thrashing would begin. Handful by handful they beat the stalks with the dry grain heads against the board with the rice falling onto the tarp. With one of the burlap bags they would fan the rice to blow away as much chaff and leaves as possible. The heavy sacks of rice would then be carried back to the village one by one on their backs.

"Leandro, who is helping you with your rice harvest?" I asked.

"Just me and my wife, Calixtra," he answered.

"Why don't you ask Juan to help you and then you can help him with his rice?" I suggested. He looked at me, with shock because the Chortí people never worked together like I was suggesting.

The next day I went out to see how Leandro was getting along with his harvest. He had two men and his daughters helping him and they were all smiling. After that we noticed several small groups of men working together to harvest their rice.

A few days into the harvest, a couple of the farmers came to Homer. "We need mules to carry our heavy sacks of rice out to the buyers in Sejá," they said. The weather during the rice harvest is cloudy and rainy. The "road" soon became a muddy, watery trail and the Colorado Jeep could no longer make it into the village.

"I know how to take care of mules and horses, because I helped don Chon, our pastor in Jocotán, take care of the church's mules," Dolores quickly offered.

"Okay, I'll see if I can find a horse and a mule in Chiquimula," Homer decided. Soon there were two pack animals moving rice from the village to Sejá.

The rice had to be moved quickly to a buyer because of the high moisture content. If delayed, it would heat up in the bags and spoil. The horse and mule hauled rice to Sejá, two one-hundred-pound sacks apiece. There it was loaded onto the Colorado Jeep and taken to Rio Dulce. At the river it was transferred to dugout canoes and ferried across to a buyer who had his truck waiting on the other side. It was weighed and paid for at the agreed-upon price and the money taken back to each owner. This was a daily affair, except for Sundays, for the four weeks of rice harvest.

"I have never worked this hard in my whole life," Santiago exclaimed.

"Yes, yes, that is true," Vicente agreed, "but look at all the harvest. And the price we have received for our harvest is a fair price; the same that everyone else in the country receives. This land so easily gives us an abundant harvest. It is hard work, but it's worth it."

With their money, they were expected to pay back what they borrowed for tools and materials that they needed for their work. We did not ask them to begin payment on the land until the second harvest. For the most part there was enthusiastic cooperation.

Lorenza

Virginia

Lorenza, an elderly mother and grandmother of one of the Chortí Indian families, had moved to the project with her son and family. She happily helped everyone who had a need and, of course, everyone loved Lorenza.

As was the custom in her former village, she always walked barefooted. She wore her simple typical Indian dress that was decorated in the style of the women of her village. Her feet were callused and cracked.

The ground in El Florido was always muddy from the constant rains. The trails, now used by the pack animals, became quagmires of deep mud, water, and the manure from the animals. Grandma Lorenza became sick with fever and tetanus.

"Are you all right with the Lord?" the village pastor asked her.

"Yes, I am," she quickly replied in the Chortí language. "I'm going to grind corn for my Lord," she added.

After two weeks of suffering, she died. This was a sad time for her family and the whole village. This illness might have been prevented if we had administered the immunizations to the people earlier. There was so much work for us to do but we were frustrated because we lacked the physical energy, time and resources to complete it all.

Guatemalan law required that burial must take place within twenty-four hours after death. There was no way Lorenza's body could be taken back to her village in Jocotán and El Florido did not yet have a cemetery. The nearest cemetery was in San Felipe at the mouth of Lake Izabal and Rio Dulce.

The next morning her body was wrapped in a *petate* (a sleeping mat made out of tule reeds). They took her body by dugout canoe up the river to San Felipe. The petate with Lorenza's body was lowered into the grave and covered up. Before long, that grave at the edge of a distant village's cemetery and marked by only a simple wooden cross, was overgrown by vines and swallowed up by the jungle.

The El Florido auxiliary mayor and his helpers soon made a trip by dugout to Livingston to report the death. At the same time they made a request for an official cemetery in El Florido, which in due time was granted. A piece of land outside the village was marked off for the cemetery, with a sketch showing how the plots were laid out.

The Establishment of the El Florido Friends Church

In February 1969 the El Florido Friends Church was officially established by the denomination in Guatemala. Our church would fall under the jurisdiction of the church district of Morales. Representatives from the district came to officiate over this registration process. These church officials were Ladino businessmen who lived in the urban areas. They had probably never been in such an isolated place as El Florido. They expressed their approval of the Chortí people and were very impressed by the amount of development that was occurring in that area. The Chortí people appreciated the encouragement and affirmation from these church leaders. This was another event that was reshaping the thinking of the Chortí people as to who they were and how God had heard their cry and was helping them come out of their sufferings.

Church meetings were being held regularly in one of the homes. However, plans were quickly made to erect a church building. In the center of the village, three lots were set aside—two for the church building and one for a pastor's house. The church building was constructed like their houses: four corner posts, beams, thatch roof, dirt floor, but no sides. The pulpit was a wooden table, and light came from a kerosene pressure lamp suspended from a beam by a wire.

The church in El Florido rapidly became the center of village life. By early 1970, thirty-five families had moved to the project. Church services there were like any of the Friends churches throughout Guatemala: Sunday School followed by the worship service; Sunday night preaching service emphasizing salvation and deep spiritual living and commitment to Christ; Tuesday night prayer meeting; and Thursday night a teaching service on Bible doctrine. Later, a women's meeting, a men's meeting, and a youth meeting would be added. The singing was accompanied by one of the men playing his guitar.

Since church attendance was large and growing, and most of the members had limited experience in church leadership we decided to invite a Bible school graduate pastor to help shepherd the congregation. Romolo Hernandez and his wife, Melida, were both graduate pastors from Berea Bible School, and they had a little daughter, Corina. Romolo had an agricultural background and was a great help in many ways. They loved the Chortí people, worked hard, and fit in well.

Long ago our mission decided that the missionaries would not take positions as pastors in local churches, but instead, missionaries would disciple and equip Guatemalan leaders to pastor their own congregations.

What we envisioned as the strength of the village was the church life as well as a school to educate the children. We already had a church building, but plans still needed to be made for a school. The temporary solution the people came up with was to hold classes in the church building. The challenge would be to find the right teacher.

The failure of schools in the villages around Jocotán was well known. Chortí parents witnessed the frustration of their children who could not understand their teacher, and the teachers who could not understand their students. So it seemed logical to have a Chortí-speaking teacher. Could we find an educated Chortí Indian who could teach? God heard this cry and had already begun answering.

Years earlier, a young Chortí believer, José Antonio Vásquez, from the village of Pellio Negro, had come to Evelyn and asked her, "Would you teach me mathematics? I just sold some coffee to a buyer out there in the street and I think he robbed me. But I can't do the math to figure the right price."

After that, every Sunday before church, Evelyn taught José and two other youth mathematics. José became an avid learner not only of arithmetic but of geography, simple science and other subjects.

About this time the different evangelical missions in Guatemala joined with the national church leaders to write a curriculum for a primary adult-education course, grades one through six. This course was eventually approved by the Guatemalan government. José studied all the classes with dedication and graduated with a sixth-grade diploma. So, yes! God had helped the El Florido people find an educated Chortí who spoke the language, and as a huge bonus, he was a Christian in our Jocotán church.

When El Florido invited him to come and teach the children, José enthusiastically moved with his family to El Florido. Another big advantage was that he and most of the families knew each other so a trust was already established. Several things contributed to Jose's success: he spoke the children's language; he was at school every day; and he had a passion for teaching the children of his people.

This would be a private school and José would be paid by the mission out of the relocation budget. Even though it was a private school, the Ministry of Education of the Guatemala government provided all the study materials. If the kids did not continue in their studies, they would at least be functionally literate and could defend themselves in the marketplace. The school offered first through third grades and José later added grades fourth through sixth. To everyone's surprise, now El Florido offered a full elementary educational opportunity for its children, even though José himself only had a sixth-grade education.

The success rate of the El Florido students passing their grade exams was far above the average for rural schools. Again, God was leading in ways we had not even imagined. A great hope was growing in the hearts of the Chortí settlers as they saw their children prosper intellectually and advance through the grades.

A Harrowing Trip to Livingston

One month after José arrived, fifteen Chortí settlers needed to register their personal identification cards at the county seat in Livingston. Their trip began at Rio Dulce in the early morning dawn. Two dugout canoes were loaded with seven men in one and eight men the other. It would be a slow, easy trip down the river since the dugouts had only ten-horsepower motors. The men were excited and scared at the same time, but since Homer was with them, they felt safe.

The trip to Livingston was uneventful, but exhilarating as they saw the magnificent scenery on both sides along the Rio Dulce. They arrived at Livingston at 9:30 a.m., just in time for the office to open. The business began with the men one by one signing in and answering many questions, and the official signed the bottom line of each paper. Homer noticed that this procedure was taking longer than he had anticipated, but they had to continue.

They finished at 12:30 p.m., and then he wanted to take the men to a lunch before they started back. It was 2:00 p.m. when they went down to the dock and found their dugout pilots pacing back and forth.

"Where have you been?" they demanded. "Don't you remember we asked you to be back by noon? Look at the sky. We are going to be in a storm!" All the men and Homer meekly and quickly climbed into the dugouts and began the return trip.

As they came out onto El Golfete Lake, the sky was dark, and a strong wind had come up. The dugouts rose to the top of each wave and then fell back down into the troughs. Soon the waves began breaking over the bow of each dugout. Streaks of lightening and loud claps of thunder added to their terror as the heavy rain pounded their backs.

"Get those cans and start bailing water out!" the pilots yelled. There were two one-gallon empty cans in each boat just for this purpose. Two men in each boat started bailing water as fast as they could, but it did not seem like they could keep up. The rest of the men hung on and prayed. All of the Chortí men were sure they were going to die that day as the wind howled and the rain poured down.

Suddenly—**SWISH BOOM!**—the pilots had run the dugouts into a marshy island in the middle of El Golfete to wait out the storm. The Chortí men were so frightened they did not have the strength to climb out of the dugouts, so they just sat still in the rain while they waited for the storm to pass. Two hours later they continued on their return trip home drenched with rain, but rejoicing that they were saved from drowning in the storm.

Several men related this story to us later. Homer agreed that it had happened, but he did not want to talk about it!

9

El Florido Becomes Home

Virginia

It was about noon when we looked up to see Homer and Evelyn driving up to our house in Jocotán for an unexpected visit. We quickly put two more plates on the table and shared our chicken and rice. We were so glad to see them.

After a little while of catching up on the news of our Chortí brethren in Jocotán and in El Florido, Homer slowly began to explain the purpose of this visit. "We have decided that we are tired and need a rest," he explained. "We would like to go home to the United States for three months and then we will return to El Florido."

There was silence while we pondered this idea of Homer and Evelyn leaving. The work of setting up an entire village in the middle of the jungle and then relocating a large number of families to live there was truly daunting. We just had not stopped to think that Homer and Evelyn might need a rest.

"That sounds reasonable," Ray reassured them, knowing they were in their mid-sixties and had carried extremely heavy responsibilities in Jocotán as well as in El Florido.

"We would like for you both to go to El Florido at least once a month to keep an encouraging eye on the work there," he said. "Your family can stay in our home and use our provisions."

"Yes, we are glad to go to El Florido on a part-time basis!" we agreed. Both of us were excited about the relocation project and all the hope it held for the Chortí. At the same time, Ray still had chicken projects, agricultural classes, and church visitation responsibilities in the Jocotán area. And I had ongoing clinic work to do there.

Really? I thought. I was excited about this opportunity as I remembered my childhood dream of being a missionary nurse in the jungle—and here it was!

One week after the Sharplesses returned to California, we packed one suitcase apiece for our family, a few supplies, and two more Chortí families in the back of our pickup truck. We drove down the Atlantic coast highway to the Morales turnoff and on to Rio Dulce.

We made the usual trip across the river in dugout canoes together and then boarded the Colorado jeep to ride on to Sejá. Parking the Jeep, we could see that the Indian people who were with us were exhausted from the trip, but they picked up their belongings and we began the trek together.

No sunlight came through the canopy of the jungle trees. The smell of moist, decaying leaves on the floor of the jungle reminded me of the musty smell in the damp dirt floor of our farmhouse basement in Iowa. We heard strange bird calls. In the small areas where jungle had been cleared away it was sunny, humid, and stifling hot, and I wondered what kind of animals lurked nearby. *There must be snakes,* I thought.

As we approached the Sejá River we saw that Homer had left a small log across the river for us to cross, but the log was so small you could only step one foot in front of the other foot. As more people crossed, it became more slippery from the muddy feet making it especially precarious for the people bringing up the rear. The sure-footed Indian people walked across the log barefoot, grasping the log with their toes while carrying their *kaites* (sandals) and all of their other belongings. Ray carried Kenny on his shoulders as he crossed; Tad and Linda were very agile and got themselves across. All of the experiences of this journey into El Florido built our anticipation of what lay ahead.

There it was—our temporary home in an exotic paradise! It was a green building on low posts with a red, corrugated tin roof. It had everything we needed to live comfortably in the jungle. There were many comforts I could live without, but I was glad this house had a wooden floor instead of a packed-dirt floor. I was also glad that the house was elevated on posts to keep the snakes and rats out.

We slept in American-style beds with mattresses and sheets instead of slat beds on sticks with a *"petate"* over the slats like our neighbors had. I was so thankful Homer and Evelyn and the Friends Mission thought these things were important for our family to be comfortable and healthy.

Of course there was no electricity in the village, but Homer had left a small Honda generator that could light the two light bulbs in the house. We still chose to use Kincaid kerosene lamps for light at night, moving them around the house as needed.

We were thankful for the Maytag wringer/washer that had a Briggs and Straton engine mounted under the tub to run it. Now the only problem with washing clothes was trying to get them dry. It rained at least every other day. So we put up rope lines inside our house to try to dry jeans, shirts, and dresses. Sometimes it took four days to dry them.

Evelyn's kerosene-powered freezer helped us keep meat frozen so we could eat meat two or three times a week. When someone butchered an animal, whether it was a chicken, a pizote, or an iguana, we would buy a pound or two of the meat and freeze it for later.

Once in a while it did not rain for five or six days and we would run out of water. When that happened, we walked down to the Sejá River and bathed and washed the clothes we were wearing. Linda, Tad and Kenny thought it was so much fun. Families from our village did this daily. I enjoyed getting to experience their way of life and understanding their perspective on things such as bathing and washing clothes. They were curious to see if our skin was the same color under our clothes as it was on our arms and faces.

At this point, we started understanding the extent of the fears and uncertainties that the Indians were feeling, so we decided to spend most of our time in El Florido. Our presence reassured the families that they would not be abandoned.

Strange Animals

"Mommy, there's a funny-looking cow on the trail behind our house," Linda exclaimed as she ran inside.

A funny-looking cow? I asked myself. *Wait—there are no cows around here. I must go see what my five-year-old is talking about.*

Standing just beyond our house was a tapir. We had looked up the description of animals in our area and found that the tapir was more like an overgrown pig with a long nose that almost resembled a trunk. They have very poor eyesight, move slowly and eat vegetation. I was not too fearful that it would harm our three children who were playing in the backyard, but I gave them strict orders to stay clear away from the animal. After a while it slowly meandered back into the jungle.

Before long the farmers were complaining of rats in their fields. They were having difficulty raising their corn crop due to the invasion of rats that ate corn off the stalks at night. They were able to find a poison that helped a great deal and the rat population seemed to decline.

Then a pack of pizotes attacked the cornfields. The pizote is a member of the raccoon family that would pull the stalk down and eat the ear while it was still attached to the stalk. There were two reasons the farmers began to trap these animals, one was to save the corn crop, and the other was that they ate the pizote meat. Before long the remaining pizotes moved on and there were no more problems.

A pair of colorful toucans came to the tree by our front door every morning to pick the little red berries. Their beaks were so heavy that they dived downward whenever they slowed their speed. It was a treat to watch them.

Oh, what was that streak of blue that I just noticed in the corner of my eye as it went by? I asked myself. After a second look, I realized it was a large, bright, metallic-blue butterfly loping along. "What a beautiful sight!" I exclaimed. "It's much larger than my hand."

"Mommy, I just saw a big black cat," Linda gasped as she came running into the house.

"Really, how big was it?" I asked.

She motioned about one and half feet from the ground. "It had a long tail and was black all over," she said. "It ran into the bushes on the other side of the trail." We had heard that there were a few big cats in the area, but we could only guess what she saw.

One evening we heard loud chattering in the jungle behind our house and we went out to see what was up in the trees. A large flock of colorful parrots scolded each other loudly, and after a while they left.

We caught a walking stick insect that measured eight inches long, and we mounted it on a board to admire. The click beetle had two large lights on its head that shined at night. The kids of the village liked to tie a thread around one of its legs to keep it tethered as it flew in circles, shining its headlights in the darkness.

Some of the Chortí farmers told us they saw wild pigs in their parcels. They were wreaking havoc with their corn crops by making mud holes to wallow in, and destroying some of their corn. We suspected they killed the pigs for meat.

One day in El Florido, Ray called me outside to see something. It was a dead snake, but it was no ordinary snake. It was a beautiful twelve-and-a-half foot glistening black snake with a white belly. We measured it because I usually exaggerate sizes and Ray minimizes sizes, and we wanted this one accurate.

Since childhood I have had a fear of snakes. But as I looked at that creature, I realized this was a beautiful wild animal, and it would slither away from people if at all possible. My exaggerated fear of snakes left me that day.

We discovered that the very poisonous fer de lances, green vine snakes, rattlesnakes, and yellow beards lived in and around El Florido. I realized the possibility of seeing snakes and experiencing snake bites was a reality. The nurses in the Wycliff Medical Dispensary helped me acquire two vials of anti-venom, which I kept in the clinic. This would be enough to keep the bitten person alive till we could get him to the county hospital in Port Barrios for continued treatment.

Howler Monkey

A warm breeze was felt in the quiet of the dark night. The three kids were sound asleep after we read from the Narnia series. Ray and I were in bed. The chirps of crickets and night-bird calls resounded in the nearby jungle.

Suddenly we heard the "humph-hm-hm-hm, humph-hm-hm" sound of an animal.

"Listen," I said to Ray, "that must be a gorilla." I could just imagine a seven-foot-tall black gorilla standing on his back legs pounding his chest with his fists.

"No," he said. "It's a monkey the size of a dog."

"I can't imagine a monkey that size with such a deep loud voice," I stated as we continued to listen to the animal call. The call was getting gradually louder, indicating it was coming closer to our house.

Almost every evening at the same time we heard the monkey's call. And I was sure it was a gorilla. "No one will believe me; I've got to record this," I declared. So I got out our small cassette recorder and recorded it for ten minutes. The recording was successful, but I had held the microphone so close to my chest that it had also recorded my pounding heartbeat. *Well,* I thought. *We have just recorded two monkeys!*

Knowing how unbearable the heat was under the tin roof of the church, I made a deal with our kids. "If you sit quietly through the three hour church service, I will take you to the river for a swim and a picnic." They liked the idea and tried very hard to be attentive in church.

We had just finished our picnic lunch at the Branche River when the kids jumped in for a swim. Suddenly we heard the same monkey call in a high tree about eighty feet from us. The call was loud.

At first I could not see the animal because he was hiding in the foliage. Then he began climbing down the tree. He had spotted us and we got a good look at him. He was the size of a large black dog with a long tail and a monkey head. He had a white throat. It was, in fact, a howler monkey. We had no idea what it would do next.

"Okay, kids, get out of the water and bring your clothes; we're going home," I called.

They were having so much fun in the refreshing water that they acted like they had not heard me.

"I mean *now!* Get out of the water and we're going home," I repeated as I began walking home with the picnic basket on my arm.

This time they grabbed their clothes and followed me. We looked back to see that monkey down on the riverbank right where we had eaten our picnic. He was probably looking for some food we might have left behind.

It was good for me to actually see the howler monkey fairly close and to realize Ray's description was accurate. The encyclopedia told us the call of a howler monkey can be heard a kilometer away. You can imagine how loud it sounds only two hundred feet from your bedroom window.

Two months later we were taking two visiting pastors from California with us on a walk through the jungle and out to the parcels of land. We noticed some large monkeys in a tree and stopped to watch them. Tad and Kenny ran to the tree to get a closer look. Ray and I stood back with the pastors to watch. The Indian farmers enjoyed the monkeys. But the little boys of the village liked to tease them by throwing rocks and the monkeys evidently felt threatened. We watched one big monkey swing on a vine down toward Tad and Kenny, and then it grabbed another vine and swung right above them.

"Tad, Kenny, look out! Run!" we yelled. Just then the monkey defecated and urinated, trying to hit them. They ran and the monkey just missed his target. Watching that scene was entertaining for us, but Tad and Kenny did not think it was funny.

Gloria

Evelyn had realized she could not do all the household work, minister to the needs of the villagers and make trips out with Homer by herself. So she wisely chose Gloria, a sixteen-year-old daughter of Silverio, one of the farmers of the project, to help her.

Evelyn taught Gloria how to wash dishes the 'Gringo way' and rinse them with scalding water. She taught her how to mop the wooden floor, and to wash the clothes with the Maytag washing machine. Evelyn also taught Gloria how to read the Bible and sign her name.

When Evelyn left El Florido for the U.S. she recommended Gloria to help me. I was more than happy to have her help since I had three little children, which made three times more dirty dishes and clothes than the Sharplesses had.

So I hired Gloria to work for me. Arriving at eight o'clock every morning, she would always slip her muddy shoes off at our front door and work barefooted. I immediately appreciated her very capable help and quiet manner.

I divided up our work so we both knew what we had to do and we did not duplicate our efforts. I prepared all the food and baked bread. Gloria washed the dishes and the clothes while I taught Linda kindergarten and later taught all three children in grade school. She mopped the floors in the afternoon while I took care of sick patients who came to me for help.

As we worked side by side, Gloria taught me much about the Chortí life and culture, and I taught her about the Lord Jesus. My curiosity about her life in her former village and the changes we were seeing in El Florido led me to ask many questions.

"Gloria, what did your family eat in Guareruche?" I asked one day.

"We had tortillas and coffee every day and black beans three times a week," she answered.

"What do you eat here at El Florido?" I asked.

"Now we eat plantains, fish, bread, black beans, eggs and rice," she answered. "Oh, yes, we eat Incaperina every day also, and we like it a lot!" she added. (Incaparina is a nationally produced product that can be cooked and eaten like cooked cereal. It is very nutritious, high in protein, and sold very cheaply—about one cent per serving. The Co-op store in the village sold it, and we encouraged the families to use it, especially for the children.)

"But Gloria, why do you have eggs here when you didn't have them in Guareruche?"

"Here there are lots of plants and green grass, as well as many insects like ants and termites for the chickens to eat," she answered. "We also feed them corn. We didn't have enough corn for them in Guareruche."

"Your father just put in a new cement latrine. Do you use it?"

"Yes!" she answered as her eyes lit up.

"Did you use a latrine in Guareruche?"

"No, we just used the bushes," she answered, showing embarrassment.

"Did you have a school in that village?"

"Yes, but only part time. My sister went, but she didn't learn to read or write. The teacher would never be there regularly, and she didn't finish the year."

"Your brother, Moises, can read and write. Where did he learn?"

"He sat in on classes given by the priests at the Catholic Church. He liked them."

"Is your brother a Catholic?" I asked.

"No, and he wants to accept Christ as his Savior and become a Christian. I became a Christian here at El Florido last year with doña Evelyn. My sister also accepted Christ as her Savior here."

"What about your parents? Have they changed?" I asked.

"My father, Silverio, has always been a Christian, but he had lots of problems in Guareruche. He would fight his brother, Pedro, (who also lives in El Florido), and then he would backslide in his spiritual life."

"I feel that your father is a strong Christian here. Is that right?" I asked.

"Oh, yes he is!" she explained with excitement. "Don Romolo, our pastor, has explained the Bible and the Christian life and we understand it."

"Gloria, I thought you spoke only the Chortí language when you came. Can you understand the Spanish messages in church?"

"Some words I don't understand, but I understand most of it."

We quickly developed a deep friendship, and even today she is like a member of my family. She has a unique sense of humor and helped us faithfully. Kenny, our youngest, was two-and-a-half years old when Gloria began helping us and she became as attached to him as he did to her. Gloria's mother and sister were quite steeped in the Chortí belief system which made them fearful and timid toward us missionaries. But Gloria was outgoing and trusting toward us for which I was so grateful.

Jeff's Visit

When Homer and Evelyn left for the United States in March 1970 for a three-month recovery from their health problems, they planned to return to continue the ministry in El Florido. While in the United States, Evelyn was diagnosed with pulmonary tuberculosis and treatment was begun. The therapy was effective, but the medical advice was for her to not return to Guatemala. Homer was treated for a gastric ulcer but then felt he must return to Guatemala to help Ray and me.

Jeff Hoffman, a seventeen-year-old high school graduate from Garden Grove Friends Church, asked Homer if he could serve on the mission field with him for the summer. Homer agreed to bring Jeff to Guatemala with him when he returned.

Jeff was enthralled with the sights on his 5-hour trip to El Florido. Homer and Jeff arrived just in time to join us for the evening meal. Ray was away giving Bible and agriculture classes to churches in Honduras. I knew the men in El Florido were very excited to see Homer again and visit with him, so I suggested he go to bed early and rest up for the next day.

Very early the next morning I found Homer lying on the floor in the hallway of our house. "Virginia, I think I'm having a heart attack," Homer said. "I've had pain all night and have not slept at all."

"Let me check your pulse and blood pressure," I said, grabbing my stethoscope. I noted his heart rate was only slightly elevated. However, he did not look very well and his restlessness concerned me.

"Homer, it is a long distance to the nearest doctor or hospital, so it is probably a good idea for you to go get checked by a physician in Guatemala City. But how are we going to get you to your pickup truck in Sejá?" I wondered out loud.

"Well, I guess I'll just have to walk out," he reasoned.

"Jeff, would you please walk out with Homer to his truck?" I asked our young volunteer who had been in Guatemala less than twenty-four hours. "And then would you please stay with him until he sees a doctor or gets to the hospital in Guatemala City?"

"Yes, I will be glad to do that," Jeff replied. He was so willing to do anything we asked him to do, I noticed.

I made sure they had water and Jeff carried Homer's bag. I stood at the door as I watched them walk out of the village. I prayed, "Lord, please help Jeff get Homer out to Guatemala City safely. And Lord, when is Homer going to return to us here? Is he going to come back?"

"No, he will never be back to serve Me in El Florido," I sensed the Lord reply. I wondered if that was truly the Lord preparing me for things ahead or if it was my imagination.

Jeff and Homer walked back to the main road where the truck was parked and Jeff drove Homer the long and arduous trip back to Guatemala City. During the long drive, Homer was in pain and frequently dozed off. Jeff had to wake Homer at intersections to ask for directions. On the way to the city, Homer decided to go all the way back to the U.S. So Jeff drove him straight to the airport and Homer caught the next flight to California.

Jeff knew very little Spanish and was not sure about the way back to El Florido. He was not, however, overly concerned or afraid. This was probably a combination of his youthful naiveté and an immense gift of faith. His successful return alone was nothing short of a miracle.

Later, we realized that the Lord was preparing us to do the work in El Florido by ourselves. We had moved to the village in the jungle for three months while the Sharplesses were in the United States for a rest, and we ended up living and working there much longer. Thankfully, doctors determined in the U.S. that Homer's pain was due to a gastric ulcer and not a heart attack.

Ray

It was hard to gauge the Chortí's response to what was happening in El Florido. On the one hand there was a sense of overwhelming amazement at what the land could produce. On the other hand there was an underlying feeling of uneasiness, or maybe fear or disbelief.

One day as we worked together widening the trail into the village, Cruz and Nicolás, young Chortí farmers, approached me and said quietly, "Our wives are not happy here. They want to go back to their village above Jocotán."

"What seems to be the problem?" I asked. "What don't they like?"

"They don't like all the rain and mud," Nicolás said.

"And the whole jungle environment is strange and seems hostile," Cruz added. "They feel so isolated and miss their families. They say they feel trapped here because there is no way for them to go back."

"I'm sorry to hear that, but what about you? How do you feel about making this move and living here?" I questioned.

"I see a future here that I would never have had in Guareruche where I grew up," Cruz said. "This is the hardest work I have ever done, but I can see the great reward for the effort. However, to be perfectly honest, it is difficult to believe that this is really happening. Will someone come and take all this away from us or in some way take advantage of us like they always have?"

Nicolás chimed in, saying, "If the missionaries stay here with us we will stay. If not, we will find some way to leave and get back to our villages. We want to trust you. We have trusted in Christ and our lives have changed. Has He heard our cry in that wilderness and brought us here? We want to believe, but perhaps our faith is too weak. Will you stay with us?"

These two men made it clear that many of the families felt the same way. Their sense of being a forgotten people from a desolate land was too strong to overcome in a few short months. They were saying, "We will wait and see."

An uneasy and almost scary feeling came over me of just how dependent these people were on the missionaries. Their fears were real because of the generations of being mistreated. They had been looked down upon as a second-class people, resulting in a life of dire poverty with no way out.

We had conceived the relocation project as a radical way to help at least some of the Chortí people out of their misery. "We are committed to the project," I assured Cruz and Nicolás. "And, yes, you have our word that we will stay here with you!"

There was a great need for trust between the Chortí people and the missionaries. Trust is difficult to establish and often difficult to keep. It takes years to be confident that a deep, lasting trust has been developed, especially in cross-cultural relationships. Sometimes it never happens. Sometimes it is pretended or assumed but is not real.

The Friends Mission had a spiritual ministry with the Chortí Indian people for almost thirty years. We had worked directly with them in agricultural and medical assistance for several years. We felt we had earned their trust when they agreed to be relocated to the coast. Was that trust in question now?

Because of what we were hearing, we knew we had to be honest and transparent in everything we did. In the first two or three years, every time we left El Florido for more than a day, they would ask us, "When will you be back?" We planned our trips very carefully and told them exactly the day and approximate time we would return.

No matter what, to the best of our ability, we would show up on the day we had told them. We would usually arrive in the late afternoon, and there would be several men and a few children hanging around our house to greet us. Then they would slowly disappear back to their houses.

It was alarming to see the dependence these people had on us and the extent of their fears of being left alone in that place. Strengthening our bond with the El Florido people in those first two years was crucial to the success of the settlement. Our trust in each other would be tested again and again during that time.

10

Medical Ministry in Our Kitchen

Tuberculosis

Virginia

Tuberculosis had become a concern to us because the disease was endemic in the Chortí villages. Since Evelyn Sharpless had contracted it recently, we wondered how many of the El Florido people had it. We met Dr. Cesar Margarin, a Chiquimula doctor, who was supportive of the Friends missionary work.

Dr. Margarin became interested in giving his services when he heard about the medical needs in El Florido. He and his wife, Marina, visited us in El Florido and assessed the medical needs. He directed a plan for diagnosis and treatment of some patients while helping me in our clinic. He ordered chest X-rays for twenty-eight people who showed signs and symptoms of TB. Seventeen of them had positive chest X-rays for active TB.

Dr. Margarin followed up on the care of the sick people by helping us acquire medical treatment for those with TB. I administered the treatments daily in El Florido, and all of the patients cooperated by regularly coming to me for their medicine. After two weeks, they each said they were feeling much better.

Due to the advanced stage of his TB condition, Pedro Damian was ordered to go to the hospital in Chiquimula for treatment. When he finally consented to go, Ray and I took him to Chiquimula to be treated until he recovered.

After one month in the Hospital, Pedro ran away to Pelillo Negro, a village above Jocotán. Three months later I met him walking into El Florido.

I greeted him. "Hello, hermano Pedro." ("Hermano" means brother.) "Buenos dias," he replied glumly and continued on.

Later I visited him in his home. "What happened in Chiquimula?" I asked.

"Well, they kept me in a hospital, the tortillas were cold, and they never gave me enough beans," he replied.

"Then what happened?"

"They would not give me my clothes, so I left in a white shirt when the door was open," he explained.

"Did you tell the doctor you were leaving?"

"No," he replied, "it was so bad I would have died there if I had stayed."

I realized the medical personnel of the hospital did not understand the Indian culture and how to apply treatment within that culture. I wondered how I could take care of Pedro in El Florido and protect his family at the same time.

Dr. Margarin advised me to go ahead and treat him in his home with daily medication. I asked Pedro to come to my house every day to receive his medicine. I knew I could not trust him to take his medication properly if I sent a dozen tablets home with him.

After the first week he stopped coming in. When I visited him in his home, he told me the medication made him sick and he felt worse when he took it. I advised him to eat a piece of tortilla with the medicine, but two days later he did not return for treatment. I struggled with the dilemma of trying to treat his advanced TB condition and respecting his right to decline treatment. And I continued praying for him and asking the Lord to show me what to do for him. Days and weeks passed and I did not see him.

One day his wife, Catalina, came to see me and asked for medication for Pedro.

"What's his problem?" I asked.

"He has a bad cough and it is difficult for him to breath," she explained.

"I need to see him before I can send some medicine, so please bring him here," I pleaded.

"Bueno, I'll see if he will come," she replied.

Three days later Pedro walked to our house looking just terrible, and his hair was uncombed. I listened to his lungs and the breath sounds were congested with fluid. His breathing was labored. I gave him some decongestant expectorant, but I knew this medicine could not help him very much. I also wanted him to know I still cared for him, even as frustrated as I was, and I was sorry he was suffering so much. I prayed with him before he left that day.

On the next trip to Chiquimula I consulted Dr. Margarin about Pedro's condition. "Here is what you can do to temporarily relieve his labored breathing," he explained. "Take this large-barrel syringe with the large needle and insert the needle between the right lumbar ribs. Slowly withdraw a syringe full of fluid, and he will be more comfortable."

Oh my goodness, I thought, *I have observed doctors doing a thoracentesis in sterile conditions in the hospital, but—.*

"I'm not sure I can do that out in El Florido," I said.

"Yes, you can do it," he said, "and here is the necessary equipment."

Can I do this? I wondered. *Should I do this?* Frankly, I was doubtful.

Back in El Florido I visited Pedro and Catalina. I explained that I had consulted Dr. Margarin and he told me to put an injection between Pedro's ribs (I used this word because they would not have understood any other explanation).

"Will it hurt?" Pedro asked.

"Yes, some," I answered, trying to be honest.

Two days later Catalina came to me and said, "Pedro is ready for his 'shot' in the lungs."

I prepared and sterilized the equipment and walked over to his hut with the dirt floor, stick sides, and thatch roof. They had an old metal barrel in their home that I used as a table for my drape, sterile field and sterile instruments. Then I prayed, *"Lord, please help me do this, and please help Pedro breathe better."*

Still with much trepidation, I proceeded. A small amount of local anesthesia was injected first under the skin. Then I began introducing the large needle that was connected to the large syringe. The needle was about one inch under the skin when I saw movement out of the corner of my eye. I looked at the floor and saw a small green snake coming toward my feet. Tremendous fear and disgust filled me, and I froze. The animal slithered between my feet and out between the sticks of the wall on the other side of the hut and was gone.

Slowly my nerves calmed down, and I regained my attention to the procedure that I was attempting. With the needle in place I tried to withdraw fluid but nothing came into the syringe.

Pedro was exhausted and so was I. I decided I had honestly given it a good try but was unsuccessful. I explained to Pedro and Catalina that I was unable to help him. And they kindly said, "It's all right, we understand." I put a Band-aid on the injection site and left.

One week later Catalina came to tell me, "Don Pedro is in so much agony. All the medication you have given him has made him much worse." I knew that I had lost the confidence of my patient. In their eyes, I was now the cause of their problem instead of a solution. And when this happened I discovered there was nothing more I could do that would help him except pray. This truly was a humiliating and helpless feeling that I had learned to accept on a few occasions.

Catalina returned two days later and asked me for a bottle of iodine to cure a "sore" Pedro had on his chest. I gave her a half-ounce bottle of iodine and prayed with her for Pedro.

That afternoon I went to Pedro's house to see the "sore." The TB infection had formed an abscess on the upper left chest. This abscess had broken through the outer skin so that I could look through the chest wall right into the pleura sack of the lung and pulsating heart. The opening was the size of a quarter. What an awful, helpless sight! Pedro was conscious, talking, and short of breath. Instruction was given to Catalina to maintain a bandage over the hole at all times. I prayed with Catalina for the Lord's help and touch. Don Pedro and Catalina thanked me for the visit.

Two days later Catalina came to tell us that Pedro had died. The men and women from the church immediately went to help the family. The men dug the grave in our village cemetery. The women washed the body and wrapped it in a large muslin sheet I donated. The women began the process of making tamales for the people who would spend the night at the vigil in the home. It was the custom for neighbors to spend the whole night with the family in their home and the burial was the next day. Since Pedro was poor, they wrapped his body in a new woven reed mat and placed it in the grave and covered it with dirt.

Homer and Evelyn had always welcomed the Chortí people into their home to visit or talk about their crops or to pray. So when we moved into the Sharpless home, the pattern was already set, and we were delighted that our friends felt free to visit whenever they wanted. I realized I did not need to feel guilty about our comparatively nice home as long as we shared it with our Chortí neighbors. We enjoyed the friendly camaraderie with our Chortí friends.

I quickly discovered they had many medical needs, so I diagnosed and treated them in our kitchen. Often spiritual needs and medical needs are closely related. If a patient was too sick to work on his parcel of land, he also would be discouraged and fearful that he would not be able to provide food for his family.

I made it a practice to always pray before treating the patients, "Lord, please help me understand what is happening to this person, please help me discern the physical needs and help me to communicate Your love to him." Then I took a good verbal history from the patient, did a physical assessment and kept those records in a simple notebook.

The indicated medicine was administered with careful instructions on taking the medication and on the necessary care of the patient. Then I prayed, "Lord, Help this medication work properly in his body. Only You can heal and encourage him. So Lord, use this to touch him and to bring glory to Your name. Thank you, Lord."

Each patient was charged twenty-five cents per visit. Visitors from the United States questioned why I charged these people who were so poor. I had decided to charge a fee because in their minds, "free" medicine could not be very effective. The second reason they paid for the medicine was because our goal was to keep the medical work self-supporting, not dependent on foreign funds.

Medicines and supplies were purchased from a Wycliff mission medicine warehouse in Guatemala City. Wycliff bought medicines wholesale from pharmaceutical companies such as McKesson, Abbot and Wyeth, and others. Their nurse administrator would sell the medicines wholesale to about fifteen of us missionary nurses who had rural primary-care clinics in Guatemala.

I had just called the family to dinner one evening when don Juan, the oldest man in the village, came into our home with his hand and arm wrapped in a bloody shirt. I carefully unwrapped his arm and found that he had a deep six-inch cut on the inside of his left arm that happened when his machete had slipped. It needed to be sutured. I did not have the necessary suturing needle and silk suture thread on hand, but had read in a medical manual that a sewing needle and thread could be used in an emergency.

"Don Juan, I do not have any anesthesia here, do you still want me to suture this?" I asked. "Maybe you should go into Puerto Barrios to the hospital there," I suggested. (It was a four-to-five-hour ride on a public bus after walking more than a mile out to the road.)

"Go ahead, doña Virginia," he said with a grimace. "Let's get it done here, please?"

So I wrapped a couple of my sewing needles and thread in a white dish towel and placed it in my pressure cooker on a rack above the water. It was sterilized for ten minutes.

The truth of the matter was that I had never sutured before. In the United States, the doctors always did the suturing while we nurses assisted. But I knew what needed to be done for Juan. So I prayed, "Lord, please help me help Juan. Guide my hands. Please, heal this arm. Thank you, Lord."

The pressure-cooked towel was my sterile field. I put on sterile gloves and started the procedure with the needle and thread.

What a surprise! His skin was very tough, and it was difficult to get the sewing needle through the skin. Finally I got the first stitch finished and tied. Since I had not heard a sound from Juan, I looked up. Sweat was rolling down his face, and he had a towel in his mouth to clench his teeth on.

"What do you think, don Juan, shall I do anymore?" I asked.

Juan answered, "Yes, please go ahead and finish, I can take it."

The skin was like leather and the suturing was tedious. My family was trying to eat their evening meal on the other side of our kitchen table from where I was working. The suturing had taken much longer than I had anticipated, and they could not wait to eat any longer. Finally I finished the job with six stitches and bandaged the wound. I gave Juan Tylenol and antibiotics and sent him home.

Upon reflection of the episode, I decided I would not do that again with a sewing needle and no anesthesia. On our next trip to Guatemala City I purchased suturing equipment, local anesthesia, and sterile gloves. I kept all the medical equipment and the medicines for coughs, diarrhea, and infections in our bathroom.

Five days later Juan returned to have the stitches taken out and his arm had healed beautifully. It was amazing. "Thank You, Lord, for Your healing touch," I prayed with him.

Human Botfly

One day Rosa and her husband came to visit me in our kitchen. They began by casually asking about our children, especially our youngest, Kenny. I asked them about their children and how they were. We talked about the corn harvest and the scarcity of rain in Jocotán this year. This friendly conversation went on for over thirty minutes until finally they broached the real purpose of the visit.

Rosa quietly said, "Doña Virginia, I have a sore that has been bothering me for some time."

"Where is your sore?" I asked.

"Here," she said, as she discretely showed me the swollen sore on her thigh.

"Oh, I see," I said. "How long have you had this sore?"

"For two weeks," she answered, smiling all the while.

"Does it hurt when I touch it?" I asked as I slightly touched it.

"Yes. At times something moves inside the sore, and that really hurts."

"Hmmm." I thought, *What is this?* At first glance it looks like an ordinary boil that is raised, red and warm to the touch. Then I took a closer look. The top of the "boil" had an opening where I thought it must be draining the pus.

"Wait a minute," I said mainly to myself. "It *is* moving." I could see a tiny maggot-like piece move when it was probed.

At this moment I was remembering my microbiology lessons in the university laboratory. We had observed many slides and specimens of tropical parasites. I had studied them and identified them for the exam, but now wished I could go back and review what now had become very pertinent information.

So I decided to apply my basic wound care techniques. Following the technique for treating an abscess, I applied hot packs for twenty minutes but there was very little drainage. Then I applied some pressure thinking the "thing" could be quickly squeezed out.

"Ouch, that hurts," Rosa groaned.

I decided to not try that again.

I cleaned the wound, applied antibiotic skin ointment, and a bandage.

Rosa graciously thanked me for helping her.

"I know, Rosa, but really, I was not able to remove that 'thing' in the center of the boil," I explained.

"It's okay, doña Virginia, I'll be better," she said as they went out the door.

I wondered what kind of boil I had just seen. I wondered what the cause of it was.

Months later, Ray's uncle, Dr. Merritt Canfield, gave me three *Manuals of Tropical Medicine*. I was deeply grateful for those books that aided me in the diagnosis and treatment of tropical diseases.

In *A Manual of Tropical Medicine* by Mackie, Hunter, and Worth, I found the description of the disease that Rosa suffered. It was the human botfly, an insect that gets a mosquito to plant the egg under the skin. The egg grows into a larva that stays under the skin fifty to one hundred days. The treatment is to open the boil under sterile technique, surgically remove the larva, and then cover the wound with an antibiotic ointment and a bandage. When this is done, the wound heals very quickly.

But this pest continued to attack us. Tad had a large larva on his back that I had to remove. Ray had one on his stomach. The people in El Florido were getting them fairly frequently. I was alarmed at the prevalence of the botfly and uncertain as to how it could be prevented in this mosquito-infested region.

Within a year's time, however, the number of botfly cases in my clinic tapered off till finally it seemed to have stopped altogether. I wondered if the villagers were still suffering with the botfly infestations but were no longer coming to me because their home remedies for it were less painful than the nurse's.

The Planned Parenthood Dilemma

While we were in Jocotán planning the relocation project, it was decided that Planned Parenthood should be taught and encouraged. The theory went something like this: Since high birth rate was one of the causes of poverty among the Chortí, it was felt by missionaries and the mission board that birth control should be taught. This was also a popular point of view from the U.S. public health. Consequently, the health classes that I was preparing for the El Florido women included the birth control plan that I had learned in the United States and in Guatemala City.

During my preparation of these classes, Pedro, one of the leaders in El Florido, came to me to talk about his family and his wife's current pregnancy.

"Pedro, do you know there is a way to plan your children's birth a little further apart so each one has better nutrition?"

"Yes," he answered. "I have heard about that, but I don't think it is right."

"Oh? Why?" I questioned.

"God tells us in Genesis 1:22 to be fruitful and multiply the earth, so I don't think God wants us to control births," he told me very quickly. His reply to this question was immediate and based on a specific Bible verse.

"Where in the Bible does it tell us to plan our children's birth?" he asked me.

I thought for a moment and quickly asked God to help me in this debate. I considered the Bible verses that give instructions on raising children.

"Hermano Pedro, you may be right. I can't think of a verse that tells us specifically to plan our families," I slowly answered.

"So," he said, "I don't think it is good to control birth rate; it's not God's will."

I did not want to give in to his reasoning so I reminded him how he plants his corn.

"Why do you put spaces in between the seeds that you plant in your corn field?" I asked.

"So it will grow better and produce better," he replied. "But the Bible does not tell us to control the birth of our children. Now I need to go to the field," he said matter-of-factly. "Adios."

"Adios, my brother," I responded. I was really surprised at Pedro's adamant explanation of his point of view. I also felt deflated about my theory that the Chortí needed to practice birth control to get out of poverty. I had lost this debate, and I knew I had not convinced hermano Pedro of the benefits of birth control.

I decided to examine the Scripture closer to see what God was telling us about birth control. Ray and I love God's Word and the Chortí brothers knew that. They knew we wanted to obey God's Word all the way. We had taught them many Bible classes. It was important for us to be consistent in everything we did and to "walk our talk" every day. We prayed that they would see Jesus in our lives and follow Him. Interestingly, during my search I could not find any Scripture that specifically supported birth control, but I continued preparing classes to teach it.

In the meantime, Teofila, a very precious friend and prayer warrior, visited me. She felt called to visit one or two families a day until she had visited every family in El Florido and prayed with them. Then she started the cycle of visitations again, sometimes with her little daughter, Felipa, in tow. I appreciated her praying for me and our family. She was loved by everyone.

"How many babies have you had, Teofila?" I asked.

"Thirteen," she quickly replied.

"Thirteen!" I exclaimed. "But you brought only three with you to El Florido—Felipa, Andrés, and Carlos.

"Yes," she said quietly.

"Where are the others?"

"They died," she replied, smiling.

"How did they die?" I humbly asked.

"Well, a little girl died at birth, two died about a month after their births, my Juanito died just before he turned two years old, Carlos died when he was five years old with whooping cough, Juana and Rosa died when they were eight and ten from measles, Luis died from dysentery when he was twelve, Maria died a month after she was born, and Mario died when he was two years old," Teofila explained.

"Oh, no," I sighed, "You have experienced such horrible grief!" She had lost ten children. She had named them, loved each one, cared for them, prayed for them, and then they died. My heart was heavy and tears came to my eyes as I thought about this suffering. I asked myself, *How would I walk through all this grief if I were in her shoes?*

"Oh God," I cried with a broken heart, "how can I help these families who have suffered so much?"

Suddenly the answer came: *"Help the children live!"*

I asked some of the other mothers in the village the same questions about their children that I had asked Teofila. I learned that every one of the families had lost three to five children before they came to El Florido. I estimated that more than 50 percent of all the newborn Chortí babies that were born in the villages around Jocotán died of tetanus before they were one month old. I began to ask myself the questions, "How do they get tetanus?" and "Why do they die then?"

I learned that the next most dangerous stage, after their first month of life, was when they were being weaned. The prevention of childhood diseases and improvement of child birth practices became my focus. All the Planned Parenthood classes about birth control were canceled. "Help the children live" became my theme.

Introducing a New Birth Practice

One day, Lázaro's wife, Macaria, who was eight months pregnant, came to visit me after I had finished giving a hygiene class.

"Doña Virginia, would you help me when I deliver this baby?"

"Oh, yes," I replied, "I would be very glad to help you. You call me when the labor pains begin and I will come to your house."

"Very well," She agreed with a sparkle in her eyes.

I prepared the usual equipment such as the sterilized cord clamps, scissors, and string to tie the umbilical cord. The sterile gloves, sterile sheet, and a nurse's jacket and mask were ready. Since I had worked in obstetrics and had helped deliver many babies in the hospital in the United States, I was comfortable with the anticipated procedure of a home delivery.

I planned to train a midwife to help with the deliveries in the village, since I knew my load would be heavy. Doña Rosa was the acceptable midwife already for most of the deliveries in El Florido. So I asked her if she would like to work with me on the birth of Lázaro's child.

"Oh, yes," she replied with a smile. "I would like to assist you."

In my kitchen I taught her the sterile technique of delivering a baby. During one of these classes, I asked, "Doña Rosa, how do these Chortí people cut the baby's umbilical cord?"

"With a machete," she quickly replied. "The husband runs the blade of the machete through a fire and then cuts the cord," she explained.

This was the explanation for tetanus of the newborn, I quietly realized. I am sure the Chortí had not made this connection.

Three weeks later Lázaro came to our house and said, "It is time, doña Virginia, Macaria is going to have her baby." When Lázaro asked me to come, I sent a neighbor's child to call doña Rosa to attend this birth with me. I grabbed my bag with the sterilized equipment and put on my white jacket and followed Lázaro to his hut. I found his wife in labor and sitting on a small log on the dirt floor of their hut.

"Hello, Macaria," I greeted her. "Here, let me help you lay on your cot, you will be more comfortable." She complied. I watched her contractions, and her labor was progressing normally. Then suddenly she wanted to get up and sit on the log again.

"No," I insisted, "you stay on your cot and I can help you better."

Again she laid back on her cot. After several of these conflicts, Lázaro said to me, "Doña Virginia, you go back to your house and I will call you when it is time for you to come."

I was sure I knew how to help, but I also knew I must respect Lázaro's wishes. So I reluctantly returned to my house knowing it could be a long process for a baby to arrive.

Several hours had passed when Lázaro returned and told me, "Now you can come."

I walked into the hut and saw a shocking sight. The newborn baby girl was lying in the mud with her umbilical cord still connected to her mother, who was sitting on the log. I just stood there dumbfounded and could not decide what to do with all my sterile equipment. Thankfully doña Rosa had arrived at the same time I did.

In this situation, I decided to forget the sterile mask, the sterile drape, and sterile gloves. Doña Rosa picked up the muddy baby and held her. We found the sterile string, tied the cord, and then cut the cord with the sterile scissors. Then I told Macaria to lie on the cot and I would help her deliver the placenta.

"Oh no, my placenta never comes until four or five days after the birth," she said.

Again I was shocked. "Well, just lie down and I will help you," I said.

She finally agreed. And with a couple more contractions the placenta was delivered. She was so excited and grateful that it was delivered so quickly. She was happy about her new baby but was equally pleased with how easily her placenta was delivered. We washed the mud off the baby, removed the log and put sand over the mud so there was a dry floor.

Slowly walking to our house with many thoughts swirling in my head, I felt defeat and failure because this was far from the sterile delivery that I had planned. There was a huge chasm between my idea of childbirth and that of the Chortí women. But wait, what were the essentials? I knew the fewer changes one makes to a cultural practice the more successful one would be to improve that practice.

So I developed a very simple plan to help the Chortí women deliver their babies and keep them alive:

- I felt that the position of delivery—a squatting position on a log—is okay. It is a quicker delivery and much of the world delivers babies in this manner.
- The mud was *not* okay. A piece of clean plastic or newspaper could be put on the floor for the baby to arrive on. And this was readily available.
- The string was available and could be wrapped and boiled in a clean cloth or plastic ahead of time for the birth.
- Instead of a machete, a new Gillette razor blade should cut the cord. This was also available in the village store.
- Iodine was to be painted on the cut umbilical cord of the newborn to disinfect it. This, too, was available in my clinic and could be obtained ahead of time.

Since the Chortí were usually receptive to new ideas when there was a tangible incentive to change their practices, so I used bribery in the subsequent childbirth classes. I told them, "Use clean plastic on the floor, use a sterilized string on the umbilical cord, cut the cord with a new Gillette razor blade, and paint the cord with the iodine. And if you use all these things, I will give you a new set of baby clothes for your baby the women in our churches in the United States have made." As I told them this, there were giggles and murmurings of agreement.

Every time I met with one of the expectant mothers, I reinforced the importance of getting ready for her new baby. I had the small kits with the sterilized string and Gillette razor blade and iodine available in the clinic. The expectant mothers and fathers made sure I knew they were going to use the Gillette and *not* the machete. Amazingly, there was not one death of a child for the following seven years. The parents in the village were astounded.

One night Benedicto came to Ray and wanted to talk to him in private by the light of the Kincaid lantern in our kitchen. Benedicto said, "Don Mundo, all of my children live, not one has died since I came to El Florido. I have seven children and there are only seven places around my table. Is there anything I can do to not have any more children?"

"Yes, there is something you can do to plan the births of your children," Ray said. "You and your wife can meet Virginia in the clinic and she will explain to you both the plan."

"Good, we will meet doña Virginia," Benedicto said. And they did.

I did offer counsel to Benedicto and all the others with this concern regarding the responsible way to plan the birth of their children. But just as important, however, was that this conversation came as a welcomed testimony to the success of the improved delivery plan to help the babies live.

I Have Decided to Follow Jesus

Often, the trail in to El Florido from Sejá was very muddy since it rained nearly every day. Ray, our three children, and I used tall rubber boots to help us walk that muddy trail out to Sejá and back.

Tad and Linda never complained about the mud unless their boots got stuck in it. Sometimes, as they walked, the mud was so deep that their boots got stuck and their feet pulled out of their boots and into the mud. When this happened they had to trudge back to their boots and put their muddy feet back inside. When we reached the river they would wash their feet and the boots. Then they would put their wet feet back into their boots and continue on the trek.

I usually carried Kenny because he was learning to walk, and walking in the mud was more difficult for him.

Clemencia Melara, the nurse who worked in Jocotán came to El Florido to help me in the clinic work for two weeks, giving immunizations to all the villagers. She lived with us, helped me with the kids, and treated patients with me.

We were walking together through the deep mud out to Sejá on our weekly trip to Morales for groceries and supplies when Clemencia stopped and asked, "Virginia, why are you doing this? It is difficult to live here, care for your three little children and try to help the Indians at the same time."

"I have decided to follow Jesus," was my simple answer. Then suddenly the old hymn "I Have Decided to Follow Jesus" flooded back into my heart, and I sang several verses. "No turning back, no turning back."

Clemencia was quiet the rest of the hike. But my heart was very happy as I sang the hymn of commitment to the Lord. Yes, that was my sincere answer.

11

Visitors and Twelve Faithful Men

Virginia

Cliff and Elizabeth Marshburn came to Guatemala as representatives from the California Friends Churches to the Central America Friends Church Annual Sessions. Being successful farmers and business people from Yorba Linda, California, they had spent their lives giving generously to missionary work worldwide as well as to El Florido. They were genuinely interested in missionaries and found many ways to encourage us.

These annual sessions of the Friends Churches of Central America would last five or six days with four hundred people from eastern Guatemala, western Honduras and El Salvador attending. This particular year, the delegation from California was giving autonomy and independence to the Central American body of Friends churches. After the meetings, Cliff and Elizabeth wanted to visit El Florido with us. This was exciting for us because at last, we could take the Marshburns to visit the Project. On the other hand, we felt intimidated because we feared that El Florido might not meet their expectations.

They had only one day available for the visit so the plan was to drive to El Florido and back on the same day. It was a sunny, warm day as we left in the mission vehicle. We left our children in care of the Jack and Waynel, our missionary friends. We enjoyed getting better acquainted with Cliff and Elizabeth as they asked us questions about the Chortí people and Jocotán.

As we drove along the highway east toward the Caribbean coast, the clouds began covering the sky. My heart sank because I could guess what might be ahead. Cliff and Elizabeth had high expectations of seeing the relocation project because of their sacrificial investment in the purchase of the land. I wondered how we would adequately show them how the

Chortí Indians were developing the land and how grateful they were for the opportunity to improve their lives.

As we turned north toward Rio Dulce, the clouds now were dark and ominous. This was normal weather for this region in November, but we dreaded the thought of a thunderstorm interfering with Marshburn's visit.

Thankfully, the region was developed enough there was a vehicle ferry to transport cars across the wide Rio Dulce. Our ride across the river was uneventful but now it began to rain. It was a light rain to begin with, but it soon became a heavy rain. We arrived at Sejá without umbrellas or boots. All our boots were in our house in El Florido. It continued to rain. Ray and Cliff were in the front seat and Elizabeth and I were in the second seat. We waited about twenty minutes to see if the rain would let up, but it was still coming down.

Ray and I knew we had a time limitation. We had to walk in to El Florido, visit the village and return to the ferry before it shut down for the night at 6:00 p.m. Things were not working out well.

So we stepped out in the rain at Sejá and walked up to the shop where Marcario, the shop owner, was standing and purchased thirty feet of plastic sheeting with the gaudy flower print on it. This plastic was plentiful on the coast, and the local people used it for everything from tablecloths to raincoats. He cut the plastic in four pieces and we each used our piece as umbrellas/raincoats. Then we bought plastic bags that we pulled over our shoes and tied around each leg. We were now ready to walk the long muddy trail into El Florido. Meanwhile, the Marshburns were carrying a large video camera with a tripod to record as much of this adventure as possible.

The rain had let up to a drizzle, now. Ray and I were amazed at Cliff and Elizabeth's enthusiastic attitude and sincere determination to get in to visit the project. I tried to gently explain to them the distance we had to walk through the mud, but that did not deter them. They were ready to go.

The first third of the walk was only slightly muddy. The horse and mule that were carrying two sacks each of rice out to a truck in Sejá passed by. As we began the descent to the Sejá River the mud got deeper. Sometimes we would have to hang on to the plastic bag to pick one foot out of the mud in order to take the next step. There was that moist sucking sound as a bagged foot was pulled out of the mud.

Finally we arrived at the Sejá River. The single log was there across the river. We took the long stick to put down to the bottom of the river to give us balance. All four of us got across without anyone falling in.

The last third of the trail was more deep mud. At the top of the next rise we entered the edge of the village. Stick-sided thatch roof huts lined both sides of the trail that led toward the center of the village and to our house. Finally we reached the green missionary house with the red corrugated-tin roof. We were glad to get in the house, rest for a while, and lunch on sweet rolls and water.

Cliff and Elizabeth were anxious to see the village. They put on a pair of rubber boots from our house and hung on to the plastic sheets for cover as Ray showed them the village. We passed by a store in one of the homes, several thatched huts, and a stick building with a corrugated-tin roof that served as a church on weekends and nights and a school during weekdays. There were logs, brush, and uncut jungle between the houses in the village.

As we walked through the village, the settlers and their children came out to greet us. Ray introduced Cliff and Elizabeth to several of the farmers. He would interpret the villagers' messages to the Marshburns, and they in turn very lovingly gave the villagers words of encouragement.

Cliff wanted to visit the parcels of farmland that belonged to the members of the relocation project. The dilemma for Ray was how to get them out to the farmland. Also, he constantly had in his mind that we still had to trudge back through the mud to Sejá and then to Rio Dulce to catch the ferry before 6:00 p.m.

This was one of the most frustrating times we had ever had bringing visitors into the tropical weather. Cliff was an important participant in making the Chortí Relocation Project a reality. We cringed at the thought that this unprecedented visit was so hampered by such a miserable rain.

He just had to see some of the farmland. It was unthinkable to use the main trail that went north out of the village where most of the cleared land was because the animals and people had made the mud holes even deeper. As an alternative, Ray took Cliff on a trail east out of the village where we stood at the edge of the cleared land so he could see what the men had done.

For a North American farmer, this was certainly a unique experience. The Chortí had cut down the jungle just one year earlier, and the logs were lying in crisscross patterns across the land. They planted their rice and corn between the logs and branches.

We stood there and talked about what we were seeing for maybe fifteen minutes, and then Ray softly said, "We have to go." We had wanted them to spend one or two full days with us in El Florido, but it ended up being only one or two hours.

We began our return hike back to Sejá through the mud and drizzle. We got to the carryall and drove to Rio Dulce just in time to make the last ferry crossing for the evening. The Marshburns had to get back to Chiquimula because they were leaving the next day. Cliff would probably never have an opportunity to visit El Florido again.

On the way back, Cliff and Elizabeth were quiet, and we could not imagine what was going through their minds. With the quick trip, the rain, mud, and limited exposure, we could only wonder what they thought about the progress of the project. But for the most part the whole day was enjoyable for Ray and me because we got to spend the day with our special friends, who we admired. It was a joy to introduce them to our place of service for the Lord among the Chortí people. We arrived back at the mission headquarters in Chiquimula about 9:30 that night and found that it had not rained there at all!

Ray

Although the work of clearing the jungle to plant corn and rice was daunting, the Chortí farmers also had interest in yard animals. Most of the families had brought two or three chickens with them from Jocotán.

"Don Mundo, I would like to raise a pig here in El Florido," Lázaro stated. He was a young farmer who had a pretty wife and two young sons. As he eagerly worked in his parcel of land, he had dreams of getting ahead. He was a deep thinker and it was easy for us to work with him.

"Well, Lázaro, we need to plan how you are going to care for a pig and where you will keep it," I explained.

"Okay," he responded. Now the families lived in a town setting with very close neighbors. The pig had to be kept near their home in a closed structure at all times, a big difference from their custom in the villages above Jocotán of letting pigs run loose and forage for themselves.

"Very well, we will help you design a ten-foot by ten-foot pen with a cement floor, stick sides and a thatch roof. And drainage is important since you will need to clean the pen daily," I instructed.

After Lázaro had finished his pig pen, we bought a young purebred Duroc sow at a government animal breeding station near Chiquimula. We built a wooden crate especially for this pig and carried her in the back of the pickup to Sejá. Four Chortí farmers carried the crate with the sow in to El Florido.

Months later the sow came into heat, and we had to get her to a breeding station near Port Barrios. So we put the sow back into the same crate, but now she weighed more than two hundred pounds and it took six men to carry her. They put the crate with the sow in the "Colorado" Jeep and started down the rustic road to Sejá. The truck broke down, and by the time we got it fixed, it was too late in the afternoon to catch the last ferry. So she spent the night in the crate along the trail in the jungle.

The next day we delivered her to the breeding station. We returned two months later, picked her up, and Lázaro and his five friends carried her in the crate back to El Florido. Everyone was hopeful and excited that they would have a new breed of large, healthy pigs, which Lázaro had agreed to sell to the villagers once they were weaned.

Delivery day came, and the sow delivered *one* piglet. Maybe the traveling and the strange surroundings were just too traumatic for her. Who knows?

After that ordeal of getting the sow bred, I decided we did not want to repeat it, so we bought a young boar from the breeding station in Chiquimula. He was going to be my responsibility. So we built another pen and I fed it, watered it, and cleaned its pen daily.

Vicente, a young Chortí farmer, was a natural leader and the villagers trusted him for advice. They named him as their first town mayor.

One day, Vicente, who had a quiet manner and a gentle voice, came to me. "Don Mundo, I would like to use part of my land as pasture for a cow. I used to have a cow in my village near Jocotán, and I would like to have one now."

Interestingly, we had just received information that Heifer Project International had opened a chapter in Guatemala. This organization received donations of animals to be distributed to poor farmers around the world. Homer and I attended a couple of their meetings, and they became interested in our relocation project for the Chortí Indians.

Before long, one of the committee members, a wealthy Guatemalan dairyman, announced that he would like to donate a heifer to our project. This would be the first time in Guatemala that a Ladino donated an animal to a needy Indian.

We felt again that God had arranged for us to come in contact with this organization and this man who lived on the other side of the country in order to bless His people. When we picked up the animal on the Pacific coast, we were surprised that it had a young calf and had already been bred again. So we were receiving three animals from the one donation.

This cow was a mixed breed developed in Guatemala for the low, hot climates such as ours in El Florido. It was a combination of five-eighths

Brown Swiss and three-eighths Brahma. It had enough Brown Swiss to maintain a reasonable milk production and enough Brahma to give the animal resistance to the hot tropical climate. Vicente took good care of his cow and calf from the very beginning and they grew to be very healthy animals.

All the men in El Florido worked on the demonstration plots of unfamiliar costal crops, such as rice and pineapple. They saw the potential for a wider variety of food for their families and for a cash income at different times throughout the year.

Each of the families asked for fifty to a hundred pineapple shoots to plant on their land. The pineapple shoots were purchased from a plantation owner just across Rio Dulce. Jeff drove Homer's pickup and I drove mine to haul these shoots home for the Indian farmers. Pineapple grew exceedingly well in our climate. The crop of huge, beautiful, delicious pineapple was harvested in six months.

Everyone on the project wanted to plant plátano, the cooking banana. We found a plantation near Port Barrios that wanted to sell plátano seed (the bulbs). Again, Jeff and I loaded the pickups with sideboards as full as we could with the plátano seed and drove the seventy miles back to El Florido.

Each bulb was between the size of a softball and a soccer ball. We stopped on our way in, unloaded all the seed, and washed them in the Sejá River and in a barrel of fungal and nematode disinfectant. Then we loaded them on the Colorado Jeep, which carried the plátano seed the rest of the way. We made these daily trips for two weeks.

Jeff was a big help for me in the physically demanding work and life of the early days of the Project. He fit in well living with our family of five with limited space and he never complained. Jeff would be the first of many young men and women to spend part of their lives helping in the development of the Chortí Relocation Project.

Cocoa Trees

Virginia

One hot, humid Sunday during the long church service, a young boy walked in and leaned over Ray's shoulder. He said, "A trucker is waiting for you on the road from Sejá. He says he has cocoa trees that he wants you to *hurry* out to unload *now*."

Cocoa trees? Ray was wondering, and then he remembered that Homer had ordered three thousand cocoa trees from the government nursery before he left for the United States. "Oh yeah, I had forgotten about those trees," he responded. Because it was Sunday, Ray did not want to take the men out of church to help him. So he said, "Come on, Virginia, let's go unload the truck."

We found the truck near Sejá loaded with all those little trees. The plants were in one-gallon black plastic nursery bags, and weighed five pounds each and averaged about two feet tall. Ray climbed up in the truck bed and began handing me the trees one or two at a time. I would put them neatly together by the side of the road and then reached up to receive two more. We worked like that for an hour at a time, rested for a few minutes and then continued our labor.

"Ray," I said, "no one has come to help us. Maybe we should go get help."

"No," he replied. "We can do it. Look, just a few more and we'll be done."

Finally, we had unloaded the last of the 700 trees and carried them to the nearby shade. We were exhausted. We realized that not a single Chortí farmer had walked past us. I was sure they knew we were there but were avoiding us.

Cocoa production was part of our plan to help these people diversify their farming. But here was another one of those awkward situations. Cocoa has to grow under partial shade—like coffee. These men had not forgotten what it was like to be starving because there was not enough land to grow the corn they needed. They were clearing *all* their land as fast as they could in order to plant enough corn for their families and rice to sell for income. Neither of those crops grew in shade, and they did not want to leave part of the jungle intact just to shade cocoa trees, a crop they knew nothing about. It made no sense to them. Later we found that not a single farmer wanted a cocoa plant.

"*Lord,*" I prayed, "*is this El Florido project going to succeed? How will we know if we are doing Your will? What is Your purpose in all this?*"

Understandably, the Chortí people were sometimes skeptical of our new projects. Sometimes they did not want to follow our advice. Ray and I began wondering that afternoon if this endeavor would ever succeed.

During our walk back to El Florido my thoughts of doubts were transformed by a profound vision from God. The impression was clear:

"Twelve Faithful Men." God told me, "If at least twelve faithful men finish well, My purpose is accomplished."

After that vision, in every church service or meeting, I was able to count at least "twelve faithful men" who prayed, read their Bibles and attended church. When I saw them, I felt a strong encouragement from the Lord. Most of the time there were many more than twelve, but at least there were always twelve.

Latrines

Julio brought his little five-year-old daughter, Juanita, to the clinic in our kitchen because she was tired and had occasional bouts of diarrhea. First I did a physical assessment. Juanita was small for her age, her hair was sparse, her little legs were very thin and her abdomen was slightly protruding. She was listless and her eyes lacked the usual spark of a five-year-old Indian girl. I checked her eyes and found that she was suffering anemia.

"Julio," I asked, "do you have an outhouse, or where do you go to defecate?" These were embarrassing questions to ask, but I must ask them to be able to adequately assess the child's illness.

Julio was embarrassed also, so he quickly glanced around to see who was listening and then whispered, "We don't have an outhouse; we just use the bushes behind our hut."

This information helped me diagnose Juanita's problem since I did not have a microbiology laboratory to examine stool or blood specimens. The apparent anemia led me to ask myself, *What are the most common causes of anemia?* I knew they were intestinal parasites, TB or malaria.

Since little Juanita did not have a serious fever or debilitating cough, I diagnosed her as having anemia due to severe infestation of large intestinal parasites. Remembering the life cycle of the intestinal hookworm and roundworm, I knew she had probably picked up the hookworm in the bushes behind her house. The large roundworm, which often coexists with the hookworm, was probably ingested through the drinking water from the rivers.

I needed to help Juanita quickly because she could die of the anemia or succumb to the flu or bronchitis due to her debility. I prayed with Julio and Juanita as I did with all my patients, asking God to give me wisdom and that He would heal her.

So, right there in our kitchen, I administered the first dose of the bitter medicine for the large roundworms. Often the parents had difficulty, administering medications to their children. This way I knew the treatment was begun.

"Don Julio," I insisted, "please bring Juanita back tomorrow and tell me how many worms she got rid of as a result of this medicine."

"Okay, doña Virginia," he replied. "Maybe my wife can bring her tomorrow."

"Very well," I assured him, "you follow the instructions and she will be better very soon."

Don Julio paid his twenty-five cents for the medicine and hurried on his way.

The next day Juanita's mother, Anna, brought her to me. "She got rid of forty large worms!" Anna exclaimed.

"Good," I replied, knowing the diagnosis was correct. "Now we will give her another medicine for the smaller worms."

The next day Anna returned to my kitchen/clinic with little Juanita. Her eyes were brighter and Anna reported she had a better appetite. I instructed Anna to continue the treatment for three more days. Then I gave Juanita a multivitamin with iron to take every day. Juanita was giggling, smiling and promised she would take her vitamins.

As they left the clinic, I prayed, *Thank you for helping little Juanita. Help her to know You as I touch her life.*

But as I reflected on my help to little Juanita, I also realized that giving worm medication for an infestation is only a stopgap, a short-term cure. El Florido was new land, uncontaminated by humans. We wanted to keep it unpolluted for as long as possible. Virtually all of these Chortí people moving from the Jocotán villages would have parasites, so as each family moved to El Florido, I would give each member a treatment for worms. Now they needed an improved latrine system in order to preserve the uncontaminated condition of this land.

The Guatemalan government had a latrine program throughout the country. In Sejá, we saw cement latrine platforms and seats that were leaning against the wall of a shed used by the road construction company.

We had a meeting of the El Florido people to tell them that latrines were available and that using a latrine was one of the agreements they had signed in order to become members of the Project. They were actually very excited about this possibility. They said they had wanted latrines even when they were up in the Jocotán villages, but they were not available to them.

Ray went back out to Sejá and looked up the foreman. "What can you tell me about these latrines?" he asked.

"If you want them you can have them," the man replied. "They have been here for months and no one in Sejá wants them."

There were fifteen or twenty of them, and Ray said, "We can use them in El Florido. Can we take them all?"

"Help yourself," was his response. "We will be glad to get them out of our construction yard."

These cement platforms and seats were heavy. It took the El Florido men a couple of days to get them moved into the village and put in the warehouse, but now we had our latrines.

The government had published a pamphlet on how to build the latrine, which we insisted every family follow. "Each family has to dig a hole six feet deep and two-and-a-half-feet wide first," we said. "Then you can get one of the platforms and seats out of the warehouse."

My assignment was to measure the holes that were dug, and when they had the right measurement they got their latrine. The families then built a stick hut around the latrine, and even the children learned to use them.

We instructed the women to put one teaspoon of chlorine in a clay pot of drinking water and let it sit for at least one hour to kill parasites in the water. With the combination of latrines and clean drinking water, the incidence of intestinal parasites dropped greatly.

Our Kids' School

Linda turned four while we were in Jocotán, and she was interested in books and trying to write, so I knew she was ready for kindergarten. My sister, Alice, who was a public school teacher in Iowa, sent some school materials to us. Ray built a special table and painted it pink and white, and Linda was ready for school!

I was her teacher. We had school two hours a day, three times a week. Linda was highly motivated to learn. Our only difficulty was Tad, her little brother, who felt left out during school time. Tad wanted Linda to play with him. We gave him a piece of paper and a crayon, but he quickly lost interest because he wanted to play outside. When we moved to El Florido, the school table came with us and Linda continued working on her schoolwork.

The philosophy of educating the missionaries' children was to send them to a boarding school when they entered first grade. From where we lived, the boarding school in Huehuetenango, near the Mexican border, was a twelve-hour drive. I was feeling led to teach my children at home as long as possible.

Our house did not have a ceiling. When you looked up, you saw the underside of the corrugated tin roof. The heavy rains on the tin often made such a loud roar that it was impossible to hear each other speak. At other times the hot tropical sun beat down on our tin roof, radiating heat like an oven. All of this made concentration on schoolwork difficult.

The Stress on Our Marriage

Suddenly we faced the daunting task of the work in El Florido that Homer and Evelyn had been doing in the new settlement. Ray and I have distinct personalities and differing philosophies of leadership. For the first time in our marriage, we had to figure out how to work together in order to help the Chortí be successful farmers.

We continued the difficult tasks before us. I loved caring for my children and became close to each one. I tried to keep the household running smoothly and attended to the five or six sick people who came to our kitchen every afternoon for medical help.

Meanwhile, Ray was in his element. Moving more families and purchasing supplies for the families already living on the Project consumed much of his time. The on-going struggle over the land survey resulted in frequent trips to the capital and it seemed like he was always gone.

I felt lonely and isolated. Because of the difficulty of getting in and out of El Florido, especially with the kids and the muddy trail, I left home only once a month or once every two months. We had no means of communication with any of the other missionaries. I also wished that Ray would talk to me more, and I thought he was not handling the Chortí farmers' accounts as well as I could. Unfortunately, Ray and I did not attend to the smoldering resentments we held inside. And on and on it went.

Our only hope and our only help was the Lord. We began every day in family worship. We read a portion of Scripture and each one prayed out loud. We also faithfully attended the church services held in the village four times a week. My private Bible study followed a basic daily Bible study program, and the Lord taught me many new lessons each day. We were assured He had a plan to relieve the stress on our marriage.

12

Rice Seed, Renegades and a Replacement

Ray

By early 1970 there were twenty-five families in El Florido and twenty-nine eight-acre parcels had been surveyed. We could still only use part of the land because the conflicting surveys had not yet been resolved. We prayed that the survey dispute would be resolved quickly and equitably. Soon we would have to put a hold on moving the rest of the families.

The time for clearing land was in March and April. Using the experience of the first families, the new families were facing their daunting challenge of cutting down jungle growth. Year after year more rice was going to be planted.

The following story is only humorous as we retell it now, years later. It was a blessing and a nightmare for the El Florido men. It was an embarrassment and a tragedy for the Guatemala Ministry of Agriculture, as well as to some people in the United States.

We planned to provide certified rice seed each year to help the men produce and harvest the best rice possible. Certified seed was the highest quality of seed available to farmers. A week before the planting time I went to the Ministry of Agriculture warehouse in Guatemala City, bought the seed and distributed it to the men in El Florido. On the right day they all started planting and in a week they were done. We saw the excitement in the men and women as the sprouting of the seeds brought hope for their future.

The next week a young man, obviously from the city, appeared at our door, having walked in from Sejá. He introduced himself as a representative from the Ministry of Agriculture and needed to talk to us about the rice seed we had purchased.

"There has been a mistake, and the rice seed we sold you is registered seed, not certified seed," he nervously explained. "I need to take that seed back to Guatemala City." The registered seed is a pure seed that the government purchases from the United States for the purpose of reproducing and selling the next year as certified seed.

"Well," I said, "we do have a problem. All of that seed has already been planted."

Our friend was obviously disturbed, and I wondered if he had not been the one who had made the mistake and was sent out to rectify the error. All he could do was turn around and return empty-handed. At this point I knew that we would have a *really* good harvest.

A week later another man walked in and presented himself at our door. He was also from the Ministry of Agriculture. He was a little older, very agitated and perspiring profusely. After the introductions he got right to the point. "We have made a big mistake, and we have a huge problem," he said. "The rice seed you bought was not certified seed, and it is not registered seed either. It is *foundation* seed that was not even supposed to leave the United States. They are wondering where it is. We have to take it back."

"Well, sir," I said. "I can show it to you if you want to walk with me out to the farm parcels." He consented and we walked down the muddy path through the buffer of jungle separating the village from the farmland and stepped out into the clearings. We stopped and stood there in silence, viewing the neat rows of young rice plants stretching out over the rolling hills.

It was a couple of minutes before he spoke. He had obviously been thinking very hard. Finally he said, "We'll be in touch with you regularly in regard to the harvest, which we will control." We turned and walked back to the village and our friend just kept going to Sejá and the road.

Rice is a four-month crop, and at first our friend, and others, came to El Florido monthly. But after the third month they sat down with us and all the Chortí farmers to outline a plan.

First he asked, "Did you plant *only* the foundation seed from the U.S?"

"No," was the answer. "We also planted some certified seed from another supplier."

Now the situation was more complicated. Because of the danger of cross pollinating, each field of foundation rice would have to be identified, and the men from the capital wanted to personally supervise that. The foundation rice growing next to other rice could not all be sold as foundation-quality rice.

They insisted on marking off about thirty feet all around the foundation rice, and that strip could not be sold as foundation. It had to be sold as commercial rice. As a compensation for the extra work, the government offered the men a 30 percent bonus for selling them the foundation harvest. It did not seem like fair compensation to me but it did result in quite a windfall profit for our men.

It took two long days to mark off the rice that could be sold as foundation. We had to climb over burned logs, under dead tree limbs, over hills and across streams. Everyone was soaking wet from the waist-high rice, watered by the nightly rains. The men from the Ministry of Agriculture had never experienced anything like this and were utterly exhausted when they finally left El Florido.

The government officials stayed with us from the first of October until the end of the rice harvest in mid-November. There was no place for them to stay except in our house, since we had no extra bedrooms or beds, so they slept on the floor in the hallway. By mid-November the plants were chest high and we could only see the eyes and hats of the shorter Chortí men. I could not even imagine rice growing that tall.

The sight of the rolling hills covered with ripening rice was beautiful to behold. I could not help thanking God for His care and provision for His people. We had no idea of the high quality of rice that we had purchased for the project, but God did. This was one more way He was unfolding His gracious plan to bless those faithful Chortí followers of Christ. And what a joy and blessing it was for Virginia and me to be part of what God was doing in their lives.

The rice harvest of 1970 was huge. The Chortí had never experienced anything like it before and had never worked so hard in their lives. A *bodega* (storage barn) was built in the village as well as one in Sejá at the road. The rice was carried from the fields on the men's backs, weighed and tagged with the owner's name, and piled in the bodega. The pack animals carried two sacks at a time to the bodega in Sejá. They could only make so many trips in a day and were not keeping up, so men were carrying sacks out as well. They took turns guarding the rice in Sejá at night.

The vehicle ferry at Rio Dulce could carry the loaded trucks across the river. The government men arranged for a truck to haul their foundation rice to the capital. We had arranged to sell the rest of our rice to a processing plant near Port Barrios at the Caribbean coast about four hours away.

The harvest lasted about six weeks. It was a flurry of exhausting activity. The trails to the fields and from El Florido to Sejá had become quagmires of deep, sloppy mud from the light, drizzly rains that persisted day and night in October and November. The thick cloud cover kept the sun from breaking through and drying things out. This miserable weather continued for weeks.

We made contact with a truck owner in Morales through our church leaders. When a load of two hundred sacks was ready, I would notify him. I always followed the truckload of rice with my truck to the processing plant, where it was weighed and stacked. They would give me a receipt for the weight, which I took to the office of the owner, Mr. Oliva, in town. There he paid me in cash and I took the money back to El Florido. Shipments of rice would be made every three to five days. When that harvest was over, the men of El Florido had marketed 525 sacks of foundation rice and 1,163 sacks of commercial rice.

Usually I arrived home about dark, carrying the fat envelope of money from that day's sale of the rice. For a few quiet moments, Virginia and I would stare at the money that I had taken out of my pocket and put on the kitchen table. For us, this was both a miracle and a journey into unknown territory again. My thoughts turned to these families and the poverty they had experienced for so long. In my mind I had many questions, such as what were they going to do with this much money? How would their lives be changed? Would they be faithful in paying for their debts and their land? Would they be faithful in following Christ? We would soon find out.

Each time I got home from a shipment, even though it was already dark, the men began to arrive at our door. One by one I would have them come in. I first had them verify the amount of rice that they had shipped according to the log book. Then I carefully counted out their money and gave it to them. It was usually late at night before all the business was finished.

This was the first harvest for many of the families and we did not ask them to make a land payment but to pay off their personal loans and crop expenses. Virtually all of them, at the time they received their money, asked how much they owed and handed back the money to cancel their debt. This was entered in their personal account folder and a receipt was issued. These were "God moments" for the Chortí families as well as for Virginia and me as we witnessed dreams being fulfilled through God, the faithful Provider.

It was astounding to consider what this foundation seed debacle had brought about. There was really no way to know for sure if all the rice the men said was foundation rice was really from within the marked-off area

144

or whether they had included some from the buffer zone to get the bonus. Also, the government representatives could not accurately supervise the harvest that was taking place simultaneously over such a large area. But when it was all over, they were satisfied that the product was indeed pure enough, and they were thankful for the cooperation from the El Florido community. Perhaps it was the best possible outcome from a very bad series of mistakes made by the U.S. and Guatemala agricultural officials.

The Ministry of Agriculture was so pleased, in fact, that our next saga with them began almost immediately. They asked, "Would you be interested in raising corn seed?"

"Well," I said, "what do you have in mind?"

They had observed that El Florido was surrounded on three sides by jungle. Corn is easily cross-pollinated, and to keep a variety pure, it has to be kept at least one-third of a mile from any other corn plantings. El Florido qualified as land for this use.

I was pondering their proposal.

"And of course there would be a financial benefit for doing this," they added. "The farmer would receive a bonus over the market price for corn at the time of harvest."

This meant, however, that if they agreed to do this, no one in El Florido would be allowed to plant their own seed and each farmer had to agree to the plan. So, I called a meeting of the Chortí farmers to make sure that they clearly understood what was expected. I then gave them time to discuss it among themselves.

"Yes, we are willing to become corn seed producers," they replied.

With their agreement, I informed the ministry that we would proceed with their plan.

The time for planting was only about a month away, and the men were already busy preparing the land. About two weeks before the planting date I was in the capital taking care of business and stopped by the government warehouse to pick up the seed. I was informed it had not arrived yet, but they were expecting the shipment any day.

A week later I went back to the capital, this time solely for the purpose of getting the seed. The men were getting anxious and had told me that I had better come back with the seed. Time was short. Following their planting cycles, they needed to plant in three days. They knew that there is a very small window of time that is considered ideal for planting.

Arriving at the warehouse, again I was told that there had been a delay. The seed would arrive here "any day now." I went back to El Florido with no corn seed. Gathering the men, I asked, "How many days can you wait to plant?"

"Two," they answered. I was tired of making that six-hour trip to the capital, especially for just one thing and not sure I could get that.

I had a phone number of the ministry warehouse. So with one day left, on my trip to Morales to get mail and supplies, I used the phone in the post office to call the warehouse representative with whom I had been dealing.

"Hello, I am Raymond Canfield from the El Florido project. Is the corn seed available for me to pick up?"

"Fíjese" he began. When you hear that word you know you are not going to get the answer you wanted. It is a very descriptive word that the speaker uses to buy time for making excuses and to give an explanation of what went wrong. And for the other person it braces them for a setback and time to think quickly of an appropriate (or inappropriate) response.

"Fíjese, the corn seed is not in yet," he stated simply.

"The men have to plant. The time to plant is now. We MUST have the seed!" I almost yelled into the phone.

"Tell them to wait just a little while longer," he replied.

"I'll tell them, but it probably won't make any difference." I knew the urgency for the Chortí farmers to plant now.

Back in El Florido, the men said, "We are going to plant our own corn seed."

I agreed that they should plant, knowing that their belief in planting times was usually right. We were not going to let the government's failure to deliver the seed on time hinder the El Florido men from planting their own crops and providing for their families.

A week later when I went into Morales to pick up our mail, there was a telegram from the warehouse representative saying the seed had arrived. "Come pick it up as soon as possible," it said.

I placed a call to the man, and when he answered our conversation went like this:

I said, "Fíjese, the men have already planted, the planting time had passed, and they had to plant their own corn seed."

There was a pause, and then in a desperate voice he said, "Tell them to dig up their seed and plant only ours."

"The corn has already sprouted," I responded.

"Have them pull up the plants," the warehouse agent demanded.

"I am really sorry. We had looked forward to working with you and being seed producers. However, it looks like you will have to plant that seed in your warehouse because it is too late in our fields," I responded with some sarcasm. We continued to have many important and cordial dealings with the government over the years, but this was the last time we received an offer to be seed producers.

Toward the end of 1970, when things were going so well in El Florido, the ugly head of an enemy began to bring conflict and dissention. For some reason, which I will never be able to figure out, two of the men we had moved to El Florido, Domingo and Balbino, decided they wanted to take control of the village. They were just like the other men: humble, non-assuming, Chortí-speaking subsistence farmers who had been given a wonderful opportunity to better themselves by taking part in the relocation project. But they wanted to have authority and power over the others.

Since El Florido had not yet named auxiliary military commissioners for the village, these two men went to the army base in Port Barrios and asked to be named as military commissioners. In order to be issued this title by the military, they falsely claimed that the village had given them this responsibility.

As soon as they received their credentials, they began to demand people accept their authority and obey their orders. The people did not know what to think of this because these two men were their neighbors, and no different than any of the others. But things continued to escalate, and soon the village men and women were intimidated and threatened. At one point these "auxiliary military commissioners" arrested two men of the village, took them to the military post in Rio Dulce and accused them of a crime. There was no evidence of the crime so they were not detained and were able to return home. This really put the village on edge.

Two Men Waiting for Ray

Virginia

One evening, I stayed home while Ray walked out to Sejá to help in a church service. A small boy came knocking at our door. In the light of the Kincaid lantern I could barely see his face.

"They're waiting to kill don Mundo!" he exclaimed breathlessly.

"Who?" I asked as fear shot through me, "Who is going to kill don Mundo?"

"Domingo and Balbino are waiting along the path with their machetes to kill him."

Well, I thought, *what can I do?* The Chortí were known to kill with their machetes. *What should I do?* I pondered. *We do not have a telephone, the closest police station is six hours away and I cannot go out and leave our children alone.*

Then it came to me. "The power of heaven is available and eager to help us in whatever we ask." So I opened my Bible to Psalm 37 and meditated on the promises (verse 1): "Do not fret because of evildoers." (verse 9) "Evildoers will be cut off, but those who wait for the Lord, they will inherit the land." (verse 14) "The wicked have drawn the sword and bent their bow, to cast down the afflicted and the needy, to slay those who are upright in conduct." (verse 15) "Their sword will enter their own heart, and their bows will be broken."

"Oh thank you, Lord, for these wonderful promises," I prayed. I knelt in prayer in the kitchen with my head on a wooden chair. I continued in prayer, asking the Lord's divine protection over Ray and the men with him. I asked Him to bless the new fledging church in Sejá. I asked for His direction and blessing over the El Florido church. I asked the Lord to solve the delicate problem with Domingo and Balbino's desire to control our village.

Two hours later I heard the men's low voices talking to Ray as they trudged along the dirt path toward our house. As Ray stepped into the kitchen, I said, "Hi, honey, I am so glad to see you! I thank the Lord for His wonderful, powerful protection over you." I continued. "Did you see Domingo or Balbino on the trail?"

"Yes, I saw Domingo sitting on a log on the trail, and that's all," he said.

Then I relayed the story to him.

There was a victory that night for me. I learned that in whatever need, we can call out to the Lord. He wants us to depend on Him on our knees. He is ready and able to answer that prayer.

A promise for the work in El Florido also came that night: "The wicked man will be no more; and you will look carefully for his place, and he will not be there. But the humble will inherit the land, and will delight themselves in abundant prosperity." Psalm 37:10, 11.

Ray

The five members of the project committee, representing the whole village, came to me late one evening with fear and urgency. They said, "Many villagers are thinking of leaving the project. If Domingo and

Balbino are not removed from their authority and from the village, we will probably all leave."

Adding to the urgency of the situation was that Virginia and I were leaving in a month on our first furlough and would be gone for a whole year. The village knew this. If this situation did not get resolved before we left, there was a possibility that there would be no relocation project to come back to. It was that serious.

It was common knowledge that these two men had not been selected and named as military commissioners by the village residents, which was against the legal procedure for establishing village authority. Fortified by that fact, I decided to go to the regional army base in Port Barrios the next morning. I took with me the El Florido pastor, Romolo Hernandez, who was a Ladino and who knew protocol for this kind of thing and Vicente, the auxiliary mayor of the village.

The army base was expansive, housing the army for all of eastern Guatemala. The military in Guatemala was very intimidating, and the people had a respectful fear of the soldiers. The people always tried to keep their distance from them. Certainly no civilian would go out of his way to engage the military.

As we approached the base I began to question whether I was doing the right thing. It was good that I did not have the history with the army that the Guatemalans had. This allowed me to have more confidence and boldness to do what I knew must be done. We had prayed about this problem. We knew the Holy Spirit was going before us and would be our Guide.

At the gate we briefly explained who we were, where we were from, and what we wanted, and we asked to speak to the base commander. We waited while the intercom call was made to the main office. Shortly the reply came that two of us—the missionary and the pastor, but not the Chortí auxiliary mayor—could be escorted into the command center.

Interestingly enough (but not coincidentally), this was the day all the outstation army officers had their monthly gathering on the base. Their meeting had just ended and we were ushered in.

The commander received us cordially and asked, "And what is the problem that brings you here?"

"We are from the village of El Florido," I explained. "Two men from our village acquired their credentials on their own but had not been named by our village."

The commander turned to his assistant and asked if the officer in charge of the Rio Dulce post was still there and if so, could he be brought in. The assistant left the room and soon returned with the officer whom we both recognized immediately.

"What do you know about the village of El Florido?" the commander asked him.

"They are a group of families who had been brought in to clear and farm the land. They are Christians, hard workers, and a peaceful people," he explained. His answers blessed our hearts.

"And what do you think about those two commissioners in El Florido?" the commander asked the officer.

"They seem to be overstepping their duties as military commissioners and in general, causing a lot of trouble for the village's people," was the officer's reply.

"Bring those two men here tomorrow," the commander ordered the Rio Dulce officer.

Turning to us, he said, "We will take away their authority. You tell the residents to select two of your men that the village approves of, and we will appoint them as your military commissioners."

We thanked the commander from the bottom of our hearts for his understanding of our situation and for his resolution. As we stood there, an unusual sense came over me, a thought that had never entered my mind until that moment. I did not know what I was going to say or how it was going to be accepted, but I knew I was supposed to speak.

I said, "Sir, if you have a minute I would like to ask a favor."

"Yes, go ahead," the commander said.

I explained about the background of the Friends Church as a people of peace and that our objective here was to help impoverished Christian families attain a reasonable standard of living in a peaceful manner.

Then I said to him, "I would like to ask that you grant permission for the village of El Florido to function without military commissioners."

When I finished, he looked at me intently, and then turned to the Rio Dulce officer and asked, "What do you think?" Obviously this would be a unique exception to the way law and order was enforced in Guatemala.

"I think El Florido would function well without military commissioners," the officer answered.

"So be it," the commander said, getting to his feet in a dismissive manner. "Your village does not have to have military commissioners."

We expressed again our heart-felt gratitude and we left his office. As we walked through the base and back to the truck, we were giving thanks to God for yet another evidence of His hands on this project and on these faithful Chortí families. As far as we knew, El Florido was the only village in all of Guatemala that did not have the required military commissioners. (Note: El Florido remained without military commissioners for nearly six years, until the political unrest began to escalate.)

A meeting had been planned with the project committee at night when we had returned from the army base. There was a visible relief when the outcome was explained. It was agreed that as soon as the men returned from the army base the next day, without their credentials as military commissioners, I would tell them they had to leave the village. We prayed that everyone would be safe during the next twenty-four hours.

Early the next morning, Domingo and Balbino were summoned to immediately report to the base in Port Barrios. After they returned in the late afternoon, I went to each of their homes. I made it very clear that the consensus of the village and of the project committee was that their privilege to be a part of the relocation project had been revoked. I told them they were to move out of the village as soon as possible. I cited infractions of articles number five and ten of the bylaws of conduct that they had signed. They assured me that they would leave immediately.

Domingo and Balbino were frightened, reasoning together that without their authority, they were probably in danger from reprisals by the other families because of the awful way they had treated them. But that did not happen. The families were satisfied to know that the men would be leaving, and they trusted that in God's mercy their lives would be peaceful again in El Florido.

Most families stayed out of their way while others offered to help during the three or four days it took them to exit the village. There was a great deal of grace shown, an evidence of how God can change the heart and character of individuals who have turned their lives over to Christ.

Who Will Come to Help?

Virginia

Homer and Evelyn had returned to the United States, and they and the mission board decided they were not able to return by January 1971, which was when we were scheduled to go to the States for a year's furlough.

It hardly seemed possible that four years had passed since we had embarked on this missionary venture.

The mission board and we determined that someone needed to be present to help and encourage the Indian farmers while we were away. A call was made in the Friends churches for a missionary couple to serve in El Florido for one year and longer if possible. A pastor in the Walnut Creek church advised his nephew, Larry Kirk, of the need. Larry and his wife, Ina Jo were excited about this possibility and contacted the mission board.

Phil Martin, chairman of the mission board, and Keith Sarver, superintendent, recommended Larry visit El Florido first. They wanted him to see the situation and then decide whether he wanted to take his family there.

It was October and a busy time with the rice harvest. Larry was an excited visitor with all the usual questions of "why," "how," "where," etc. Ray showed him the parcels of land. He introduced Larry to the Indian farmers and their families. He explained to the Chortí that Larry was a missionary who would take the Canfields' place for a year. Ray and Larry walked side by side while Ray tried to explain and orientate Larry to the purpose and goals of the project.

Larry and Ina Jo loved the Lord and were anxious to serve Him. Larry had many talents and expertise in construction and mechanics, which would help him continue the development of the project. Ray gave him a detailed orientation that went into the night when the kids were asleep. Ray had a peace about leaving the project in his hands.

David Hamm was living with us at the time while he measured and marked the boundaries between the parcels of land with his surveyor's transit. One sunny afternoon, David was doing his calculations in the house and I was caring for the kids when our village neighbor, Vicente, dragged a very large dead green snake to our house.

"Would you like to have this?" he asked. "It's pretty good to eat."

"Yes," David responded without hesitation. "I think it would be good for supper." Then David came into the house and asked, "Virginia, do you know how to fix snake to eat?"

"My jungle cookbook says it needs to be skinned first," I replied.

After it was skinned, we cut the body of the snake into four-inch long pieces and placed five of them in my pressure cooker. I cooked it for more than an hour, making sure it was thoroughly cooked.

Carrots, potatoes, and an onion were diced. I pulled long strands of cooked meat off the ribs of the snake and diced them. Then we put the vegetables together with the meat, added seasonings, and cooked it for twenty minutes. When I tasted it I found it to be surprisingly tasty.

Ray and Larry were gone for the day, and when they came home we sat down to eat. Linda, Tad, Ken, David, Ray, Larry, and I were at the table. The stew was served, and everyone thought it was delicious.

We were halfway finished eating when David asked, "What kind of meat do you think this is?" He couldn't keep the secret any longer.

Ray looked up at me with his questioning glance.

"It's chicken," Larry declared.

"No," David said slowly, "it's snake!"

"Snake??" Larry gasped. Then he jumped up from the table and ran to the bathroom and got rid of his supper.

David and I exchanged glances. I had to suppress a giggle. Maybe I should have been feeling sorry for Larry. Regardless, our new missionary's reaction was more dramatic than we expected.

But in spite of all this, Larry decided that he could use his God-given talents to serve the Lord in El Florido with his family.

13

Furlough

Virginia

*L*ord, how do we communicate what we have experienced on the
mission field to people in the United States? I prayed on the flight
from Guatemala City to Des Moines, Iowa. *We have stared poverty
and helplessness in the face. We have suffered serious illness ourselves. We
have witnessed God's wonderful grace and miraculous answers to prayer.
How can we convey all of this adequately to those who love and support us?
It seems impossible.*

Just tell them about Me and My Word, was God's answer as I walked
down the aisle of that Pan Am Boeing 707 airliner.

A new peace came into my heart. We were invited to speak at New
Providence, Iowa, Friends Church in three days, and I was preparing
myself for that responsibility. God wanted us to share the truth about Him
and His Word. Our experiences were only illustrations of those truths. We
knew God had given us His plan for these furlough messages and for all
the subsequent furloughs. God helped us take the focus off of us and put
it back on Him.

This first furlough would be for one full year. We had spent one year
in Spanish Language Institute in Costa Rica, two years in Jocotán, and
one year in El Florido.

What a shock it was for us coming right out of the tropics to Iowa in
a snowstorm just before Christmas. Mother and Dad met us at the airport
with coats for all of us. Tad and Linda insisted they were not cold and did
not need those coats. Cold was a new experience. Linda stepped outside
on the ice in the parking lot and immediately slid under a parked car. Tad
was right behind her, and he too fell down on the ice.

"This is really cold," Tad cried. "I need that jacket."

Christmas at my parents' farm home with family and friends around
us was a joyous celebration. While there, Ray and I were invited to a

Bible study in the Nelson farm home, and we shared what God had been teaching us on the mission field. At the end of our talk, Mrs. Nelson asked us, "Well, Canfields, how can we pray for you?"

I immediately knew the answer. I hesitantly replied, "You could pray for our marriage and that we learn how to communicate better with each other." The unresolved conflict about how to work together with our distinct personalities and differing philosophies of leadership was still fresh on my mind.

"Okay," she said. "We would like the two of you to sit here in the center, and we will form a circle and pray over you." That is exactly what they did. We felt uplifted, encouraged, and hopeful that God would help us.

After our two weeks' visit in Iowa, we flew to California where Keith Sarver, the superintendent of California Friends churches and his wife, June, met us. He presented us with keys to a 1952 dark-blue Chrysler sedan for our use on furlough. This car was spacious and seemed like a limousine to us.

When Marlin Davis, a good friend of ours from Whittier, saw the car, he named it The Blue Sherman, referring to the Sherman Tank. The name stuck, and we heard many jokes about the missionary's car. We were grateful for the Blue Sherman and the generous people who donated it for our use.

Keith Sarver also gave us keys to the parsonage next to a closed church in Montebello, California, where we lived for a year. This little house had three bedrooms, a fenced yard, and plenty of room for our children. Various friends from different churches furnished the parsonage with furniture, dishes, and toys. A small TV was included, and our kids could not have been happier since they had never watched TV before. We were delighted.

We visited all the Friends churches in California and Arizona at least once, and many of them two or three times to visit their small groups. We usually showed the slides of our life and ministry in Guatemala. After each service a family from that church invited us to their home for a meal along with a few others from the church. They were always kind and considerate toward our children. This time of visiting churches was enjoyable because we could put faces and personalities to the cards and notes of encouragement they had sent us. They taught us much about culture, life, and church as it was evolving in the United States.

Prayer is essential to the missionary endeavor. We knew we really could not accomplish the huge task of the agriculture/nursing ministry that God had called us to unless we had people holding us up to the Lord in prayer. New friends promised to pray for the Central American missionary work and the faithful ones recommitted their support.

One Sunday evening we were speaking at Granada Heights Church. We felt like we had conveyed our excitement about the work and how God was guiding us to help the Chortí Indians. After our presentation which included slides of the beautiful jungle and the Chortí people, a man walked up to Ray.

"That is what God called me to do," one man stated. "When I was in high school, God called me to go and serve as an agricultural missionary," he explained. "But I told God I did not want to do that; maybe later. Then I married and my wife does not want to be a missionary. Now I can't go," he stated. As tears welled up in his eyes, Ray put his arm on the man's shoulder to comfort and pray with him.

Just before Ray began to pray, another man walked up and said, "I knew God called me to be a missionary, but I wanted to get a good job and a new car first," he said. "Now I have a family and can't go."

Ray prayed with these two men that God would forgive their disobedience. "God, please guide their lives from now forward. And Lord, help them listen to Your Word and obey it. Amen."

"Amen," they both responded. They thanked Ray for his prayer and then turned and left the church.

For days afterward, the memory of those two weeping men caused me to shudder. It also reminded me to thank the Lord that He helped me answer His call to the mission field. I thanked Him for guiding us along the way. Since childhood, I had asked the Lord to lead me and keep me from regrets about not obeying Him.

A discipleship course, "Basic Youth Conflicts," was being offered in Long Beach, California, and Verl Lindly, the pastor of Granada Heights Church, gave us scholarships to attend. We hired a babysitter and went with our friends from that church.

The leader taught us about forgiveness and trusting God, specifically in relationship with our spouse. The leader addressed the need to trust God to lead our spouse. He emphasized releasing our need for control. These classes spoke to the exact struggles we were facing. We knelt there during the service and asked God to help us through these issues in our marriage. I lost track of how long we spent on our knees, but when the service was over I knew God had healed our hearts. And I had some answers of how to improve our ministry together.

I committed my heart to loving the Lord first above all else. Secondly, as a wife to Ray, I could leave the decisions about the work in his hands. When we disagreed I would give my input and leave it ultimately to him and then pray that the Lord would guide him. As a result, we became united as a team. Soon after we got these things figured out, our lives were happier and our ministry ran much smoother.

$12 Per Month

We decided to visit the missionaries who had retired from service in Guatemala. After our experiences of the past four years, we had a deep respect for those missionaries who had gone before us and a curiosity about them at the same time. We knew we had a lot to learn and they could teach us and answer our questions.

William and Mae Stanton had served for more than forty years as missionaries in Guatemala and were living at Quaker Gardens, a Friends retirement home in California. They had been retired for fifteen years and were around eighty years old when we visited them. A part of every missionary's support is paid into a pension plan during their service. Our denomination had endowed six units in Quaker Gardens, which is a life care facility for career missionaries and pastors upon retirement.

They invited us to visit them. When we arrived, at the Stanton's apartment, William was sitting in his easy chair. Mae was sitting across from him on a small chair. Ray and I were so excited to actually meet and talk with *the* Señor Lester Stanton (as he was called in Guatemala).

"This is a very nice apartment," I said. "Isn't it generous of the mission board to provide such a comfortable place for you?" I was remembering the usual arrangements the board has for their retiring missionaries.

"No, the mission board did not furnish this for us," William explained in his slow manner. "This is our own apartment."

"Tell us, please, how were you able to do this?" I was really curious about this, realizing how expensive it was to live there, but I tried to be respectful toward their personal affairs.

"We know that when you first went to the mission field in 1913 you were receiving $12 per month, and that only gradually increased over the years," I said.

"And some months during World War II we didn't receive any income," he added with a smile.

"Then how could you afford to buy into a place like this?" I asked.

"Well, we always tithed one-tenth of our salary first and gave it to the church. Then we saved another tenth and lived off the rest each month," he carefully explained. "Our savings grew," he said. "When we retired I bought a house in Whittier, California. Several years later I sold the house and bought into Quaker Gardens. And here we are," he simply stated and grinned contentedly.

"The Lord has blessed you as you have honored Him," I exclaimed.

We talked for a while about the missionary work in Guatemala, and they asked us more specifically about the relocation project for the Chortí Indians.

As we walked out of their room, William did not get up, but Mae saw us to the door.

On our way to the car I said, "Ray, I think we heard God's voice just now! He told us how to live on a missionary's meager salary," I stated.

"I think you're right," Ray said. "Let's put this into practice and see what God does."

That was exactly what we did. Our combined monthly salary at that time was $300, but we put into practice William Stanton's budget plan: Tithe first to the church, save the next tenth, and live off the rest.

Down through the years we have marveled at God's faithfulness and the many blessings He has given to us as we dedicated ourselves to serve Him with all our hearts and resources. Words of Jesus from His Sermon on the Mount came to us often: "Seek first His kingdom and His righteousness; and all these things, (food, clothing, lodging,) shall be added to you." Matthew 6:31, 33.

Rumblings

News from Guatemala and our friends in El Florido was precious to us while we were in the States. Telephone service to Guatemala was rare and expensive, so we awaited news from missionaries or visitors who came from Central America.

In March of 1971, Homer Sharpless visited the relocation project and returned with news that there were some misunderstandings between Larry Kirk and the people in El Florido. However, he did not have many details.

Later, David Hamm returned from El Florido with news for us.

He began, "You folks are in for a real surprise when you return to El Florido."

"What do you mean?" Ray asked.

"Well, Larry and Bruce Pinkston have built another bedroom and a living room onto the missionary house," he explained.

"Really?" We could hardly imagine the gift of more room for our family and all the guests that we anticipated visiting us there.

"He has also built a sawmill and is sawing logs," David continued. "Larry talked to the officials of the United Fruit Company in Morales, and they have donated two used Fordson tractors to the relocation project."

"Wow!" Ray exclaimed. "That will be a great help."

"And here is the clincher. You can drive the pickup clear into the village now," he excitedly explained. "With the tractors and a trailer that he built, he has graded and graveled the road into El Florido."

Ray and I were so excited we hardly knew what to say. Larry and Ina Jo, along with three short-term volunteers—Bruce Pinkston, Sam Steiger, and Paul Vore—did more toward the development of the project in one year than we could have done in five.

The Kirks were also very concerned for the spiritual growth of the village people. Part of their plan for ministry was to develop medical and dental caravan work as well.

Then David Hamm continued with his news from El Florido.

"There is just one main problem," David explained. "There is not a good relationship between the Chortí people and Larry."

"Larry does not understand us and our ways," several village leaders had told Paul Enyart, our field administrator. "We will leave the relocation project if he stays."

"How could this have happened?" we sadly asked ourselves. We also felt sad for the Chortí, who had such high hopes for a new land and a better life. They had worked very hard and put their trust in us missionaries as well as in the Lord.

Sometimes we missionaries are overzealous and in such a hurry to complete our projects that we forget to take time to build relationships of love and respect with the people God gave us to serve.

As was the practice for returning missionaries, the Guatemala Friends Church leaders approved our return to Central America. Overwhelmingly, our desire was to continue serving the Lord in El Florido but we did not want to override the work that the Kirks had accomplished there. This decision ultimately depended on the field director and the mission board in the States.

"So you will be returning to El Florido, and Larry and Ina Jo will move to Honduras," Paul instructed Ray and me.

We were excited to see our Chortí friends again and continue working on the goals we had set out three years earlier for the relocation project.

14

Title Ownership, Security and Healing

Virginia

It was an early Sunday morning as the dawn was beginning and Ray and I were up enjoying our first cup of coffee. The usual rain had come in the night, and now mist with light fog hovered over our village in the jungle. There was a sense of peace and contentment in our hearts since we had recently returned to our home from our year away in the United States.

The smell of a wood fire wafted into our house as we saw smoke from our neighbor's hut curling above their thatch roof, and I could hear Rosita patting out her tortillas by hand. The roosters, chickens and dogs milled around looking for their favorite morsels of food.

"I need to go out to check the recent survey lines to see if the neighboring landowner of the San Humberto Ranch is respecting our new survey measurements when they put in a fence for their cattle," Ray stated. "Would you like to go with me?"

I thought for a minute. All three of our children were sound asleep in their beds. I could probably leave them for half an hour. "Yes, I'd love to go for an early morning hike with you, honey," I replied.

We pulled on our boots and started out. We walked side by side in the cool fresh morning air. Then we came to an area where the grass was high and the brush was thick. I fell into line behind Ray and tried to walk in his footsteps because I hoped his feet would have scared away any snakes in the grass.

Oh my, look at me, I have even adapted to the Indians' ways, I thought. *The women who carry loads and children always walk directly behind the men when walking together.*

While Ray was meticulously checking the fence posts, barbed wire, and survey measurements, I was delighting in the magnificent beauty of the jungle, with the early morning fog and mist hovering over us. It was eerie because all the animals were silent, and the normal morning sounds were muffled by the fog. I felt a deep happiness and gratitude to the Lord for permitting me to be at this moment in such a beautiful place with my husband, who I adored.

Ray

The boundary survey work continued despite the density of the jungle and the vastness of the land we were surveying. The neighboring San Humberto land was finally officially registered with the government, which meant we could go forward with our own survey, for the second time. Two sides of our land bordered that piece of property, which made the work go quickly and reassured us that our boundaries would probably be accepted.

Lucio wrote a chronicle about the development and ministry of the El Florido project. Following is a poignant account of an experience of the survey team. "One evening, we, the survey crew of ten men and the surveyor, did not return as usual. It got dark, and the families in the village became very worried about us. So a search party with David Hamm was organized to look for us. They only had a rough idea of where we were working that day, and it was hard for them to decide which direction they should follow. They realized the chance of finding us was remote.

"As the search party walked out through the jungle with flashlights and a lantern, they began to yell as loud as they could. After three hours, they found us huddled together at the base of a huge tree. What a relief it was to see the lantern light and hear the voices of our friends from the village. We thought we were going to spend the night lost in the jungle. We didn't have a lantern, and we had heard of the wild animals that roam in the jungle at night," he concluded.

When the survey was finally finished, our lawyer started the process of the title change and registration of the deed to all twelve hundred acres that we purchased. It was officially listed with the government land department. Now all the land could be measured into farm parcels, and we could help the rest of the families move from Jocotán to El Florido.

We missionaries wanted the El Florido village to have the amenities of other villages, so we thought the village needed a piped-in water supply. We went ahead with the project even though the villagers had not seen this as a felt need nor had asked for piped-in water. The mission would put in the water system and the villagers would pay for the maintenance.

A water pump was installed at the Branche River, which was considered relatively pure, and was about a quarter mile away. It pumped water through a two-inch plastic pipe into a thousand-gallon tank on a short tower in the village. From there the water ran through pipes, pulled by gravity, through the village to four strategically placed faucets.

This water project lasted only about two years. What went wrong? First, the pump quickly wore out and replacements were too expensive for the villagers. Secondly, there was trouble at the faucets. Some of the ladies became territorial and would not let others get water, so disputes broke out. When the water stopped being pumped into the village, each family quickly found a place to get their water in nearby creeks, springs, or shallow wells. We reminded them of the need to treat their water with chlorine drops again. And there was renewed peace in the village. This particular project had taught us the important lesson that in order for a project to be successful, the people had to see it as a felt need. This one had not been the case.

Virginia

One day Dolores came into the clinic in my kitchen. Dolores and his wife, Gabriela, were our next-door neighbors and good friends who helped us in many ways. His right hand was wrapped in a bloody shirt, and he was holding it with his other hand.

"What happened, Dolores?" I asked as he sat there in stoic silence.

"Well, this *oso hormiguero* grabbed hold of my hand," he quietly explained. (An oso hormiguero is an anteater.)

I carefully removed the bloody shirt and found deep gashes and torn tissue on his right hand and fingers. It was an ugly sight. Immediately the process of carefully cleaning and examining the wounds was begun. Thankfully he could move his fingers fairly well.

Dolores continued to remain stoic. "I reached down to get some honey out of a log and I didn't see this animal. It grabbed my hand with the honey and would not let go until I kicked him and he tore my hand," he said.

I gave him a good dose of antibiotics and bandaged his whole hand. He thanked me profusely and went home. After several bandage changes, his hand healed completely.

Ray

Our coming and going was dependent on the work of the vehicle ferry and crew at Rio Dulce. The first small ferry could hold five vehicles if they were arranged just right, which the crew could do in multiple and creative ways. Consequently, the ride across the Rio Dulce on the ferry was often harrowing.

We quickly built relationships with the crewmen working on the ferry and they treated us well. The fee was $2.00 each way, which increased our operating budget, but it was a blessing to be able to get our truck across the river between 6:00 a.m. and 6:00 p.m. Sometimes the fee collector would tell me I did not have to pay, but I insisted on paying and getting my receipt. There were times when the ferry had just left the shore, but when they saw our truck come down the hill toward the landing, they would turn around and come back to pick us up.

In 1972 the rice crop was abundant. But most of the farmers made only nominal payments on their parcels of land, indicating their "wait-and-see" attitude about how things were going to work out for them.

However, Vicente Mendez, decided to use the money from his harvest to finish paying for his first eight-acre parcel. When his land was officially registered in Guatemala City and he received the title, we had a ceremony in the El Florido church honoring him. His land was now secured by a registered title that no one could take away from him.

Several months later, he decided to take his deed to the bank to see if it really was a valid title. He returned to tell us and the others that the men in the bank told him, "Yes, this is a legitimate title to a piece of property." He was so excited and the other farmers were amazed.

The following year, after another good rice harvest, virtually all the men made substantial payments on their land. Eleven men completely paid for their first parcels and received their deeds during another celebration service in the village church. It was a blessing to see God's care and provision for these Chortí people.

In this unprecedented prosperity, probably one of the things that helped their sense of dignity was that we charged them fair prices for the land, tools, seed, animals, and medicines in the clinic. We knew the richness of the soil and the size of their parcels would make it possible for them to pay for all they were receiving.

It was a new experience for the El Florido people to see that they actually had money left over after they had paid for all of their financial obligations, including giving to the church. What did they do with their disposable income? They bought things like other people had, of which they had only dreamed. They liked wrist watches, transistor radios, jackets, and leather shoes. We were happy for them.

Then we noticed Chortí-speaking men speaking broken Spanish to each other as they walked through the village or on the trail out to the parcels. *Maybe they were speaking the language of the more prosperous people around them in order to gain the respect they so deeply desire,* I wondered.

A Difficult Diagnosis and Treatment

Virginia

During this time the medical outreach was growing, and people came from outside the El Florido project for medical help. There was no clinic or doctor within a two-to-three-hour drive, and people had heard of the "missionary nurse" who could help them. I saw this as an opportunity to minister to a larger group of people.

Americo was a tall Ladino man who lived in Sejá with his wife and six children and worked as a lumberjack in the jungle. He had been raised in the Friends Church in Gualan and had been a Christian for many years.

When church services began in Sejá, Americo attended regularly with his family and was the natural leader for that new church. A lantern, a guitar, and a rustic wooden pulpit which were supplied by the El Florido Church, were all they needed to start a new church. He brought the Coleman lantern and opened up the doors to the rustic church for all the meetings.

He was introduced to me as the man in Sejá who wanted to become a member of the Friends Church. I immediately noticed a very large sore on the right side of his neck, and he volunteered the information that it was from a bite from a chicle fly. Two months later we decided to take him to the doctor in Morales.

The doctor examined him and diagnosed it as leishmaniasis, a tropical flesh-eating skin disease caused by protozoa blood parasites. The doctor promised to get medicine for him within one week. Two months passed and still there was no medicine. New lesions appeared on his knees, arms, ears and hands, and he suffered much pain.

Americo continued to serve as lay pastor of the Sejá congregation. Just before Christmas, I received the medication from the doctor in Morales and gave him the ten injections of an antibiotic. After this series of medication was finished, Americo's condition worsened again and he suffered more pain. For several days, Ray, Jim Gay, our short-term volunteer who was living with us, and I had been earnestly praying for Americo.

In February Ray and Jim took Americo to Guatemala City to see Dr. Hernandez, who sent him to the University of Guatemala Medical School. The faculty was very interested in this patient because the disease was common in the tropical jungles here, but this was the first time they had ever heard of it affecting the extremities. They took photographs and biopsies of his lesions. Dr. Hernandez sent Americo home with some pills and promised to send us the laboratory examination results along with specific medications.

In the meantime, I had learned from my Tropical Medical Manual that Antimony was an effective treatment for leishmaniasis, so Ray brought some from Guatemala City on his next trip.

Three weeks passed and Americo did not improve but became even worse. There was no word from Dr. Hernandez. We earnestly prayed, and I felt the Lord directing me to start the injections of antimony. After the sixth injection of ten doses, a letter arrived from the doctor telling me to begin the injections of antimony. That letter also stated there was no known cure of that type of visceral leishmaniasis.

But Americo was already responding to the treatments I had started and was rapidly improving. When the injections were over, we did not know what to do next because he still had a few lesions, so we prayed and asked the Lord for wisdom. I felt directed to give the antifungal oral tablets for fungal infections that I always have in our clinic. Five days after starting the oral medication, a letter came from the doctor telling me to start this exact medication. Americo's lesions were healing, and he had no more pain.

Again we prayed because we had finished the oral medication and three lesions were not healed. I felt led to give him another series of injections of antimony. Just before I had given him the last two injections, I reviewed the *Tropical Medicine* text again, which explained that antimony could cause death. Suddenly I was afraid to give those last two injections, but I finally did. All the lesions healed, and Americo completely recovered and continued leading the church. God had intervened, answered our prayers, and healed Americo. We praised Him.

Through this experience I learned much about praying, listening to His answers, and then having the courage to obey His directions. I learned how God wanted me to trust Him and not lean on my own understanding.

The Feud

We were reminded that the Chortí Indians had come from a lifestyle of violence and feuds because quarreling and fighting occasionally surfaced in El Florido. It was also evident that a few of the families had professed faith in Jesus simply in order to be part of the project.

Don Alejandro came to our house one evening after dark. We had finished supper and were getting our kids to bed. He wanted to speak with Ray.

"Don Mundo, I have a real problem," he said quietly after they had discussed the rains and crops for twenty minutes.

"Yes," Ray said, "what is it?"

"Well, my wife is very angry at Bonifacio's wife because they hate us," he explained.

"Why?" Ray asked, knowing there was always more to the story.

"Well, you see, she threw a rock at our duck," he replied.

"Where was your duck?"

Don Alejandro hesitated for a little bit and then answered, "On Bonifacio's roof."

"How did it get there?"

"Well, I guess it flew there," he answered. "But now Bonifacio's wife is so angry she is going to throw rocks at my wife, who is angry also."

"Don Alejandro, we need to come together—you and your wife together with Bonifacio and his wife so we can understand one another," Ray patiently explained. "Please go and bring all of them here to talk about this."

"Uhh, I'm not sure they will come," Alejandro explained doubtfully. "Do you want them to come tonight?"

"Yes. I will pray they come." Ray knew the sooner this was taken care of, the better.

Alejandro hesitantly went out the door and into the night. About thirty minutes later the two couples arrived at our door, sullen and in silence. Ray readily invited them into our kitchen and they sat together on a bench.

I had just finished reading a story from the Narnia series and had prayed with Linda, Tad, and Kenny before tucking them in bed for the night. Since there were two women in this group of visitors, I felt comfortable joining the group as an observer and a prayer.

Ray led the discussion. "Doña Carmencita, what happened to your duck?"

She replied, "Doña Luicita threw rocks at my duck because she hates me."

Before she had finished, Bonifacio's wife interrupted, "Her duck was destroying my roof. She needs to pay me for repairing my roof."

Alejandro's wife interrupted. "No, you need to pay me for my duck."

"Was your duck killed?" Ray calmly asked.

"No, it was injured a little bit," Alejandro's wife answered.

This heated debate went on with both parties talking at once for about thirty minutes.

Finally, Ray stopped the arguing and said, "Look, is it worth being enemies and fighting each other over a duck? Wouldn't you rather have peace and live together happily?"

All was quiet for a few minutes. Then Alejandro said to his wife, "Could you forgive doña Carmencita?"

There was more silence while we awaited the answer.

Finally doña Luicita said quietly, "Yes, I will forgive her."

Ray said to Bonifacio's wife, doña Carmencita, "Will you ask doña Luicita to forgive you?"

More silence.

Finally doña Carmencita said to Alejandro's wife, "Will you forgive me?"

"Yes," she answered.

Bonifacio said, "We need to pray together, don't we, don Mundo?"

"Yes. Talking to the Lord is the only hope," Ray replied.

So all six of us knelt on the kitchen floor around wooden chairs, and we prayed quietly at the same time. We prayed for each other and for ourselves. I could tell these dear friends were earnestly talking to the Lord about their problem.

After thirty minutes of prayer, the couples got up. The two women embraced and told one another that they would be friends again. The two men also embraced and told each other they appreciated one another as neighbors. They turned and left our house and went back to their homes in the dark. It was late and we were tired, but it was a "happy" tired. All of us were learning that only Christ could break the chains of hatred and fighting that had held them captive for so long and could bring true reconciliation and forgiveness.

Later we were surprised to learn that families who had been arch enemies in the villages above Jocotán had chosen to live on adjoining lots in the new village. This seemed as if they wanted to continue the feuds. Ten years earlier Bonifacio had lost his right arm in a machete fight with enemies of his family, who were in Alejandro's family. This living arrangement in El Florido could have fomented the feuding but God used this to unfold His purpose of peace.

One evening as the sun was just setting at El Florido, I met Benedicto Mendez, one of the Chortí farmers, on the path leading to the missionary's house. He had a smile on his face and was truly happy as he greeted me.

"I am so fortunate to be here because all of my family, except the real small children, have accepted Jesus Christ as their Savior," Benedicto volunteered.

"Do you think they would have been Christians if they had remained in their village near Jocotán?" I asked.

"No," he answered, "it was too far for the whole family to walk to church in Jocotán. Only one son and I would walk to Jocotán to attend church once a week.

"But here at El Florido, the whole family attends church and Sunday school every Sunday morning, church on Sunday evening, prayer meeting on Tuesday evening, church on Thursday evening and church on Saturday evening. And now my whole family has heard and understood the Word and accepted Jesus Christ as their Savior.

"And we have enough food to eat here. We have bananas, pineapple, eggs, chickens, platanos, beans and corn for tortillas. Everything we plant grows here. Now our needs are met and we are happy."

Another testimony came in the form of a letter of gratitude from Benedicto to Homer Sharpless:

El Florido, December 13, 1970

Mr. Homer Sharpless,

It gives me much pleasure to write to you, desiring that you are well and enjoying rich blessings from the Lord.

Homer, we here are enjoying blessings from the Lord, but we feel your absence. The purpose of this letter is to greet you and to show you my appreciation for all the help you have given us. We have harvested rice and made some money to supply our needs and are getting the land ready to plant corn. For now, only this, and I wish you a Happy New Year.

Benedicto Mendez

Homer commented after receiving this letter back in California, "I have known Benedicto for more than ten years, and this is the first time he is not asking for money to feed his family. We must pray for him and the others at El Florido that the Lord helps them to invest their money wisely."

Ray said, "Yes, Benedicto is using his money to improve his house as well as to buy clothes for his family of seven children. He also paid off his debts."

15

A Government School, New Lives and New Ways

Mr. Oliva

Ray

In 1973 the rice harvest was bountiful, and it was again sold to the rice-processing plant near Port Barrios. The improved gravel road now made it possible for the rice buyers' trucks to come all the way in to El Florido to pick up the sacks of rice. This was an improvement from the previous years when the rice was hauled to Sejá by mule or men's backs. However, I would still follow the truck to the processing plant, get the invoice for the sacks of rice delivered and take it to the office of the owner of the plant. The bookkeeper would pay us in cash.

After one of the deliveries of rice, the bookkeeper had not yet returned from his siesta break. The owner, Mr. Oliva, was there, however. He invited me up to his office to talk while I waited.

Mr. Oliva was the *diputado* (senator) to the national legislature for the department of Izabal and probably the most prominent citizen of Port Barrios. I had only met him once briefly. But this time he wanted to find out what we were doing because he had heard that all this new rice that he was buying belonged to a group of Chortí farmers.

He listened intently as I talked for maybe twenty minutes about how the Friends Mission was helping the impoverished Chortí Indians develop the land that they had bought and improve their lives. When I had finished, Mr. Oliva asked me, "What are the greatest needs on your project?"

This caught me off guard, but the needs of our village school immediately came to my mind. I knew that this could only have been an inspiration from the Lord.

I responded, "We consider the education of the children a key factor in the future of the Chortí people. We have hired a Chortí man to teach in what has been a private school for the last four years. Our goal is to establish El Florido as a self-sustaining village and one of the remaining hurdles is to have the school recognized by the government."

Mr. Oliva reached across his desk and picked up a piece of paper. He wrote a name and a phone number on it. He handed me the paper and said, "Wait one week and then contact this person in the Ministry of Education. I know him personally. You will have government endorsement for your school."

I was dumbfounded. But I felt *God was in this conversation.*

After a sincere and humble expression of gratitude, I said, "There is one more thing I would like to ask. In the village we have talked often about the future of the school. The families really like our teacher, José Antonio Vásquez, because he speaks their language and most of the kids pass their grade every year. They would like for him to continue as their teacher in El Florido, but he is not a titled teacher and only has a sixth-grade education. What can we do?"

Mr. Oliva instructed, "Write a history of the school and its success, the training, and years of experience of the teacher and his Chortí background. Then have all the villagers sign it as a petition to the Ministry of Education." So José, the teacher, complied by writing a careful history of the school and of his background and qualifications for continuing to serve as the teacher for the El Florido School.

Back in El Florido, the Chortí villagers were skeptical. They had never had success getting their voice heard in the government, and more than that, they were afraid there would be reprisals against them. They chuckled with disbelief when Ray announced that everyone should sign the petition. But finally they decided to sign in order to make don Mundo happy.

The school opened in January 1974 as a national school. Our Chortí teacher was now being paid by the government. This was visibly "a God moment". God had used that unplanned visit with the Guatemalan Senator to once again pay heed to one of the cries of the El Florido people.

The Revival in El Florido

Virginia

In 1972, the El Florido Church had planned some special services. For weeks, the people excitedly made arrangements. The families donated sacks of corn for tortillas, sacks of black beans, lime for cooking the corn for the tortillas, chickens, coffee beans to be ground, sacks of vegetables and firewood.

A big part of these special services was the mealtimes together. The church named a committee of women and men to cook the meals, which was a special honor. The planning and work began two days prior to the special services. Volunteers pitched in and helped cook the hundreds of tortillas during these meals on the large *comals* (clay cooking disks) over a wood fire.

Juan Aguilar, pastor from Olopa Friends Church, was the invited guest speaker. He preached a message in the morning services and then gave the evening evangelistic messages. A singing group from the Sabana Grande Church was invited to bring special music. They played their guitars and sang hymns and choruses with lots of enthusiasm.

People attended prayer meetings very early in the morning, ate breakfast together, attended another service at 10:00 a.m., and enjoyed a noon meal together. It usually was chicken or beef cooked in a stew and served with tortillas. Black beans and tortillas with cheese and coffee were served for both the breakfasts and the evening meals. At siesta time in the afternoon, families went to the river to bathe and rest.

The evening church service was the last activity of the day. Hymns that everyone sang were accompanied by two guitars, and Juan gave the message from the Bible. The benches were made of six-inch-thick logs cut in half and placed on sticks, with the flat side up to sit on. They were not very comfortable after thirty minutes.

More than three hundred people attended these services. Some came from other villages such as Sejá, La Libertad, and Semoux to celebrate with their friends in El Florido. The overflow crowd could hear just as well standing outside of the church as those sitting inside due to the stick walls.

Our family looked forward to eating with our friends because it was a wonderful time of sharing and fellowship. The whole weekend had an atmosphere of a happy celebration.

At the end of the last evening service, one man stood and said, "I would like to ask my neighbor, Leandro, to forgive me for getting so angry last week."

"I forgive you, Pedro," Leandro responded as he slowly walked to the front of the church. The two men embraced and knelt together at the altar in front of the church. Everyone present knew of the strife between the two men and was filled with deep emotion. We felt the presence of the Holy Spirit and the power of forgiveness.

"I want to ask doña Berta to forgive me for throwing mud on her clothes," doña Angelina said as she stood at the altar.

"I forgive you," doña Berta responded as she quickly came to the front of the church. They also embraced and then knelt at the altar. Several people knelt with them to pray.

"I want to ask my wife, doña Rosa, to forgive me for not telling her the truth about how many sacks of beans we had," don Inéz said sincerely.

Doña Rosa was still resentful but she slowly came to the front of the church saying, "Yes, I forgive you." They embraced and knelt together at the altar. I was in awe of this moment because outward affection was never shown between husband and wife in that culture.

Interestingly, most of us observers in this service were aware of the various conflicts in our community. When pardon was asked and forgiveness granted, everyone was involved and ready to forgive. That night, more than forty-five people asked pardon of one another, and others accepted the Lord for the first time. The service continued until past midnight as people prayed, asked forgiveness of one another, and praised the Lord.

After the last prayer at midnight the visitors from the other villages walked home carrying their Coleman lanterns and singing hymns as they walked through the jungle. It was an awesome sound of praise reverberating through the trees that seemed to perfectly culminate this weekend of revival. Our hearts were overflowing with joy as we felt the Holy Spirit near and dear to us.

Following this weekend of services, a vibrant church planting movement began. New Friends congregations began springing up in the entire region, stretching the 40 miles between Rio Dulce and El Petén.

The Sejá church was small and struggling so Ray helped them twice on Sundays. I gave the Sunday school lessons to the children. Our three small children enjoyed being part of this group.

The congregation in Cieniga was started by an invitation from don Vitalino to begin Bible studies in his home on Tuesday evenings. Four or five people were sent from the El Florido church to play the guitar, lead the singing and teach a Bible lesson. Our family would often accompany them in the truck. Don Vitalino invited his neighbors and friends to these meetings.

In the village of Las Conchas, a new group of people held church services in a home on Wednesday and Friday nights. They asked Ray to lead a Bible study and he always took three or four men from El Florido with him. I usually stayed home those nights to put our three children to bed earlier so they were more alert for school the next day.

At this same time, the village of La Libertad asked El Florido to begin Bible Studies there also. This congregation quickly grew and soon became an official Friends Church.

We were not doing this ministry alone. The El Florido men did most of the outreach work, such as visiting the homes ahead of time, playing the guitar, and giving messages from the Bible. When they walked the two to four miles to villages for services after a long day's work in their fields, they were exhausted and often returned in the nightly rain. We were glad to make their ministry a little easier by taking them in our truck. In this way, Ray was an encouragement in the spiritual as well as the material realms.

Considering Boarding School for Our Children

In home school, I taught Linda second grade and Tad first grade every morning, and Kenny began kindergarten. Linda loved her studies and often worked into the afternoons. I noticed the boys often gazing out at the jungle as if it was beckoning them to go fish and explore.

Keith Sarver served as superintendent of the California of Friends churches' missionary work. He usually made a trip to Central America every two years to visit the missionaries and their work. He also maintained a working relationship with the Central American church leaders.

Paul Enyart was our field director of missions who lived with his family in Chiquimula. Paul was a son of missionaries and had lived on a mission field most of his life.

On this occasion, Keith and Paul visited us in El Florido. We took them to see the village, church and parcels, and talked with a couple of the Indian farmers. They also had lunch with us. They saw the medical work and visited the short-term volunteer, Jim Gay, who was living with us at the time. We all returned together to the mission headquarters in Chiquimula for three days of meetings and fellowship.

We began each morning with Bible reading and prayer. Then we would begin two to three hours of praying together. The older missionaries knelt at their chairs and they would talk to the Lord about the concerns on their heart. We prayed for our own families and for the national church workers. The prayer meetings always closed with Matthew 9:37, "The harvest is plentiful, but the workers are few. Therefore, beseech the Lord of the harvest to send out workers into His harvest."

After lunch, Keith and Paul met with individual missionaries or missionary couples. We looked forward to meeting with them as we had their full attention and could share whatever was on our hearts. During this session, Keith and Paul made an appointment with Ray and me for our evaluation. Keith discussed the progress of El Florido and he asked about our concerns. We gladly took the opportunity to share with him the victories we had witnessed in El Florido.

Then Keith said, "And now let's talk about your children. When are you planning to send them to boarding school in Huehuetenango? We strongly encourage you to send them now."

Huehuetenango is a city in northwest Guatemala near the Mexican border. Missionaries had been sending their children to this boarding school, which offered an excellent education, for the past twenty-five years, from first to ninth grades. Children came home every three to four months. It was a twelve- to fifteen-hour drive one way from El Florido to Huehue Academy.

There was silence. Ray and I had not thought about doing this at all, because we both felt we were getting along well having our children by our side. We served others together as a family. They were developing sensitive hearts toward the downtrodden and hurting people. They loved to be with us as we visited the sick and when we had church services to attend.

Ray and I were enjoying our children who were a wonderful gift from the Lord. They helped us have fun and enjoy our work. Lastly, our children touched people's hearts in different ways than we adults could. The Chortí easily related to them.

I followed a strict routine to home school our children in the morning before the heat became unbearable, and I would attend to sick people in the afternoons in the clinic. Kenny was excited to have just begun kindergarten.

As my mind was reeling from Keith's question, Paul said, "We are concerned for the children. They need a really good education now."

Keith said, "Besides, Virginia would be free to do a lot more missionary service if they went to Huehue Academy."

Our silence continued. I was praying and quietly crying. *Lord, I remember I promised to trust you with my children. Please help us right now.*

Then Ray took a deep sigh. "You know, Keith, we just don't feel that this is the time to send our children to Huehue Academy. Virginia is getting along pretty well home-schooling them." More silence. "If sending our kids to boarding school is a requirement, I think you should probably look for someone else to work in El Florido instead of us," Ray concluded.

My heart leaped for joy because that was exactly what I felt. I wanted to jump up and give my husband a big hug and a kiss, but I restrained myself.

There was more silence. Finally Keith said, "I think that's all we had to talk to you folks about. Let's go eat supper."

I thanked the Lord that Ray shared my view that God's call for us to be loving parents for our children at home was more important to us than our exciting missionary service. And together, we felt God's assurance that we would not be forced to send our kids to boarding school now.

Another Drought in Jocotán

It had not rained in Jocotán for many months, and the Indians who lived in the mountaintop villages around Jocotán were suffering from hunger once again. The farmers planted the corn, and the kernels sprouted and the stalks grew six-to-ten-inches high before shriveling up and dying.

Pastor Chon Vargas, of the Friends Church in Jocotán, wrote to us in El Florido. "Please come back to help us." We had learned that the Jocotán Church could no longer pay Chon a salary, so he supported himself as a barber in town. We began praying about how we could help them if we did go back for a while.

When the news of the desperate situation in Jocotán reached the people in El Florido, they immediately started planning how they could help their families and friends back in Jocotán. They donated more than a ton of corn and sent it to them. They also invited family members to come live with them in El Florido for a while, and many came for a short time. We decided to live in Jocotán temporarily to help during their difficult times.

Sometimes the Jocotán families had only enough corn to eat tortillas once a day or once every other day. In normal times the Chortí men ate eight tortillas three times a day. As the Chortí grew weaker from malnutrition, they were susceptible to common diseases such as colds and measles. Children and older people often succumbed to these diseases during a drought.

Usually the Indian people bathed at least once a day. But when the creeks and rivers dried up, they were unable to bathe as often. They were unable to wash or repair their clothes, let alone replace them. So they were ragged, dirty, and lethargic during this drought.

The little children, who usually had big, bright eyes and helped their parents carry small sacks of corn up the mountain, now had matted hair, bloodshot eyes, runny noses, and noted lethargy. During these times of drought, children often developed reddish/blond hair and protruding bellies.

The Friends missionaries received and distributed food from relief agencies. Still there was not enough food. The Friends churches in California sent money to purchase additional food for distribution.

The key foods donated were dried milk, vegetable oil, flour, soy flour, and Incaparina. In 1968 I began teaching families how to prepare and eat Incaparina, a newly developed cereal, when they did not have enough corn and beans. It was amazing how well little children developed and grew eating only Incaparina! My own family liked it as well.

The dried milk was a problem since the Chortí never drank milk or milk products. We taught them to mix the milk powder with water and Incaparina and cook the mixture for twenty minutes. This was a delicious meal that incorporated much-needed calcium into the diet of the children as well as the adults.

At first the mothers were sure it was not good for their babies and little children, who loved the cereal. Then the adults decided to try it and discovered it satisfied their hunger. From that moment on they accepted the relief food products.

Because of this severe drought in Jocotán and the surrounding villages, many Chortí families were moving to the coast on their own. We accepted eight new families into the relocation project which brought the total to forty-five families, our planned capacity.

One day a poor Indian mother came into the clinic in Jocotán with her sick one year old baby. She explained, "My little Juanito has diarrhea and won't eat."

I noticed she was giving him a baby bottle filled with a white liquid. I was curious since the Indians do not give their babies milk. "Doña Angelina, what is the white liquid in that bottle?" I respectfully asked.

"Cornstarch and water," she proudly replied. The drought was so severe that they did not have corn or beans to eat. But she was giving the baby cornstarch, mixed with water since she had no breast milk.

I could tell the cornstarch was not cooked and she was probably mixing it with contaminated water from the river. The baby had fat cheeks and a protruding belly both due to a lack of protein. I wanted to cry for this young mother of three small children, who was trying to do her best to feed her baby.

My diagnosis was intestinal infection, and we gave the infant sulfa and Kaopectate. Then I gave her a bag of Incaparina and showed her how to mix two tablespoons of it in two cups of water and boil it for twenty minutes. I instructed her to go to the mission and get more Incaparina for the whole family. Within two days Junito was recuperating and drinking cooked Incaparina in his bottle.

Meanwhile, Ray visited the farmers in the villages and participated in the distribution of relief food. After those two weeks of helping the Chortí people in Jocotán, we had to return to El Florido. Five months later the rains began and the drought was over for a while.

Easter Eggs

One particular Easter Sunday in El Florido was a day full of joy and thanksgiving for all of us. It had started the night before. Ray had attended the church's monthly business meeting until 10:30 p.m., and I had delivered a baby at 9:00 p.m. in a villager's home. Tired but motivated by our excitement for Easter the next day, Ray and I colored Easter eggs for the kids until midnight. We used the set of food coloring dyes I had purchased in Guatemala City earlier in the month.

We were awakened in the morning at five thirty by our neighbor chasing a pig that had escaped the pen and wandered into our yard. This chase had become our wake-up call and I began to hide the colored eggs around our house outside while the kids were still asleep.

While I crept around in the damp grass, I hoped none of our neighbors had noticed me. As a young missionary mother, I wanted my children to learn the traditions and customs of our U.S. homeland.

All three children woke at their usual early morning hour.

"Hi, kids! Happy Easter," I greeted them.

They were a little groggy but answered, "Happy Easter."

"Here are your Easter baskets, one for each of you," I enthusiastically explained. I had acquired three simple, small baskets in the market and had put a pretty bow on each handle.

"Now go out and see how many colored eggs you can find that the Easter bunny has laid," I instructed.

They obediently took their baskets and went out the door to the backyard.

"Oh, here's one!" Linda exclaimed and put it in her basket.

"I found one!" Tad yelled excitedly.

"Me too," Kenny said as he spied one. And the hunt continued.

Suddenly I noticed some of Tad and Kenny's Chortí friends were watching all the excitement. Then one little boy just could not control his curiosity.

"What is that?" he asked Tad.

"An Easter egg," Tad answered.

"Where did it come from?"

"The Easter bunny laid it," was Tad's serious answer.

"What kind of rabbit is that?"

"I don't know, just an Easter bunny," Tad responded.

"Well, I didn't know rabbits lay eggs," he continued.

"This one does," Tad happily replied.

"Well, who cares about your colored eggs—let's look for that rabbit!" the boy adamantly decided.

I was standing outside the house watching this whole game. Then the little boy looked at me with many questions in his eyes.

Suddenly, I thought, *Wait a minute, something is wrong here. My children understand this is a fun game we play at Easter time, but the Indian children do not understand this. The Easter-egg hunt is a cultural tradition.*

"What am I doing?" I asked myself. "We are not here to teach U.S. cultural traditions, but to teach the truth about Jesus, our Savior." Often traditions do not translate well from one culture to another. We have to be willing to give these up when we step into another culture in order to avoid confusing the true messages that we are trying to convey, I realized.

Soon nearly a dozen children had gathered to see the colored eggs that were "laid by a rabbit." Probably our children shared several eggs with them who would have gone home and had a wonderful "show and tell" time with their parents. Others were still looking for the rabbit and asking what color it was.

I hustled our children into the house to get ready for the church service. I prayed, "I have tried to be very truthful in everything we do so that when I teach our children and the Chortí children about you, Lord, they know it is truth. Please forgive me, because this experience of the Easter bunny has confused the children." We never had an Easter-egg hunt again in El Florido.

16

The Clinic and a Health Promoter

Virginia

As part of our "new beginnings" on the relocation project, an immunization program for tetanus, diphtheria, whooping cough, and polio was initiated for every child and adult in the village.

People gathered in front of our house and we treated them one at a time in our kitchen. Fortunately there were two short-term volunteers helping me immunize the one hundred fifty people from our village. Six weeks later we administered the second immunization in this series.

Late one afternoon after administering the second series of immunizations, patients lined up for me to care for their various illnesses, all in our kitchen. I did not like bringing all the sickness into the room where my family ate their meals. But what could I do?

Melecio, one of the Chortí farmers, came limping to our front door and said, in the typical unemotional Indian way, "Doña Virginia, I have cut my leg with my machete."

Seeing all the blood on his pant leg, I stepped out of my house to examine him. "You sure have, Melecio. There is a lot of blood in your boot. But don't worry; you will be okay," I said with confidence. Although I was not all that assured in my own heart, he needed to hear my words of encouragement.

Grabbing some sterile four-by-four gauze pads and sterile gloves, I checked the seriousness of the machete cut. While Melecio sat on a bench in front of our house, I slowly pulled his leg out of the rubber boot, and wiped the blood away so I could see the wound. When someone would come in with a machete cut, I never knew how large and deep the cut would be. This time it was a four-inch cut on the shin bone but not deep. It just happened to be in an area with lots of blood vessels so there was about an inch of blood in the bottom of his boot. The exercise of walking almost half a mile from his parcel probably caused increased hemorrhaging.

I cleaned the wound with antiseptic soap and sterile water. After it dried I placed five butterfly bandages to hold the wound closed, and another bandage was placed on top of that. I gave him an oral antibiotic as a preventive measure and told him to return to me the next day, which he did.

The next morning during my personal devotions, I was praying about various concerns. A quiet moment alone to talk to the Lord was precious because my children or our Indian friends demanded my attention all day long. Much of my prayer time was spent telling the Lord my concerns or complaining about our various situations.

"Lord," I prayed, "caring for sick people in our kitchen goes against all my understanding of clean areas versus contaminated areas. This is bad for my family. I wish we had a clinic to care for the patients."

"Why haven't you asked Me for a clinic?" was God's instant reply.

"Oh Lord, please forgive me," I prayed. "And now, Lord, please give us a clinic," I humbly prayed. In my heart I knew He had heard me, for the words of Jesus came to me that said, "Until now you have asked for nothing in My name; ask, and you will receive, that your joy will may be full." (John 16:24).

Five days later we received an aerogram letter from the Friends Church where I grew up in New Providence, Iowa. "Do you have a need for our help there at El Florido?" the letter asked. "We are a group of men that do construction work and think God may be asking us to go to Guatemala and help you."

"Ray, look—God has answered our prayer!" I cried. "He is sending men from New Providence to build a clinic!"

"Now calm down, Virginia," he replied. "We'll see if something like that is what they have in mind," he calmly responded. But I could tell he was excited about them coming.

Ray wrote a letter to the church telling them of our need for a clinic. Within a couple of weeks the New Providence church responded, "We are sending four men to Guatemala to build your clinic."

We met the team at the airport in October 1973. "Look, Ray, there's my dad!" I exclaimed, shocked to see Dad walk into the immigration line along with three other men, Dick Talbot, Dennis Edgeton and Roscoe Nelson. What a surprise! We had no idea he was coming.

We drove directly down to the coastal lowlands and the relocation project. We hardly gave them a chance to transition from the cool Iowa fall to the hot tropical lowlands. In order to take full advantage of their help, we thrust them right into the clinic project.

David Hamm had drawn architectural plans for the clinic. Much of the lumber for the building came from trees cut down on the project and sawed at our sawmill. It followed the same design as the missionary home—on posts keeping it off the ground for dryness and ventilation, wooden sides up four feet, and screened up to the tin roof. It had two rooms—one for the clinic and one for a guest room with a bathroom in between.

While sometimes overwhelmed by the intense heat and humidity, our four builders from Iowa courageously and sacrificially persisted and finished the building in just twelve days. Cost efficiency was also their priority so the total price tag for this new building was$1,000.

My medical supplies were quickly moved out of our kitchen and into the new building, which was located across the village road in front of our house. All the villagers came to the outdoor celebration service for the dedication of the clinic.

Jim Gay, the short-term youth ambassador who was living with us, moved into the spare bedroom in the clinic. Jim had come with a group of summer short-term volunteers the prior year, and then he continued working with us for two more years.

He had graduated from UC Davis and came from the Berkeley Friends Church. Jim worked beside us and was an enormous help in the formative years of the relocation project. He always joined us for family worship in the mornings where we read the Bible passages in the children's Bible, and then he retired to his room saying, "I want to read that in the regular Bible."

Jim surveyed farm parcels, drove the tractor to haul gravel, harvested corn and operated the sawmill. He stayed in El Florido while we were on furlough in the States. He had a heart for the Lord, and he showed that love as he worked with our Indian friends and with the youth in the church. We especially noted his patience with our children.

Dan Butler, from Granada Heights Friends Church, came as a two-year volunteer to help us after Jim left. We thank the Lord for their generous help to us and our Chortí friends.

Lucio in the Clinic

One morning I stepped out of the house on my way to the clinic and Lucio, the man who had had the serious machete injury three years earlier, was waiting for me.

"Doña Virginia, can I talk with you about something?" he quietly asked me so no one could hear him.

"Oh, hello, Lucio," I responded. "Sure. Let's talk now." I knew I might not have another free moment to talk with him.

Lucio began, "Could I help you in the clinic?" By the look on his face I could tell that he had given this much previous thought.

"Well, I'm not sure," I said. I thought to myself, *He can't write and has not finished a single grade of school. Now, how could he possibly help me?*

Sensing my doubts, he continued reasoning, "You see, since my right hand was severely cut, it hurts to grip the machete when I work on my land. I am afraid that it will slip out of my hand again. So I would like to work with you in the clinic," he finished with a sincere tone of voice.

I had been asking the Lord for help with clinic work, but I had not considered one of the Chortí village men being able to help me because of their poor education.

"Lucio, can you write?" I asked. I already knew the answer, but I wanted him to realize that there were some basic requirements for the job.

"No, but I can sign my name," he quickly assured me.

"Can you read?"

"Yes, I can read the Bible," he responded. Most of the Chortí Christians had learned to read by teaching themselves how to read the Bible. So their reading level was very basic and slow.

"Lucio, let me pray about this," I said. "I need to ask the Lord about your offer to help me." I also needed some time to think about it. If Lucio did begin to help me, he had to succeed in it. If he failed, it would be shameful and embarrassing for him in the village.

The number of patients coming to the clinic was increasing daily. People came in to El Florido from villages as far away as five miles. One afternoon I looked out the clinic window and counted fifty-one people sitting on the small knoll between our house and the clinic, waiting their turn to be helped.

The afternoons were hot and humid in the clinic and the patients were so sick. To be as responsible as possible, I tried to keep written records on all the patients that came in. It was vitally important to take a careful history from the patients or their families. I learned to be patient, listen, ask the right questions and observe body language. Eventually the patient or a family member would tell me what was making him sick.

Then I gave a quick physical exam, taking blood pressure, pulse, weight, respirations and temperature. Using a stethoscope I listened to the heart, lungs and abdomen. A flashlight helped me check their pupils, and I checked for swelling in the extremities. When I found myself in a quandary, I would stop and pray. God was always faithful to guide me to the right decision.

Having gathered the necessary information, a diagnosis would be made. This was followed by a plan for treatment, which was usually an oral medication. An injection was administered if the case was serious and urgent. Or advice might be given about diet, boiling water or, in the serious cases, getting out to a doctor, which was four hours away by bus.

The patient's vital signs, symptoms, diagnoses and treatments were always written in the notebook. And then I prayed with the patient. I asked the Lord for two things. First I asked Him to help the medication or treatment to bring healing to the patient. Secondly, I asked Him to bless the patient and family and help them to love Him. I asked the patients to return so I could see if the treatment was effective, and then I would decide if more medication was needed.

The people had many beliefs about illnesses and treatments, and I needed to learn these so I could better understand how they interpreted my teaching about diseases. I also needed to be practical in my application. For example, if a very sick patient needed to take an antibiotic through the night, I told him to take it each time the rooster crowed because everyone knew a rooster crowed at approximately 11:00 p.m., 3:00 a.m., and 6:00 a.m. My patients quickly understood and the treatments were effective.

I noticed that young children were crying loudly as they came down the trail in front of the clinic and they cried until they were past the clinic. One day a mother laughingly told me that they tell their children they would be taken to the clinic for a shot from the "gringa nurse" if they were disobedient. This threat of pain in the clinic was detrimental to their children's beliefs about health care I reminded them.

I was happy to see that the mothers were abandoning their former beliefs that bottle-feeding was better than breast-feeding. Now they could see the benefits of breast-feeding as they watched their babies grow strong and healthy.

The crucial work of the prevention of intestinal parasites was a challenge. While I knew that water needed to be boiled for twenty minutes to kill parasites, most of my patients could not afford large kettles in which to boil enough water for the whole family. And then how would they cool it down to drink without a refrigerator? So we taught them to put three drops of chlorine bleach in a clay jug and wait one hour before drinking it. This was an effective control of waterborne parasites.

Arcelia—Breech Birth

Arcelia visited the clinic once a month for prenatal care. Fifteen days before her first baby was due, I noticed her fetus was in breech (butt first) position.

"Arcelia, please bring your husband and come in tomorrow to talk to me about the delivery of your baby," I insisted.

Arcelia and her husband, Moises, came to see me about 5:00 p.m., after Moises had finished his work in the field. They were Chortí members of our village, and Ray and I felt close to them. Moises was a brother to Gloria, our house helper.

"Moises, I think Arcelia's baby is in breech position for delivery, and that is dangerous for the baby and the mother," I carefully explained. "Sometimes the baby turns around before birth, but this is what we are facing."

Neither Moises nor Arcelia asked me any questions, they just sat there with their heads hung. I waited for them to speak if they wanted to, but they did not.

"Moises, would you take Arcelia to the hospital in Port Barrios to have her baby?" I asked.

There was silence for a moment or so, and then Moises said, "No, doña Virginia, I'm not going to take her to Port Barrios to have her baby. And she does not want to go either."

"Look, Moises, you need to get them to a place where there is oxygen for the baby," I pleaded. "And they could do a cesarean surgery if needed."

"No, she's not going to Port Barrios to have the baby," Moises stated strongly. "Doña Virginia, you can deliver the baby here."

I can? I asked myself. I had only observed a breech delivery but had never done one by myself. Obviously, Moises had more confidence in my ability than I had.

"Please, Moises, take her out a couple days ahead of her due date," I begged.

"No, I am not going to take her out," he stated decisively.

This resolve was not surprising to me. Once the Chortí men made a thoughtful decision, they stuck to it. Besides, this trip would have been expensive for them, and Arcelia wanted to deliver her baby in their home where her mother could help her. And lastly, the Chortí people were often treated dreadfully in hospitals due to the ingrained prejudiced beliefs of the staff toward them.

No, I thought, *Moises is right; they will get better care from all of us here in the village than in Port Barrios.*

"Oh Lord, You know I am so inadequate, I am afraid the baby might die," I whispered to Him. "Please give me wisdom to know how to help this baby live."

As I began to think more about this pending delivery, *"Prepare for that delivery,"* was the impression that clearly came to me.

"Yes, that's right. I will get my obstetrics text and review breech deliveries," I said to myself.

So in the evenings after the kids were in bed, I brushed up on the breech delivery technique. I memorized the step-by-step procedures. I prepared a sterile delivery pack with gloves, boiled string, and a new Gillette razor blade wrapped in a small sterile sheet. I prayed, "Lord, please help me deliver Arcelia's new baby."

God gave me a plan and all fear of the anticipated complications left. I felt like I was ready for Moises' baby to arrive. I did not realize this at the time, but God was preparing me for another patient that would increase my awareness of His power.

A Seventeen Year-Old Delivers a Baby

Several days later, I was trying to finish the reading and math classes for the kids, Tad informed me that there were sick patients waiting for me. So I quickly finished the classes and we had recess.

As I neared the clinic, I heard a young woman moaning with pain. She had a very swollen leg. I took her inside and began the usual process of taking a verbal history: "Your name? Your age? What village are you from? What is wrong and how did that happen?"

The young girl, Celia, who was seventeen years old, had walked in from a village seven miles away, accompanied by a young man. Three days prior her right leg began to swell, but she had not injured it. I performed a physical exam and found she had a fever of 103 degrees. Her leg was swollen from the hip to the ankle and it felt warm. There was no obvious injury or localized infection. I focused on the assessment of the leg, and my diagnosis was cellulitis of the whole leg. As was my usual custom, I prayed with the couple and asked God for wisdom and healing for the girl.

I decided that an antibiotic therapy was needed for the obvious infection. I prepared and administered an adult dose of penicillin, and I prepared a packet of antibiotics for her to take at home. As I was doing that, I noticed Celia groaning and holding her abdomen.

"What is it?" I asked.

"I am pregnant," she stated.

"Pregnant?" I asked since she did not look pregnant at all. "How many months pregnant are you?" I asked.

"Seven months," she told me.

So I proceeded to examine her abdomen. *Sure enough! She is pregnant!* I exclaimed to myself. *Oh my goodness,* I thought. I watched her for fifteen minutes and realized she was having labor pains. *We can't have a delivery of a seven-month-gestation baby here in my rustic clinic. We are so far from any professional help. We'll have a dead infant on our hands! Please, God, help me! What should I do?* I felt desperate for some help. Ray had left earlier to run errands in Morales using our pickup.

My desire was to get this girl to the nearest hospital and doctor, which was three hours away-if the ferry was running.

"Miguel, I want you to walk out to Sejá and get someone to come in a vehicle to take you and Celia to the hospital," I ordered. "Go on, quickly, and please hurry!"

Miguel, her common-law husband, reluctantly obeyed and walked out of El Florido toward Sejá. Celia's contractions intensified.

"What can I give her to slow down the labor?" I asked myself. I had stocked the clinic with a pretty good variety of medicines to treat anticipated medical needs. But at that moment I knew I did not have anything for this scenario.

In desperation, I decided to give her a small dose of phenobarbital to help her relax. "Now relax, this should help you," I stated as I administered the injection.

"Okay," she groaned.

"Now just relax," I calmly said over and over to her. I kept one eye on the clock and the other on the road hoping to see Miguel coming with a vehicle.

Suddenly Celia gave out a cry, and her contractions began strong every five minutes and lasted thirty seconds. I knew she was in real labor, and the delivery was going to happen before I could ever get her to a hospital.

"Gloria, come here to help me," I called over the small intercom between the clinic and the house.

"No, doña Virginia, I can't," she replied. She had heard the cries of pain from the clinic and already had a pretty good idea of what was happening.

"Gloria, come down now. I need you to help me." I knew she was my only hope for help.

"No, doña Virginia, I get sick in things like that," she responded.

Meanwhile, Celia was calling out, "Help me, help me, I'm going to die!"

"No, you are not going to die. Take another breath," I calmly told her. Then in her panic she again called, "Help me! I'm going to die!"

"No, you are not going to die," I reassuringly told her. "Gloria, come now, you have to help me," I demanded. Then I saw Gloria reluctantly step through our front door and slowly walk across the road to the clinic.

"Oh thank you, Lord, she is going to help me," I whispered.

She walked directly to the door since the entire crowd waiting for medical attention had left. Gloria stuck her head inside.

"Look, please bring me the empty shoe box that is on the chest inside the house. Also, put a clean baby blanket inside the box and bring it here," I instructed.

She left to do as I had asked and returned within six minutes with the box and blanket.

"Gloria, this girl is going to have a tiny baby in a few minutes, and we will put it in this box. Now once it's born, I want you to hold the box and gently blow into its face," I explained.

"Okay," she agreed, relieved that this was all I was asking of her.

The labor progressed. I coached Celia on how to breathe and then relax until the next contraction. I was concentrating so much on the birth process that I had completely forgotten about Miguel.

I donned my sterile gloves and put gloves on Gloria. With the next contraction, the water broke and two little *feet* appeared. *Oh no… this is a footling presentation on top of everything else!* I then told myself, *I have been preparing for this type of birth over the past two weeks* (because of the previous expectant mother). *I know exactly how to handle this.* Very gently I grasped the baby's tiny body and guided it out and into my hand. His little body fit in my hand and his feet rested on my wrist.

Suddenly he took a weak breath and began crying a very faint cry.

"He's alive!" I cried, amazed at that tiny body that was breathing weakly, crying and moving a little bit. I tied his umbilical cord with the sterilized string and cut the cord with the sterilized scissors. I then laid the little baby in the box, and Gloria took over very gently blowing into his face. His cries got stronger, and soon he breathed steadily.

Soon the placenta was delivered. I was preparing the injection of Ergotrate when blood began to pour profusely from Celia's body. I quickly placed my hands appropriately to put pressure on her uterus and slow the hemorrhaging. I realized I could not release my hands to give the Ergotrate, a medicine which would constrict the blood vessels in her uterus. Just at that moment, Miguel walked in, apologizing for being unable to find a vehicle and driver to help him with Celia. I was so grateful to see him.

"That's not important now; the baby is delivered. Now, you put on those sterile gloves and put one hand here and the other one here and hold them there," I instructed.

"No, I can't do that," he mumbled.

"Look, you can do this. Now put these gloves on," I demanded loudly.

He put the rubber gloves on without saying another word. He carefully followed my instructions about the positions of his hands. Slowly I released my hands, reached the Ergotrate, and administered the injection. Miguel was doing a good job of controlling the hemorrhage. After a few minutes I took his place so he could relax. The baby, still being held by Gloria in our makeshift incubator, was breathing more steadily now. About ten minutes later, the hemorrhage had completely stopped. I cleaned Celia up and let her rest on the clinic exam table.

"God has done a miracle for you two, Celia and Miguel. He saved Celia's life and He saved your son's life today. Only God could have done this. He loves you two so much! Do you love Him?" I asked.

"Well I used to be a Christian but have fallen away. I need to return to the Lord," Miguel confessed.

"Okay, let's pray right now," I said. "Let's thank the Lord for miraculously saving Celia and the baby's lives. Then let's ask Him to help you both return to Him and love Him with all your hearts."

"Oh Lord, thank you," I prayed. Then a strong sense of the Lord's presence came over us. I knew He was right there guiding and helping and saving us. This precious sense of His presence brought tears to my eyes.

After we prayed I looked up. It was dark outside, and I was surprised because I had no idea how much time had passed. I showed Celia how to wrap her new baby, how to breast-feed him, and how to carry him next to her body to keep him warm.

Ray had arrived home in the pickup. He took the young couple with their new baby home to Cieniga. The baby survived and became healthy and strong.

Two weeks later Arcelia's baby, having turned from its breech position, had a normal birth at home. God used her to prepare me for the birth of Celia's baby.

A Health Promoter

It was during all of these medical problems that Lucio had initially come to me and offered to help. Now, I was giving this much more consideration. After careful thought about the pros and cons and much prayer, the Lord gave me the answer. In church the next Sunday, I said, "Lucio, come by my house tomorrow at noon and talk with me."

"Okay, doña Virginia," he said. "I'll be there."

The next day at our kitchen table, I told him, "The main ministry of this clinic is loving people and praying with them. Can you do that, Lucio?" I knew there were lots of "clan" differences and disagreements among the Chortí. Could he minister to *all* the people equally?

"Yes, I can," he solemnly stated.

"Then you must learn to write so I can read it," I explained.

"I will do that," he replied. "I understand."

"You must take health classes with me and the classes for health promoters given by the government Department of Health in Port Barrios," I continued.

"Yes, I can do that," he readily agreed.

"And by the way, Lucio, who is going to do all the farming while you are working in the clinic?" I asked. I wanted him to consider all the ramifications of this decision.

"Well, you have the clinic open only in the afternoons, so I can do my farming three or four hours in the morning. And my sons are old enough to work now and my father-in-law helps me," he thoughtfully replied.

"Good," I said. I was glad he had already thought about the help he would need in raising his crops. "Now, Lucio, we will charge each patient twenty-five cents plus the cost of the medicines," I explained carefully.

Before Lucio joined the clinic work, I was charging each patient the cost of the medicine only. But now we would increase the patient fee twenty-five cents to pay for Lucio's salary. I had no idea if what he earned would be enough to make it worth his time.

We discovered that in the patients' eyes, the value of the medicine and care in the clinic was relative to how much it cost. For example, if it cost nothing, then the treatment was not good in their thinking. If it was costly, then it was good treatment. This was the reason patients sometimes would pay $1.50 for medicines in our clinic and then go to the pharmacy in Sejá and buy medicines for $10.00. Because it was expensive, they would value it more, even though the pharmacies would often give them an ineffective placebo.

"The first two or three weeks I want you to come to the clinic at 1:00 p.m. and just observe as I treat patients," I said, explaining our plan. "I will explain to you the process of taking histories and doing a physical for the patients. We will try to give a diagnosis and treatment."

"All right," Lucio responded.

"After two weeks you can write down the names and information while I do the assessment," I explained. In my mind I wondered if he would learn how to write so he could accomplish this basic task. Other questions lingered… Would Lucio be able to build trust and confidence with the patients? Most of them were women with children; would they let a man help with their diagnosis? I realized that I was taking a risk in bringing this man in as my assistant.

Lucio was a very quiet, soft-spoken person, and I wanted to encourage his natural humble nature. If he became prideful, his peers would be jealous. In the Chortí Indian culture, peers try to keep everyone on the same level. If one of them excels in something, the others try to bring him back down. I knew one of the biggest hurdles Lucio would face was gaining the confidence of his fellow villagers.

"It is hard work, Lucio," I said, "and the pay is not very good. But if you do this as a ministry for the Lord and for our brothers and sisters, you will do well."

"Muy bien" ("Very good"), he agreed.

That afternoon Lucio arrived at the clinic to observe. He was well-groomed and was wearing clean clothes. Twenty patients came that afternoon. I followed our plan of taking a history followed by the physical assessment, diagnosis, treatment, and prayer. I noticed his attention was glued to my every move.

During the second week in the clinic, I asked Lucio to write in the clinic log book the name, age, and village of each patient. He did, but I could hardly read it. I found that if I sounded out his written words, they were more understandable. His writing gradually improved, however.

Each day after our home school with my children ended and before the clinic opened, I taught Lucio the basics of the human anatomy and then the signs and symptoms of common diseases. Then I taught him how to use the twenty-five different basic medications we had in the clinic.

He worked beside me for two months. I examined, and he wrote the information. For training purposes, I dedicated more time than usual to discussing the signs, symptoms, diagnoses and appropriate treatment plans. We prayed with each one, collected the fee, and then saw the next patient.

Sometimes patients told us they could not pay for their treatment. We would never refuse to treat anyone because he or she could not pay. After taking care of them, we would record the amount owed in the clinic log and we encouraged them to pay it when they could. We realized the impact on a person's dignity and self-respect when he or she was able to financially take care of his or her family's healthcare. Most of the time, the patients would come back after the harvest to cancel their debt to the clinic.

Lucio was learning very quickly and proving to have a sharp mind for this work. After drilling him on how to do the physical assessment, such as take the temperature, blood pressure, pulse, respirations, and weight, he was ready for hands-on involvement. He would assess, diagnose, and treat and I wrote in the log.

One day when I gave him a new stethoscope as his own instrument, his eyes glistened with happiness, but he said very little. I noticed he took good care of it and after that he always had it with him. By now, he had learned how to take all the vital signs very well.

Ray's uncle, Dr. Merritt Canfield, who had much experience in primitive mission clinics, gave me valuable pointers during his visit. "You can diagnose anemia by listening to the heartbeat," he said. He taught me the different sounds between a heartbeat of an anemic person and a heartbeat of a non-anemic person. This was practical information I taught Lucio.

"You can diagnose tuberculosis in any place of the body by weight loss, loss of appetite, and night sweats," Dr. Canfield instructed. This was why I weighed everyone, and I conveyed this to Lucio.

We sent Lucio to the coastal town of Port Barrios where government classes for health promoters were being held. After he studied two weeks there and passed an exam, the government gave him a health promoters' certificate, which was recognized by all medical officials. He was required to take continuing education classes each year to keep his certificate current.

I quickly realized Lucio knew what was taking place in his community and culture much better than I did, including the belief systems and superstitions that impacted their health. He also understood how his people interpreted my advice and treatments for their illnesses. He was equipped to help me convince families to use the outhouse, get the vaccinations against tetanus and whooping cough, and not put ashes in wounds. The patients in our village and the villages around us slowly developed a confidence in Lucio's ability to help them.

It was again time for us to go to the United States for furlough, this time for only three months. I would leave Lucio in charge of the clinic, but I had so much more to teach him. We spent hours going over treatments and patient care until his eyes were glassy with tiredness. I set up a system for him to collect and record all fees.

Until now, Lucio and I would sit down monthly and go over the clinic income and expenses. We would also count the patients, and I would pay him a salary based on the number of patients treated. While I was gone he would do the same thing with one of our missionaries who would be visiting El Florido. I knew that the enticement to be dishonest in financial dealings would tempt anyone and I did not want Lucio to fail in this area.

The day after we had returned from furlough, Lucio came to see me with the clinic log book and a bag of money. Together we went over the patients that he had seen and what treatments he had given them and the money they paid. The amount of money came out exactly correct according to how many patients he had seen and the medicines he had prescribed. A real trust developed between us.

Lucio went to Chichicastenango in the western highlands for four weeks to take a course for rural health promoters. When we visited him, his comment was, "I have learned much, but it is very cold here and I miss El Florido." Ray gave him his sweater, a letter from his wife and money for the bus trip home. He finished the course and received a diploma.

Lucio worked in the clinic more and more while I filled in when he was not able to work. He consulted with me when he had questions or was unable to make a diagnosis, and together we would figure it out.

Twice a week, after his work in the clinic, he went with church people to hold services in the neighboring villages of Semox, La Libertad or Las Conchas. Lucio was treasurer of the El Florido Church, an officer in the regional district of churches and an active evangelist. At one point, Ray had to warn him about working too hard and spreading himself too thin. But he just smiled. All of us knew he wished he could do even more for the Lord.

Some patients told me, "Lucio isn't as good as you are."

My response was, "I trust him so you can too."

When we moved to Chiquimula in 1979, Lucio was managing the clinic and doing a very good job. In 1988 he presented Ray and me with a history of the development of El Florido that he had written. We have used some of his details to complete this book. He was concerned that we remember and record the wonders that God had done for his people.

A U.S. company that was growing trees in the area for paper pulp hired Lucio to manage their clinic in Sejá for their employees. Sejá was more centrally located to the surrounding villages from where a growing number of patients were coming. So Lucio moved the clinic there and began walking the two kilometers to Sejá and back every day.

In 2000 he suffered a severe heart attack and had limited physical strength after that.

In November 2006 Lucio passed away in El Florido. Pastor Rolando Lopez from Chiquimula called to tell us about Lucio's home-going. There was a huge funeral in the church and hundreds of people from the surrounding villages came to pay their final respects. Rolando performed the service. Since we had returned to the United States, we were grieved that we were unable to attend.

We lost a wonderful friend and servant of God. And as he entered the gates of Heaven, I'm sure he heard the Lord tell him, "Well done, good and faithful servant."

El Florido

Dugout ride across Rio Dulce

Crossing Rio Seja on a log bridge

Dedication of the El Florido Project

José Antonio Vásquez, Chortí school teacher

Homer and Evelyn Sharpless

Don Alejandro and son in a beautiful rice field

Ray and Moises sawing logs

Ray teaching Moises how to fix the tractor

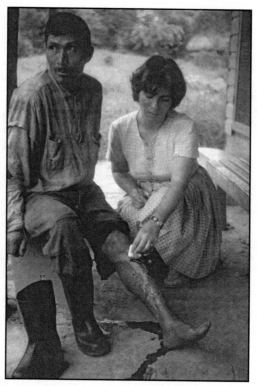

Virginia caring for Melecio's injury

Kenny, Tad and Linda with their friends

Vicente (center) receiving the first title to his land from lawyer
Hugo Morales and Manuel Estrada, a church leader

Dedication of new church building in El Florido

Patients waiting at the new clinic

Ray with nine new landowners who paid for their land

Lucio in the clinic

Linda, Tad, and Kenny Canfield

17

Building a Church with "God's Acre"

Ray

I n 1973, the El Florido church members approved the construction of a new church building during one of their monthly business meetings. This created an excitement in the village. The present church was too small and had been poorly constructed, and it still had a dirt floor and stick sides. The members named a building committee and asked me to meet with them. The chairman of that committee was Ponciano, the lay leader of the church, who was a dynamic leader among the people in the village.

I saw that the timing was good. The sawmill was operating, the road was graveled out through the land that was being cleared, and logs were being dragged in to be sawed into lumber.

"We could have a large, attractive wooden church building at little cost," I stated.

"No, we are going to build our houses out of wood," they said, "but we want the Lord's house to be better than ours. So we want to build the new church out of cement block."

"Do you know how much that would cost?" I asked the committee.

"No, but with the help of the Lord we will do it," they answered with conviction.

"No, brothers, we need to build it out of wood. We can saw up the logs off your own land. It will not cost so much," I reasoned. I could tell that the brothers did not like my idea very much, but they politely remained silent.

We were due to go on a three-month furlough in December, and no decision had been made about the new church. Just after the very large rice harvest, we left for the United States.

On January 7, 1974, the El Florido people came together to discuss all the factors involved in launching the building of their new Friends Church. They beseeched God together in prayer asking Him for clear direction. The result was that the people made a unified decision to begin building the church immediately and it would be built with cement block.

They hired Pedro Casanga, a stone mason who they knew from previous church contacts, to oversee the building of the new church. They had to bring all the sand, block and iron in from Sejá, where the trucks delivered it. Sometimes they worked late into the night after finishing their work in their fields during the day.

When we returned from our furlough, we immediately walked down to the new church site. There it was! We saw the beginnings of a cement-block structure which they had purchased with their own tithes and offerings. The block foundation covered an area much bigger than the old church building. We felt conflicted about the new church, however. We were happy that they were moving forward but apprehensive about how they would pay for it. We had always encouraged them to not depend on the mission to pay their bills.

The building committee met with me to discuss how to continue financing the church. The majority of the members were tithing (giving regularly) to the church. But this project was expensive, and they were far from having sufficient funds or even a specific plan of how to acquire them. We missionaries did not approve of a loan and debt for the fledgling farmers who were struggling in so many ways already.

I remembered how fund raising for churches was done in rural farming areas of America, where each farmer would dedicate one acre of his land for the church-building project. So I presented the idea, calling it "God's acre." The proposal was that each farmer would mark off one-fourth acre of his rice field as God's acre, and the proceeds from the sale of the rice crop from that land would go into the church-building fund. The committee adopted this plan. Subsequently, everyone in the village caught the vision and they were eager to get started. Weekly prayer meetings and monthly all-night prayer vigils were held, as they asked God for His provision and protection over "God's Acres."

The idea of the "God's Acre" was about the only suggestion I made for the church-building project that they accepted. They were making decisions for themselves, as they trusted God and boldly put their faith in Him. God was being honored.

Another contribution the men made was with their labor. They agreed to work voluntarily in groups of two or three. They made sure that no one worked more than their allotted time so that everyone had time for farming. The problem with this was that none of them had ever mixed cement or cut and tied iron for columns before, so this meant that each new group of men had to be trained by the hired builder. And this slowed down the construction and increased the amount of wages paid to the builder.

It was September, and the Indian farmers had their crops almost ready for harvest. The rice was tall and headed out.

Virginia

As I was getting the kids' breakfast ready, our short-wave radio caught my attention. The radio program we were listening to had been interrupted. "May I have your attention please? This is the American Armed Forces radio broadcast reporting that the path of Hurricane Fifi is westward from the Caribbean coast. Landfall of this hurricane will take place at Livingston, Guatemala. The storm system will travel westward across northern Guatemala, north of Rio Dulce…"

Suddenly the tinny voice on the radio was echoing in my head. We were on the very path of that hurricane, and it would be upon us within twelve hours! Ray had left the day before to get supplies for the upcoming harvest in Guatemala City. We needed help! But the only "911" available was God. We earnestly prayed.

All forty-five Indian farmers and their wives gathered in a shed near our house to discuss the danger and how to protect themselves and their vulnerable homes. The men in the group began to pray aloud one by one. They asked God to protect them and their rice crop. The prayer meeting continued for more than two hours. Eventually the couples returned to their thatched homes and waited.

Our home was built on posts with screen walls and a tin roof, a structure that would be frighteningly vulnerable in a hurricane. We had never experienced a hurricane before, so I wondered if I had enough plastic sheets to keep our things dry. How could we survive if the roof was ripped off or if a huge tree from the jungle fell on our house?

The sky was very dark. Light winds came in gusts from different directions. At noon the sky was so dark we needed the lanterns, but the expected strong winds and heavy rains were not coming. For hours that day my children and I sat in the darkness, while I read children's stories by lantern light to distract myself and them from the fear of what was ahead.

By bedtime the storm still had not hit. We went to bed thinking the storm had taken a different path. Hours later we woke to a bright, glistening sunny morning. All was well.

Then reports arrived of terrible destruction to the villages twenty miles to the south and fifteen miles to the north of our village. There was no damage whatsoever to any property in El Florido because God's powerful hand protected us in the eye of the hurricane. We had truly experienced a miracle of God!

While the entire rice crop in the Motagua Valley had been decimated in the hurricane, El Florido's rice crop stood tall. Two weeks later the abundant harvest of the rice began. The farmers were amazed at how many sacks of rice their parcels produced. Each farmer brought their rice into the community shed, where it was weighed and marked. There was very little rice harvested in eastern Guatemala due to the hurricane. The El Florido rice brought in an unprecedented $12.00 per one hundred pounds, far exceeding the usual price of $3.50.

The farmers took the money they received from "God's Acre" parcels and bought cement blocks for their new church. In one year the construction of the new church was finished, with a minimal loan of $700 for the pews and other final touches. With one more "God's Acre" project the next year, their debt was canceled. This miraculous experience strengthened their faith in God and increased their sense of worth and dignity.

The dedication of the new El Florido Friends Church was especially poignant since we had visually experienced God caring for that which belonged to Him! A faithful God had heard their cry and was honoring their trust in Him.

Several weeks later the Ladino church in the town of Buenos Aires asked the El Florido church to send them a speaker for their special church services. The El Florido church named Nicolás to go. This Chortí-speaking young farmer always had a big happy smile and was studying Bible School by extension in the evenings and on weekends.

Ray and I took him to Buenos Aires to save him time after his work in the field all day. We were absolutely amazed to listen to him speak in Spanish with joy and enthusiasm to this Ladino congregation. Then we were amazed at their enthusiastic responsiveness to his message. In former times, the Chortí would never have been invited to speak to a Ladino congregation, and the Chortí would never have had the courage to preach in a Ladino church. We were witnessing a remarkable change in the Chortí identity in Christ.

Forgiveness

Ponciano had just finished serving as lay pastor of the El Florido Friends Church. During that time, he had had a significant role in overseeing the building of the new church structure. Another church member had been named to be the lay pastor, but Ponciano continued to have a strong influence in the village.

During a monthly church meeting after the dedication of the church structure, Ponciano began criticizing each member and his or her attendance record to all the church services that month. He was concerned that the members were slacking in attendance.

In the following monthly meeting, he brought up the subject again, referring to the attendance record he maintained. There were six church services a week. He proposed that the members who missed more than three meetings a month be removed from the membership list. This would have included us missionaries because we were often absent due to ministries in other churches. The other members did not like the proposition but decided to discuss it later.

Ponciano brought this proposal again to the next monthly church meeting. Again the rest of the members did not approve and said that the better solution would be to continue encouraging members to attend more regularly and pray that God would convict their hearts.

Meanwhile, I, the missionary nurse in the village, was distressed and angry toward Ponciano for being judgmental. I had ignored him several times because I did not like his attitude of putting himself above the others.

One morning during my quiet time, I was talking to the Lord about my frustration with Ponciano and his critical attitude toward others. The Lord brought Matthew 6:14, 15 to my mind, "For if you forgive men for their transgressions, your heavenly Father will also forgive you. But if you do not forgive men, then your Father will not forgive your transgressions."

The Lord told me I had to ask Ponciano to forgive my poor attitude. But I argued with the Lord about it. Finally I prayed, "Okay, Lord, if he comes across my path, I will ask his forgiveness." I thought the likelihood of this happening was rather remote.

I got up from my prayer time, walked to the door, and there stood Ponciano! I heard the Lord's instruction loud and clear.

"Ponciano, would you please forgive me?" I asked.

"For what?" he responded with a surprised tone in his voice.

"I have had a judgemental attitude toward you for the way you are trying to take people off the church membership," I explained. "Please forgive me."

"I don't see why you need to ask my forgiveness, but if you insist, I will forgive you," he replied with a smile. Then he reached up and put his arm around my shoulders and gave me the customary hug that is done in the church when reconciliation is made between two people. I thanked him. I knew a huge burden had been lifted from my heart, as tears came to my eyes. I had no idea what God's plans were for Ponciano, but I was free.

A Morning Off

We had been convicted that the Lord wanted us to take one day for rest and relaxation. We knew we would have to leave El Florido for this because if we stayed home, there were demands on our time and attention. However, we did not have extra money to spend on entertainment.

What can we do? I pondered. *The kids love to swim, and there are some tourist resorts at Rio Dulce. Maybe, just maybe, we could make a deal with one of the owners,* I dreamed.

"Ray, what would you think about us talking to don Siguesmundo about using their pool once a week?" I asked. He was the owner of the Marimonte Resort.

"I don't think he'll let us, and you know we don't have the money for the fee," Ray replied. "Those tourist resorts are expensive."

"Well, he knows us because you bought pineapple and achiote from him for the project. He is a fairly friendly old man," I persisted.

"But I don't think he'll do it," Ray stated. "You can ask him if you want."

On our next trip to Rio Dulce, I drove over to the Marimonte Resort and asked, "Could I speak with don Siguesmundo, please?"

"Just a minute," an employee replied.

After a little while, a white-haired elderly man came out. He invited me to sit down and to have a Coke at his poolside restaurant. This was the typical friendly Guatemalan approach to business. He spoke Spanish with a European accent. As soon as I mentioned my husband, Ray Canfield, his eyes lit up and I knew he remembered him.

Finally I asked, "Don Siguesmundo, I was wondering if we could bring our kids here to swim in your pool one morning a week?"

"Hmm, would you and don Mundo come together?" he inquired.

"Yes, we would come together," I replied.

"I think that would be all right, and don't worry about paying the fee," he volunteered.

"Would Thursday mornings be all right with you?" I asked.

"Yes, that will be fine," he responded.

I was so excited and thankful that we could enjoy one morning a week together as a family. "Oh, thank you." I tried to not let my excitement be too obvious.

"Say, you are religious, aren't you?" he questioned.

"Yes, we are missionaries."

"Is that Catholic or Protestant?"

"Protestant."

"I know about the Catholic Church, but I am not Catholic," he slowly explained. "I am from Poland."

"Ray, my husband, lived in Poland for a year and I think he would enjoy talking to you about that," I said.

"Good. Bring your husband. I would like to talk with him."

"Okay. We'll be here next Thursday to swim in your pool."

"Good. I'll see you then."

I drove back to Rio Dulce and the ferry, where Ray and the kids were getting supplies. "Ray, he invited us to come on Thursday mornings," I excitedly announced.

"And what is the fee?" he asked.

"He doesn't want to charge us anything," I exclaimed. I was so excited to have five hours alone with just our family. The kids love to swim, and they needed to learn to swim better to be water safe.

Thursday morning came, and I knew Ray had forgotten about the plan.

"Let's get our swimming suits and towels to go to Marimonte," I announced after breakfast and devotions.

The kids jumped up from the table and ran to get their suits.

"I can't go," Ray protested. "I've got too much to do to take a morning off."

"Please come with us," I pleaded. "You can teach the kids to swim better, which is for their good."

"No, I can't leave."

"Well, I'll take the kids and go on to Marimonte if you won't come," I declared.

The kids and I were out the door and walking toward the pickup. They were so excited.

It was a struggle for Ray. He was focused on his commitment to help the Chortí farmers succeed. Each day he planned what he wanted to accomplish. Farming took his full attention in the daytime, and church work took most of his attention in the evenings. On weekends he taught Bible classes in other churches.

Both of us were immersed in our work and loved it, but we needed to spend time with each other as well. I knew he needed some rest and refreshment as much as the rest of us. I also wanted to have a restful cup of coffee to talk with Ray at the pool while the kids played in the water.

I started to climb into the driver's side of the pickup and he came up to me and said, "You're serious, aren't you?"

"Yes."

"I guess I'll go with you," he said half-heartedly. He went back inside the house, grabbed his swimsuit and joined us.

The ride to Rio Dulce was somber and quiet because Ray was still not convinced that we were not going to be charged the exorbitant tourist fee to use the pool. The kids, however, were excited about going to swim in the pool. An employee welcomed us into the pool area and there was no charge.

"Yeoweee, the water is so cold!" Linda, Tad and Kenny yelled. It was not cold but the air was so hot that the water felt cold. Soon they adjusted and loved it.

Ray played with the kids in the pool and made sure that they practiced their swimming. Even I, who was not a swimmer, joined them in the pool. Later, Ray and I enjoyed a cup of coffee at the poolside and talked mainly about our work in El Florido. We had a glorious morning together. "Thank you, Lord, for your provision for some relaxing family time," I quietly prayed.

During our next outing to Marimonte the following Thursday morning, don Siguesmundo was at the poolside restaurant when we arrived. We invited him to join us. That was the beginning of a friendship as he and Ray talked about their common experiences in Poland.

It was in this second visit that he told us his life story. "I am a Polish Jew. I've been through the siege of the Warsaw ghetto in Poland by the Germans in World War II. My young wife and I joined the resistance. She was killed before my eyes. It was a terrible experience. I miraculously escaped and finally came to Guatemala." As Siguesmundo told us his story, we sat in silence. We could not imagine the anguish he must still feel. Although he was now prosperous and secure, he appeared to be a sad and lonely man.

Lost in the Jungle

Virginia

It was July and we were returning from attending three days of missionary meetings in Chiquimula. We stopped in Morales to buy our usual supplies and to pick up our mail before the post office closed at noon. We enjoyed lunch together at our favorite place, the Bananera Fruit Company Restaurant. As we left the restaurant we noticed some ominous dark clouds in the north toward the El Florido project. I thought, *we never know what might be ahead of us.*

Vicente and Cristobal met us at the market with their crates of soda pop and supplies for the village store. We loaded the truck and began our trip home. Ray, Linda, and I rode in the front seat of our crew cab while Tad, Kenny, Vicente and Cristobal were in the backseat.

As we drove north toward home, the dark rain clouds got bigger and darker. At Rio Dulce we took our turn getting the truck on the ferry and riding across to the other side in the rain. "It has been raining hard all day!" one of the ferry helpers exclaimed.

And it was raining when we arrived at Sejá. "The river is really high, don Mundo," don Marcario replied to Ray's question about the status of the Sejá River, which we would have to cross. A sick man flagged us down in Sejá. He wanted a ride to the El Florido clinic to be treated, so we invited him to join us.

Ray drove us to the Sejá River crossing, but the water was high and roaring.

"Well, I guess we won't get across this river for quite a while," Ray stated. "What do you think? Shall we walk in from the San Felipe Co-op?" Ray asked me.

"Yes, let's try it," I replied. I was anxious to get home for the night. "I'm okay walking in to El Florido." The kids were excited about the adventure of hiking through the jungle to our home.

Ray drove the pickup to the Co-op and parked. He asked Isidro, a good friend, for permission to leave it there for the night with all the supplies left in it, and Isidro agreed. We did not think we needed flashlights because there were at least four hours of daylight left.

We left the truck and all eight of us started out on foot. The two El Florido farmers assured us that they were familiar with the trail into our village, so we agreed to follow them. The rain had turned into a very light drizzle.

We came to the first challenge, which was a rushing deep creek across which someone had placed a six inch wide tree trunk as a bridge. Cristobal offered to take Tad across on his shoulders. I hesitated. *Do I trust him to carry my son across?* Then I told myself, "He is strong and accustomed to walking barefoot on these logs. I will trust him."

Cristobal took Tad on his shoulders and easily crossed the creek, clinging to the muddy tree-bridge with his toes. He was across the creek in seconds. Vicente carried Kenny across the creek on his shoulders in the same manner.

They cut a thin branch off a tree and gave it to Ray to use for balance as he crossed the creek. Then they handed me the walking stick. I was shocked that the stick never touched the bottom of the rushing creek. The current was so swift that the stick almost made me lose my balance. So they cut a longer stick for me and finally I got across. Ray took Linda's hand to guide her across and we were on our way. Vicente took the lead.

We followed a narrow path through *guamil,* an area where the original jungle has been cleared, planted in corn, harvested, and then the jungle was beginning to come back. The wet grass was up to our hips and we were getting soaked. We walked single file through the grass and muddy trail an hour longer.

Suddenly we came to a divide. One trail went to the right, one to the left, and the third went straight. Our leader said, "Okay, let's take this trail to the right."

We followed him for thirty minutes, but this trail ended at a farmer's cornfield and no farther. We all made an about face and walked back to the first trail. I was beginning to lose my confidence in Vicente's knowledge of these back trails, but I knew neither Ray nor I would be better guides.

Now an argument arose between our trusted leader and Cristobal. "Let's take the trail to the left," Vicente decided. As he started down the trail, we followed. On we walked until suddenly we came to a deep ravine and jungle.

"This is not the right trail," Cristobal stated. "I knew it was not right." Again we did an about face and walked the thirty minutes back to the original trail.

By this time it was dark, and there was no moonlight. As we trudged along in the shallow mud, we followed the person in front of us by his or her light-colored shirt. I was thankful that Ray's light-blue shirt looked white in the dark. Tad and Kenny also wore light-colored shirts, which we could see. Linda was close to me, and I hung on to her hand to reassure her we were safe together.

"Mommy, there's something moving over there in the trees. I can hear it," she said in a trembling voice. "What is it?"

I knew very well that there were plenty of animals in these jungles, but I was in no mood at this moment to discuss which animal it could be. I just wanted all of us to focus on walking ahead together and getting home soon.

Finally we got back to the place in the grass where the trail divided. "I know for sure this other trail is not the right one," Vicente stated adamantly. "I know it does not take us to El Florido."

"Well, where is the trail to El Florido?" Ray asked with growing tension in his voice.

Cristobal and Vicente argued again about which way to go. They looked and looked for the right trail. Meanwhile, a gentle mist began to fall which soon grew into a gentle rain. We stood still in single file waiting for our guide to find the trail.

What are we going to do now? I asked myself. *Don't panic—as long as we all stick together we'll be safe. We have to find a safe place to sit down and rest. We can use some large leaves of guamo (a large leaved plant) to cover our heads from the rain,* I told myself.

I was getting a place ready beside a tree for Tad and Kenny to sit because they were tired.

Suddenly out in the distance I heard a wail that sounded just like a baby's cry.

"Ray, hear that? We must be close to a village because I hear a baby's cry."

He corrected me. "No, that's a night-bird's call."

"Well, let's call out for help, in case there is someone who would hear our call for help," I suggested.

"No, there is no one out there," he replied. I knew Ray was easily embarrassed. When in difficult situations, he was sure of his own ability to survive. Calling out for help sounded ridiculous to his masculine perspective and reflected admission of weakness from his point of view.

But I had none of these inhibitions in our dire situation. So I cupped my hands around my mouth and yelled with all my might, "Auxilio! Auxilio!" ("Help! Help!")

"Virginia, shussssh," Ray admonished me.

But that was the only thing I could think of that we could do besides pray. So I called again, "Auxilio, somos perdidos auxilio!" ("Help, we are lost!")

Then Vicente joined in and he called, "Auxilio, auxilio!"

We stood in the quiet darkness in a light rain for about twenty minutes, waiting and listening.

Suddenly, far ahead of us, was a pinpoint of a light, and then two small lights, as we watched in silence. Was it our imagination? Could it be people? If so, were they friendly? Vicente, Ray, and I watched the tiny lights bobbing and coming closer. We heard the baby's cry again.

Then we heard a voice call, "Hermanos?" ("Brothers?")

"Yes, we are from El Florido and we lost our way," we answered.

Then we recognized our fellow villager, Apolonio, and his son, who had heard our calls and came to find us. He used his flashlight and led us on to the right trail and on to our village.

"Thank you, don Apolonio, for finding us and leading us home!" Ray exclaimed.

We sloshed through the village and past the open door of the church, which was lit by a Coleman lantern for the weekly prayer meeting. I was embarrassed that we had been lost and needed to be found by a fellow villager. I was sorry we had missed that prayer meeting. But it was a wonderful joy to be back in the village with our friends.

And home—our wonderful home! We took our wet clothes and shoes off, showered, and fell into our soft warm beds in our dry house.

Lord, thank you so much for finding us. We were really lost and could not find the way without help. Thank you for Apolonio, who cared enough and ventured out of his dry house and hammock to look for us. Thank you for our wonderful home where we are dry and protected and can rest.

The Lord taught us to humbly call Him and others to find us when we are lost and when we need help.

(Note: That baby's cry actually was a call of a nocturnal jungle bird.)

A Call to Go to El Petén

"Come over and help us," was the message we received from El Petén. "We are a group of Friends believers, and we would like help in organizing a church in our area." The region of El Petén represents about one third of the total area of Guatemala. This vast land was isolated from all but air and water travel until the early 1970's. At that time a new road (passing near El Florido) was constructed, allowing access to El Petén and a rapid migration had begun.

One Sunday right after church in El Florido, we packed a sandwich lunch for our family and drove up the new road toward the location of this group of Christians in El Petén. The road was recently graveled, and heavy cargo trucks had begun using it instead of the air cargo system to transport supplies for economical reasons. The trucks dug deep ruts in soft spots of the new roadway after the heavy rains.

We found much of the road in very bad condition, and driving over this rough road was hard on our pickup and on us, although, the pristine scenery was beautiful. The dense jungle lined the road on both sides.

Only two towns had gas stations within the one hundred miles between our house and Las Flores, the capital of El Petén. All the other settlements were small villages where the inhabitants lived in rustic, thatched stick huts. After an hour of tedious driving, we arrived at the town of El Chacté. Ray had the name of one man who had moved there from Gualan.

A man was in the corral outside his hut. We stopped, and Ray asked him if he knew a man by the name of Felix Jones.

"Yes. Don Felix lives right over there." He pointed across the road.

Suddenly we heard, "don Mundo! We wondered when you would come see us," don Felix exclaimed. "We knew you lived down near Sejá somewhere, and we have been hoping to see you." He quickly invited us into their rustic hut and his wife prepared a lemonade drink for us.

"We have been here for almost two years," don Felix explained. "We are having pretty good crops, and the Lord has been blessing us."

"Do you have family or others from Gualan with you here in El Chacté?" Ray asked.

"Yes, there are four families who were members of the Friends Church in Gualan," he explained. "We try to have worship services together, but they are not very regular. We meet maybe once a month."

"What would you like for us to do for you?" Ray asked.

"We need your help to organize a Friends Church here."

"I will communicate your request to the church headquarters in Chiquimula," Ray promised.

Don Felix and his wife thanked us profusely for the visit. "I'm so glad you came, don Mundo," he repeated. "Please come back to visit us soon."

All was quiet in the truck as we began the difficult trip back to El Florido.

"We must make another trip there soon," Ray said, thinking out loud.

I am glad that Ray will be supporting this new church, I thought to myself. I also felt a burning desire to take the truth of God's Word to the scattered families there. After this visit, El Florido became a launching pad for outreach and church planting into El Petén.

18

Gratitude

Virginia

A man came into our new clinic with a gangrenous toe. I was so grateful I could treat him in the new clinic instead of our kitchen. We were thankful for this clinic that was serving more and more people every day, even from villages as far as seven miles away. I cleaned and bandaged the messy, ugly toe and sent him to the public hospital in Port Barrios.

The refreshing cool air that came with the rain in the evenings was a welcome reprieve from the intense, humid daytime heat. One evening I turned the gasoline generator off early in order to conserve fuel. I continued writing letters at the kitchen table by the light of the Kincaid lantern. You should have seen the two hundred or more tiny insects flying around the lantern, on the paper, and on my arms. I couldn't stand those pesky things any longer, so I gave them a shot of "By-Gone," an insecticide. It did all of us some good. I continued writing letters and they lay upside down. We all had peace.

We made a trip to Guatemala City to take some visitors to the airport and we stayed there one extra night to purchase supplies. The next day, we celebrated Ray's birthday at the Pan Am Hotel restaurant, our family's favorite place to celebrate special occasions in the capital.

The next day we drove back home. The new clinic was in service, the kids and I would be starting our new school year and Ray and the village farmers had finished building the two mile road out to the parcels. The rice harvest was beginning, and the price they were receiving for it was higher than usual.

Ray and I felt tremendous joy seeing these Chortí men and women growing spiritually and materially. We were grateful to the Lord, who was answering our prayers for these dear brothers and sisters to succeed in this new life.

One day don Inéz and his wife Rosa came to our house to talk with Ray and me. We never knew what he might have on his heart to tell us. We always had to have patience while he talked about crops, the church work, or the weather for about twenty minutes before he brought up the purpose of his visit.

"Don Mundo, we are so grateful to you for all that you have done to help us," he said humbly. "We have enough food and a large rice harvest. We want to tell you "muchas gracias," don Inéz finished.

"It is not us, don Inéz, it is God who is answering your prayers," Ray answered. "God gives the rain and sun to make the crops grow. And God has given you and me the strength to do the hard work."

"Yes. That is right—we want to thank God," Inéz agreed. "I never have had the strength I have now to cut down big trees,—he motioned with his arms and hands the circumference of the jungle trees—and the strength to work in the field all day. *Si, gracias a Dios*" ("Yes, thanks be to God"), he finished.

Inéz whispered something to his wife, Rosa. She then got up and stepped just outside our kitchen door and whispered to a little granddaughter who was standing out of sight beside our house. Doña Rosa took a bundle from the girl's arms and came back into the kitchen.

"Here, we want you to have this," she said as she handed me the bundle. "For me?" I exclaimed.

It was a beautiful live hen. This bird had reddish-brown fluffy feathers, a healthy comb, and bright eyes. She was a big, healthy hen, a precious property of their whole family. Chickens provided eggs and baby chicks for the family. When the chicks were grown, they provided meat for the family. Doña Rosa, the wife and mother of her family, was the one responsible for caring for the chickens.

Now they were giving us a precious, costly gift to show their gratitude. Until now we had never thought how to receive gifts appropriately. Our focus had been to help and encourage the Chortí to get more food and improve their lives in every way.

My first reaction was to say, "Oh no, we don't need the chicken. You keep it. You need it more than we do."

Thank goodness I modified that reaction and said, "Are you sure you want me to have this?"

I could tell by Rosa's eyes that she was disappointed by my reaction. I might have offended her a little. *Oops! I think I have offended her,* I thought. "Lord, give me wisdom," I prayed.

I tried again. "Doña Rosa, thank you so much for this beautiful hen," I said with honest, deep feelings, "It is so pretty!"

Rosa's eyes immediately lit up. "I'm so happy you like my hen!" she exclaimed.

I wanted to give her a hug of appreciation, but this was not the accepted gesture in their culture. I knew I had to express this gratitude only in words and by carefully holding the gift.

"Doña Rosa, I'm not sure what to do with this hen. Should I kill and cook it, or should I let it live and lay eggs?"

"You can do whatever you want with the hen; it is yours," she happily explained.

I continued to hold our hen, which was wrapped in a sack on my lap, while don Inéz and Ray discussed a few more things. Then Inéz and Rosa said their good-byes and left.

"Now, Ray, what do I do with this chicken?" I questioned. I put it in a box in our kitchen for the night until we decided.

In the meantime, Linda had fun giving it kernels of corn and watching it eat. She informed us she would like to have it for a pet and told us she had given it a name already, Bubblegum.

"Why are you calling the chicken Bubblegum?" I asked.

"Well, I just dropped my bubblegum in the box and she ate it," she answered.

At this point I knew the chicken had been saved. Now an instant pet, I could never kill it and expect the kids to eat it.

Over the next several months our neighbors gave us a beautiful rooster and two more hens. Linda raised a flock of chickens as pets.

Often one villager or another brought us gifts of eggs wrapped in corn husks, dressed chicken, roasting ears of corn and tamales. They were generous and loving toward us, and we often felt indebted to them. Our love for the Chortí grew deep as we lived with them and walked through joys and trials with them. I was reminded often that our lives were enriched because we had the privilege of sharing life with our Indian friends.

A Night Trip down Rio Dulce to Hold Services in a Home

I had finished taking care of the last patient in the clinic for the day and was getting supper on the table for my family.

Ray came in and said, "Would you and the kids like to go with us to a home service tonight on the Rio Dulce?" This friend had invited people from the El Florido church to come and hold a church service in his home as a birthday celebration.

I looked at the kids. Their eyes widened and I knew they wanted to go. "Yes, we'd like to go," I replied.

"Good," Ray said enthusiastically. "We will leave in about forty minutes."

We hurried through supper, and the kids changed into clean clothes. I washed their faces and picked up the bag of life jackets for them.

The three Indian men took two Coleman lanterns, a guitar and their Bibles. One was going to lead the singing of hymns and the other was going to bring a message. It was a privilege to be able to accompany them on such an occasion.

Ray took us to the river in the pickup and bargained with a canoe driver to take us two miles downriver to a certain house. The plan was for the canoe driver to stay with us for the two-hour service, enjoy tamales and then bring us back to the truck.

"Oh, now that will cost more, don Mundo," the driver declared as he began to hedge and bargain. Finally a price was agreed upon and we climbed in the boat.

I had never been out on the big river at night, in the total darkness. It is a very different scene from the daytime river rides. There was no moon, just blackness. The canoe driver turned off his flashlight, and we began the trip in the dark.

This is foolishness, I thought. *How can he see the other boats?* It was an eerie ride. Suddenly we heard another outboard motor off in the distance. But we did not see any light. When the other boat was closer, our pilot turned on his flashlight and signaled our position, and the other driver did the same. I realized they were guiding their boats by their sounds in the night and signaling their positions with flashlights. They knew exactly what they were doing.

Soon we arrived at the rustic home on the river. Several neighbors were waiting for us to join the celebration. In the home we sat on boards that were nailed onto two-foot posts stuck into the ground.

Vicente led the singing of several well-known hymns out of the hymnbook. We prayed, and Pedro brought the message from the Sermon on the Mount. There were probably twenty-five of us attending.

It struck me as interesting that this family was from another Indian tribe of Guatemala, the Kekchí, which used a different indigenous language than El Florido's tribe, the Chortí. This service was in Spanish, the second language for both groups.

During the service, a busy spider decided to weave its web between the two Coleman lanterns. It was a sight I will treasure forever. Very carefully back and forth she worked to form a perfectly symmetrical design. She chose the ideal location because the bugs went to the lantern light where they were quickly entrapped in the web. When they landed, the spider quickly wrapped them in its webbing and then continued its task of weaving. She worked rapidly. The sight was so fascinating that I did not remember any of the message.

After the message, a father and his teenage son said they believed in Jesus as their Savior for the first time, and we prayed with them.

Then we had tamales and hot chocolate. Our canoe driver attended the whole service and was ready to take us back to the crossing where we left our pickup. Kenny fell asleep on the way back, so we carried him to the truck and then into the house.

That river ride at night for a birthday celebration was meaningful because a Kekchí man and his son were led to a new life in Christ by Christians from a different Indian tribe, with a different language. We had witnessed God perform a miracle between two distinct tribal cultures of Guatemala.

Crossing the Flooding Sejá River

Ed and Martha White, founding pastors of Diamond Bar Friends Church in California, came to Guatemala with their two boys, Tim and Dan. They were coming from visiting the mission fields in South America. Ed and Martha had been our friends since our high school days on the youth council of Young Friends of California, so we were looking forward to their visit.

We drove with our children to Guatemala City to meet them at the airport. After the joyful reunion, we drove back to El Florido, trying to get home for the night. The Whites were tired from their long trip throughout South America. Martha was sick with fever and lower back pain and she was feeling worse as we neared El Florido. I was anxious to get home in order to start her on medication.

We noticed all the rivers and streams were at flood levels as we got closer to El Florido. We stopped in Sejá and Ray found his friend, don Macario.

"Has it been raining today?" Ray asked.

"Oh, yes, don Mundo. It has been raining intensely over the past two days," he replied.

"Can we get across the river?" Ray asked.

We always had to ford the Sejá River in order to get into our village. "Well," don Macario slowly answered, "no trucks or cars have been able to get across all day. You probably will not be able to cross."

Ray calmly explained, "We will drive down and check it out."

It was 8:00 p.m. and very dark and drizzly. The narrow, small road was muddy. We were four adults and five children in the crew cab of our pickup. As we drove toward the river, we could see the water rushing over its banks.

Ray stopped the truck and contemplated what to do next. He then backed the truck up a little bit. "Come on, Ed, let's go check it out," he said in a reassuring voice.

"No, no, Ray, we can't cross it tonight," I fearfully begged. "Let's go back to Rio Dulce and stay in one of those roadside rooms."

We knew at least two vehicles had been overturned and washed downstream in the past year because of high water. Ed, who is six feet, five inches tall, and Ray, who is six feet, took their shoes off and rolled up their pants. With the light from the headlights of the pickup they carefully waded out into the river. The water came up to Ed's hips.

"Ed, I think we can make it," Ray exclaimed.

"Yeah, I do too," Ed agreed.

"What are we going to do, Ray?" I asked when they returned.

"We are going across," he answered matter-of-factly.

"Oh no," I moaned. "Okay then. Let's pray and ask God to protect us."

"Yes, let's pray," Ray said. Anticipating what lay ahead, everyone was somber. Even the kids closed their eyes and were quiet.

"Oh, God, please help us now, help us get through the deep water. Please keep all of us safe. Please guide us through the river and keep all large rocks and floating trees from our truck. Thank you, Lord. Amen," I prayed out loud. A sense of peace came over us. Ray took the brake off and drove slowly toward the water.

"Virginia, what do we do if—" Martha began as we entered the water.

"Sh-sh-sh. I have no idea," I interrupted her to quiet her and my fear. I knew what the rest of her question was, and I did not have an answer.

The crew cab went steadily down into the water—deeper and deeper. Everything became dark as the headlights went underwater. But the engine kept running smoothly and pulling the truck along. It never faltered. Suddenly there was light again as the headlights came out of the water. Ray steadily drove the truck onto the road on the other side of the river.

Once we were on the opposite shore, he stopped to let the water drain out of the bed of the truck and check the engine. All was okay. Only a little water had seeped into the cab.

The five kids were so happy that we had made it through, and we adults were praising the Lord for His help. Our house was truly a welcome sight. I was able to get medicine for Martha out of the clinic and she responded to the treatment. We enjoyed a wonderful visit with Ed and Martha for three days.

Gloria—More of Her Story

Gloria, my nineteen year-old house helper, faithfully continued to provide much-needed help. I realized however, that she was getting past the age for marriage in the village. Usually girls would marry between the ages of fifteen and seventeen, but since she was receiving a regular wage for working for us, she seemed content to not marry. But I knew her job would last only as long as we lived in El Florido.

I began to wonder if my hiring her as my helper would keep her from marriage. I prayed about this dilemma and asked God what He wanted me to do. I felt I should dismiss her to go back into her culture even though it would break all of our hearts.

Two nights before I was going to dismiss Gloria, I was working late in the clinic since I had more than fifty patients that afternoon. I was caring for the next to the last one when Tad, my five-and-a-half-year-old son, came bounding down to the clinic to check on me.

"Hi, Mom," he energetically exclaimed. "Whatcha doin'?"

"This sick baby has a fever and I'm going to give it a shot," I replied. "Tad, I'm so sorry that I have not fixed supper for you yet."

"We've already eaten!"

"What?" I exclaimed. "Who fed you?"

"Gloria did," he replied matter-of-factly.

"What did she feed you?" I was uncertain what to think.

"We had fried chicken, mashed potatoes, and green beans," he said, and then exclaimed, "It was delicious!"

Deep gratitude filled my heart for Gloria, who cooked a good meal for my family when I needed her to, even though I had never taught her how to cook.

Suddenly I looked up to God. "Thank you, Lord, for my dear Gloria. She is an angel."

Then I sensed the Lord say to me, "I have sent you an angel to help you now, and I will take care of her. You do not need to worry about her future."

"Oh Lord, please forgive me," I called to Him. "I will no longer worry about Gloria."

After my last patient, I hurried up to the house. "Gloria, you are an angel! Thank you so much for fixing food for my family," I said as I gave her a hug. Tears of gratitude came to my eyes.

She responded by lowering her head and quietly saying, "It is okay," in the typical Chortí way. I now would look forward to seeing how God would take care of her future.

Swinging on Vines

"Hey, Mom, we need a ladder," Tad announced as he and Kenny came into the house one afternoon after I had finished caring for all the patients in the clinic.

"Why?" I asked, hardly waiting for an answer.

"We need to climb up higher to reach our swing," he explained in a too-brief manner.

"Now wait, wait a minute. Slow down and explain to me what you are talking about." I was trying to focus on what my boys were saying.

Tad, now eight years old, and Kenny, seven, made an impatient sigh as they were frustrated with their mother, who seemed to be taking too much time asking too many questions. Tad did not want to divulge too many details. Kenny was suspiciously silent about the situation.

Finally, he explained. "Well, Mommy, we found a really neat vine swing and I can reach it but Kenny can't. We need a ladder so Kenny can reach the vine to swing."

"How high is the vine?"

"Not too high," he quickly answered.

"We don't have a small ladder for that," I explained. "Maybe you should take me along and show me your swing."

"Okay, we'll show you," they replied. "Come on, Mommy."

A couple of their village friends were outside ready to return to the swing with them. I grabbed the camera and followed Tad, Kenny and their friends. We walked down the road to the sawmill, past the cemetery, and into the area that was cleared of undergrowth and planted with cocoa trees. Tad led us to a 150-foot-tall tree at the top of a deep ravine.

A long vine hung down from the top of that tall tree. It had been cut off from its roots the day before and they had been swinging on it. Hanging from the tops of the trees, the vines would root themselves when they reached the ground. When they are cut from their anchor in the ground, as this one had been, they quickly dry out. In two or three days it will crumple and fall in a heap if any weight is put on it.

"Wow." I gasped. "You kids have already swung on it?" I couldn't believe my eyes. The vine was high and the ravine was deep.

"Hey, Mommy," Tad yelled. "Watch me!" He climbed as far as he could up one of the trees' steep roots which fanned out from the trunk about six feet up. One of the boys retrieved the vine with a long pole and pulled it over to Tad.

He grabbed it with both hands and pushed away from the tree, sailing out over the ravine. On the other side he came close to another tree, which he used to push himself back out over the chasm again to the takeoff point. My heart nearly stopped and I yelled, "Watch out! Hang on!" I really did not want to watch, and then again I wanted to see where he would land if he fell.

Kenny and their two friends grabbed Tad to stop him, and then he climbed down.

"It is fun, Mom!" he exclaimed. "We did get Kenny on it, but it would be easier with a ladder."

"It is so much fun, Mommy," Kenny exclaimed, trying to reassure me. "Do you want to go for a ride? You would like it."

One thing I knew for sure was that I did not need to take a swing on that high vine. "No thanks," I adamantly replied. "But I do want to take some photos of you on the swing."

We walked back to the house together. I listened as the four boys excitedly talked about the great time they had swinging together.

The next day Tad and Kenny came home quiet and downcast after playing with their friends.

"What's the matter?" I asked.

"They cut the vine off way up high and we can't reach it now," Tad explained.

"I'm sorry, but maybe that was for your own good," I consoled him.

"Why?" he asked.

"Probably one of the men in the village cut it higher so you kids would not get hurt on it," I explained.

"We wouldn't get hurt," Tad argued.

"Well, we all know that after three days, those cut vines crumble and fall. They did not want that to happen to any of you," I carefully explained. Quietly I prayed, *Thank you Lord for some wise Indian friends who were protecting our children.*

They never lacked exciting adventures in the jungle.

Full Moon

It was a warm June night and all was quiet. Ray and I and our three kids had just gotten home from the Thursday evening church service.

The kids were tucked in their beds after the usual bedtime story and prayers. The Kincaid lantern was our only light. The night birds gave their eerie calls in the jungle. Our neighbors' soft voices could be heard in the distance, and the crickets were chirping in the grass.

"Ray, look at that moon." I gasped. Usually we have rains during June evenings, but this night was clear, and there was a big beautiful moon.

He blew out the lantern and took my hand. We stepped out of the house into our front yard. Ray stood behind me and embraced me; nothing needed to be said.

Here we were in the bright beautiful moonlight, surrounded by the soft warm breeze, swaying palm trees and the night sounds of the jungle. Our kids were in bed. Our heavy cares for the villagers were put aside for the night. All was quiet and well.

The only thing that mattered for now was that we could enjoy this beautiful hour with the person we loved the most.

"Yes, honey, this is beautiful and I love you so much," Ray whispered in my ear. He squeezed me just a little bit tighter as we stood together soaking up the enchanting sights and sounds under the full moon on our "tropical isle."

19

Difficult Days

Virginia

One day as I was walking toward the clinic, Ray came by driving the tractor and hauling a load of *manaca*, palm fronds, from the jungle for a villager's new roof.

A neighbor, Antonio, said to me, "doña Virginia, I know you and don Mundo are getting rich off us, but I can't figure out how."

I was shocked and hurt by his words. I did not know how to answer him, so I simply said, "Antonio, we are here because we love the Lord our God and because we love you, your family and everyone here."

Antonio looked at me with a doubtful expression, hesitated and then walked away, saying no more.

The first reaction I had when I heard his accusation was to defend myself. I thought, *I'm a missionary, giving up so much to be here. You have no idea how much money we could be making back home in the United States. You have no idea the sacrifice that we are making. If our goal was to make money, we would not be doing this.*

Then I stopped and tried to see things from his point of view. These people had always been taken advantage of by others around them. So he is thinking we were no different than them. It makes no sense to him, that someone would come and do all this work and not receive a large compensation for it. Also, he was having a hard time understanding this love that I was talking about, and he was suspicious. *He will only be convinced of our love by our consistent actions, not by our words,* was the perspective that God gave me that day.

"Oh Lord, help them to only see Jesus in us," I prayed.

God's answer came through a new realization soon thereafter.

We began hearing the people say, "don Mundo says," or "doña Virginia says." They had started taking our teaching about farming, health and the Bible to heart. We lived in their village, and they were glad that we lived close. We could never look like them or take on all their culture, but we would assimilate into their customs, as much as possible for the sake of Christ and the Gospel message.

I noticed the women started wearing a ring on their fourth finger of their left hand like I wore my wedding ring. They also had stopped wearing their usual earrings to identify with me, since I never cared to wear them. Suddenly the realization of their imitating our habits and wholeheartedly accepting all our teaching weighed as a heavy responsibility on us. But this level of trust and confidence had taken years to earn; it did not come naturally. I was no longer just another "medicine man." We prayed that they would believe what we taught about Jesus most of all.

Our Children's Letters to Their Grandparents

"Dear Grandma,

"We have two new pets," Linda wrote. "One is a parrot and the other is a black cat. Lupe, one of the farmers in our village, caught a young parrot and brought it to us as a gift from his family. The parrot was the kind that could talk, but it couldn't talk yet because it was too young. It was a big bird. It had bright green feathers on its head, neck, and back and bright red and yellow feathers in its wings.

"One day it flew away into the jungle. We looked for it and called it, but it never answered us. That night we prayed and asked God to help us find it. The next morning a lady came to the door with our parrot. I guess the Lord really answers prayers."

Love, Linda

The parrot referred to in her letter was named Panch, short for Pancho. Eventually Panch learned to say several phrases like "Pretty bird," "Hola," and "Quiere comer?" ("Do you want to eat?")

Linda kept working with Panch, trying to teach it to say, "You dumbbell" in English, but the bird would not repeat it for her.

One day I noticed Panch was not on his perch and I began calling for him. Suddenly I heard, "You dumbbell."

Hearing him say this made me laugh out loud.

And then I heard someone else laughing. Panch was imitating my exact laugh, and it sounded as if two people were laughing. Needless to say, his own crass remarks exposed his hiding place and he was quickly put back in his cage.

"Dear Grandpa,

"Thank you for the dollar that you gave me. I bought a car with it. I really like it.

"We have three goats. The nanny goat is Linda's. The billy goat is mine. The small nanny goat is Kenny's. My goat bucks all the time when anyone gets near him. I throw the soccer ball to him and he hits it with his horns back to me.

"Write when you can.

"With much love, Tad."

We purchased two doe rabbits and a buck so we could raise rabbits. Our plan was to show the Chortí people how to raise rabbits and kill them for meat for their families. Ray built rabbit hutches and they were soon filled with baby rabbits. Linda and Tad and their friends enjoyed feeding the rabbits and carrying them around.

The young rabbits grew up, and it was time to butcher several to eat. We invited three women to observe the process of dressing the rabbits. Ray chopped the head off of one and began to dress it. He turned around and all the observers had disappeared. Later they told us they could never do that to such a cute little animal.

We also found our own children did not want to eat cooked rabbit at all. So the project was not successful for the purpose we had in mind. Meanwhile, the rabbit population grew and the kids loved them as pets.

We purchased a nanny goat and her twins for our family to raise as an experiment. There was one problem—the nanny did not like to be milked. It took three of us to hold her while the fourth person milked her. We did enjoy the fresh goat milk and our neighbor made delicious goat cheese for all of us.

We soon learned our goat experiment would be disastrous. We had planned for them to be our natural lawnmower but they refused to eat the grass in our yard unless we tethered them and forced them to eat it. They preferred to eat the leaves off corn stalks, bean plants and sugar cane in our neighbors' fields. Tad's goat climbed up on top of our field director's new car when he visited. The other goat climbed up on a thatch roof and nibbled away. Needless to say, these goats were not popular in the village.

No one grieved when our goats died. This had been a bright idea to help the Indian people, but these goats had not worked with the program.

A Houseful of Visitors

As life became somewhat easier in El Florido, we began having a regular stream of visitors. Word had spread about how God was answering prayer and how a desperate people were being helped. Miracles were happening, and people wanted to witness this.

Ray's nephew, Phillip, came to help us for six weeks. Dan Butler, a two-year youth ambassador lived with us and helped Ray. Loren Hawkins was with us to overhaul one of the tractors.

Two young Guatemalan medical students wanted to have experience in a rural clinic and asked if they could work beside me during their December school break. Carlos Ramirez was the son of our mission caretaker, Alfonso Ramirez, in Chiquimula. We always were focused on training Guatemalans to serve the Lord and work ourselves out of a job. So we invited them to be with us. They were eager to work in the clinic all day but still lacked several years of training, so I needed to supervise them closely. And that meant our home school was neglected.

During this particular November and December we had the normal incessant rain and no sun. I counted forty consecutive days without sunshine. There was mud everywhere, and our washed clothes would take four to five days to dry inside the house. Our three children loved to play "house" in the rafters of our home. During this rainy season, I wondered if God would send another rainbow promise.

One evening Ray slipped and fell into a small hole on his way to the church. He skinned up his shin but it was minor, he thought. He did not mention it to me, however.

Twenty-four hours later he had severe pain and swelling on the leg he scraped. He also had chills, fever and nausea. I prayed and considered the options. It was decided to treat him at home. I gave him an antibiotic for the spreading infection and hot-packed it for twenty minutes every two hours. His nausea and fever persisted, however, so a second antibiotic was begun for typhoid fever. He began to improve in four hours. The hot packs and antibiotics were continued for ten days. The infection had localized into an abscess four inches in diameter.

I took Ray to the Banana Fruit Co. private hospital in Morales because it was time to lance and drain the abscess. I knew I could never do that procedure for my husband. The doctor took one look at Ray's leg and said, "You have done a good job caring for him."

"Thank you, Lord!" I prayed.

The doctor drained half a cup of pus out of the abscess and placed a drain in the wound so it would heal. He instructed me on how he wanted the drain and bandage maintained.

Lupe Perez, one of the El Florido farmers, built crutches for Ray to use while he recovered. Ray preached at the Christmas Eve services in the church, and by New Year's day he was able to do his regular work. Linda was my second hand through all of this, and she gladly helped me with the big job of writing our Christmas letters.

On Christmas Day only Dan was with us. All the other visitors had returned to their homes. The beautiful sunshine was drying things out. Suddenly it dawned on us that Christmas had come and we had not bought any Christmas gifts for each other. The celebration of Jesus' love and care over our family was special, and that was what we celebrated that year rather than gift-giving.

A Cold Day in January

Normal weather for us on the relocation project was: tropical, hot, humid and wet. In the inland areas of Chiquimula and Zacapa there were two seasons—rainy and dry—each about six months long. Where we were it rained almost every day. In El Florido we jokingly called December, January, and February "the dry season," which only meant it rained less.

The temperature varied from the seventies at night to the nineties in the daytime. It seldom was hotter than ninety-five or cooler than seventy. The humidity was usually 80% to 95%, and that made the heat seem oppressive. But after two years we acclimated to the weather and did not notice the intensity of the heat.

However, in January 1976 the temperature cooled down to sixty-two degrees, and one night to fifty-eight degrees. We were freezing. Our tin roof radiated the cold temperatures in January just like it did the heat in April and May. The damp, cold air was penetrating. I sat in the kitchen in a sleeping bag sipping hot tea, trying to get warm. The kids put on their sweaters and jackets that we dug out of the storage closet. This cold made it difficult for me to do my regular work of teaching home school and attending to patients.

My friend, Calistra said, "Come to my house, doña Virginia. I have a fire on my floor and our house is warm."

I accepted her invitation. "Oh yes, your home is nice and warm," I exclaimed as she, her three children, and I huddled around the fire. It was delightful to share the fire and the friendship in her cozy little rustic thatch hut. We talked about the weather, our kids and what the Lord had done for us.

I spent an hour with her and returned to my home truly refreshed. On the way back, I understood why they loved their cozy homes on days like this. Often the villagers told us they thought our house was too cold in January and too hot in April.

Linda Leaves for Boarding School

Our dear ten-year-old daughter needed a better education than we could give her through home schooling in the jungle. But there was a sense of dread in our hearts as we considered the possibility of Linda going to boarding school.

Nine years prior, I had bargained with the Lord about serving Him on the mission field, because I did not want to send our children to boarding school. He had asked me, "Can you trust me?"

"Yes, Lord, I will trust You," I had promised.

But now the conflict and doubt was thrusting its head into my heart again.

Linda was such a happy girl who loved to help me cook in the kitchen and write letters for us and entertain guests. She was and still is my closest friend, and we discuss everything. She was a great asset to our missionary ministry because she bridged relationships.

Sometimes Linda lost patience with her two younger brothers, but most of the time they had a good time playing together.

She had been studying grade school by correspondence and received good grades. But now the fifth grade would require more instruction time while I also had Tad in third grade and Kenny in first.

We discussed the decision as a family. "Mommy, I'm excited to go to school at Huehuetenango," she said, "but I might miss my family."

"Linda is excited about going away to school next year, and we are thankful she feels this way," I wrote to Ray's folks. "But, I don't know how we're going to manage without her. If we decide to do this, it would be strictly for the purpose of giving her a better education." I felt sick every time I thought about her going to boarding school.

"Lord, we love You and want to obey You, but… oh my lovely daughter, I love her so much," I told Him. "Please, Lord, help me down this difficult journey. Is there some other way? But if this will benefit her, then give me a changed heart and help me accept her going to boarding school."

"This is so hard, Lord. I confess I could feel angry about her going away. If she goes, I'm going to trust You to take really good care of her and bless her all her life. Please, Lord, help us through this," I begged.

We sent the application to Huehue Academy in April, and she was accepted as a new student for September.

The school gave us a list of clothes and supplies they required the students to bring. My mother had sent me nametags which I sewed on all her clothes. Ray and I bought a new Raleigh bike for her to have at school.

On Ray's birthday, Sept. 3, 1975, we set out for Huehuetenango, Guatemala, to the Central American Mission boarding school for missionary children. We drove to Guatemala City the day before and stayed at the Bodin Guest House overnight. We then drove the last five hours to the academy.

We found her room and roommate. We met the schoolteachers, who were welcoming and friendly. It was a modern beautiful school with lots of American kids and teachers around.

Finally we said our good-byes and drove off the school grounds. A deep pain filled my heart, and I began to cry and cry. Ray was driving but I saw tears sliding down his cheeks. Tad and Kenny were very quiet in the backseat of the crew cab. I did not dare look back at them because I would have burst out crying again. Sobs welled up all the way back to Guatemala City.

"Lord, where are You?" I prayed. "I am so sad, I don't like being a missionary anymore," I cried. "This is too hard. I don't have the courage to go on," I complained to the Lord.

Back in El Florido I missed Linda at every turn. The next Sunday morning I thought about her helping me teach the girls' Sunday school class and the deep sobs started once again. Our Indian friends understood our sadness but were careful to not ask about Linda. I guess they did not want to see us cry again.

All the students at the academy had to write a letter to their parents before they could eat Sunday evening supper. So we received a letter from Linda every Wednesday or Thursday in Morales. We made the two-hour drive to Morales once a week to get supplies and pick up our mail, including our letter from Linda.

Linda wrote, "I like my new school. I have made some new friends, and I like my teacher."

Ray and I continued to have difficulties because we missed her so much. We were thankful there was such a lovely school for her to attend and there was a place for her to make new friends. We would see her in three months for Christmas vacation, which would last three weeks.

20

The Earthquake

Virginia

It was 3:05 a.m. February 4th, 1976, when suddenly we heard a loud, deep boom off in the distant jungle. And then another was closer, and a third was very close. Then our house rolled, shook and rocked like a ship on a stormy sea.

"It's an earthquake," Ray declared. The shaking and rolling continued. "It's a very big earthquake!" Ray stated louder. We both tried to get out of bed but were unable.

"Mommy, Daddy!" Tad yelled.

"Daddy," Kenny cried. They were in another bedroom trying to get out of their beds.

"It's okay, we're right here," I tried to reassure them as we tried to reach them.

After thirty-three seconds of shaking and rolling, it stopped. Then we heard the loud, deep, rhythmic booms get fainter, until we heard no more.

"Come to our bedroom and sleep here with us," we told the boys.

"What happened?" Tad said with panic in his voice.

"We're so scared," Kenny cried.

Ray calmly comforted our sons. "It was an earthquake, but it's okay now, it is all over."

It became very noisy outside our house. Dogs were barking loudly. The chickens and roosters that had been shaken from their roosts were squawking and crowing. Many villagers arrived and were talking in hushed voices near our front door. They did not call out "don Mundo, don Mundo" as they usually did if they needed us for an emergency in the night. They were just checking to see if the missionaries were still there.

Our house was intact—no dishes had fallen out of the cupboards, and our short-wave radio stayed on its small shelf on the wall. Surprisingly, nothing was broken.

In the early morning dawn, Ray and I got up to see what had happened in our village. Several men were waiting for us outside. They explained that they feared the Rapture had happened and they had been left behind. They had come to see if we missionaries were still there. If we were, then they knew that the Rapture of the Christians to heaven had not happened. We chuckled to ourselves when we heard this. "Yes, we never know when Christ might come again. But it wasn't this time."

The concern about possible damage to the new church structure was on all our minds, so we took a quick walk down to see. We met several other villagers there. The church walls had only two small cracks, but otherwise all was intact. Thank you, Lord!

Our transoceanic short-wave radio was reporting that a strong earthquake had happened in El Salvador, and they were reporting much damage and many deaths. We tried to find a Guatemalan radio station but found *nothing. How strange,* we thought.

That earthquake in El Salvador must have been very bad, we concluded. We tried to find a Honduran radio station but those, too, were silent. It was an eerie feeling.

We had breakfast as usual. One of the villagers told us that the road between Rio Dulce and Chiquimula was closed because of the bad condition, and we should not leave El Florido.

Before the earthquake, we had planned to go to Chiquimula that day. We decided to start out and go as far as we could with the option of turning back, if we needed to. We felt an urgency to let the mission headquarters know we were okay and to check on the status of the mission and missionaries. We had no means to communicate this by telephone, radio or telegram.

As we drove to Morales we saw much earthquake damage such as walls of houses fallen into the streets, and the highways were nearly blocked with dirt and rocks.

Then as we drove farther toward Chiquimula, the damage along the Motagua River Valley was worse and worse. We found crossing the bridges was a problem, because the ground had sunk and there was about a five inch rise on to all the bridges.

Nearly the entire town of Gualan was destroyed, and the few buildings left standing were too dangerous to be occupied. The Friends Church was still standing, but the parsonage had fallen. We found the pastor and his family sitting in the yard under some makeshift plastic shades like everyone else, seemingly in shock.

"Chiquimula—what will we find there?" we wondered as we drove on. On the highway we saw a whole village destroyed. We were so relieved, however, to find all the mission buildings in Chiquimula standing and all the missionaries in residence there uninjured. A closer look revealed the adobe block administration buildings were severely cracked as well as the guest building, and the home of our caretaker.

The next day a group of pastors and missionaries drove to Gualan to visit the pastor and church people to pray with them and find out what kind of help they needed. Eighty-nine people were reported dead in that city.

Our daughter, Linda, was at Huehue Academy on the other side of Guatemala. "How do we get word to her that we are O.K.?" we wondered. All the phone lines were not working due to the destruction of all the communication towers.

Ray and Paul Enyart drove to Metapan, El Salvador, and called the mission office in Whittier, California. They talked to Keith Sarver, and reported that all the missionaries were safe. Keith then informed our family members in the United States. Keith told Ray that they had heard from Huehue Academy and that all students there were safe, but they needed to hear how Linda's parents were.

Early the following morning Ray and Paul drove to Guatemala City by way of Ipala and Jutiapa because the highway to Guatemala City was closed due to fallen bridges.

In Guatemala City they found a mobile phone system on a truck outside the central telephone offices. Ray called Huehue Academy to let them and Linda know we were okay. The school principal told Ray we were the last parents they were waiting to hear from.

"Let's drive to Huehuetenango and visit Linda at school," I suggested to Ray when he returned. He agreed.

Early Friday morning Tad, Kenny, Ray and I began the long trip on mountainous gravel roads through the southwest towns of Esquintla, Mazatenango, Quezaltenango and finally Huehuetenango. It was a ten-hour trip in our crew-cab pickup.

Linda was surprised and happy to see us, and we were elated to see her. We were glad we made that trip because we wanted to console and comfort her after the shock and fear of the earthquake she suffered while being so far from home. Tad and Kenny attended one day of classes with her while we were there.

We drove back to El Florido the next week to continue the home school for Tad and Kenny and clinic work. However, the realization of our helplessness after the terrible destruction of this earthquake had brought all of us to our knees before our merciful God.

The El Florido people also felt burdened to help in some way. Ray and the men of El Florido sawed up a truckload of lumber from the trees in their parcels to help rebuild the parsonage in Gualan. A contingency of El Florido men was sent by the village to deliver their lumber and encourage their brothers in Christ.

The Trip Down Rio Dulce to Livingston

We received an order for all foreign residents to register at their local county seat. For us that meant the town of Livingston, on the Caribbean coast.

We were looking forward to this canoe ride down Rio Dulce because it was such a beautiful trip through the heavy jungle to the Atlantic Ocean. We decided I would make the trip with Linda (now home on school vacation), Tad, and Kenny, leaving Ray behind. I needed to register us and pay the county tax for the El Florido land. Ray wanted to stay home and work with Dan to build the road out to the parcels of land. This road was essential for the upcoming rice harvest. Ray took us to Rio Dulce and bargained with a canoe driver to take us to Livingston.

It was early morning, and the sun had not risen yet. I had a couple of umbrellas to protect us from the sun and rain, two bottles of water, and life jackets for the kids and me. Now, equipped with the essentials, we set off on our river adventure.

Suddenly our boat rocked from side to side. We grabbed the sides of the canoe to hang on. The pilot throttled the boat down, killed the engine and lifted it out of the water. I looked into the water and saw a huge gray creature.

We saw it go under our boat, and we rocked back and forth again. We felt its hide rub slowly against the bottom of our vessel. Again it came up alongside our boat. Its body was almost as long as our boat. We were petrified!

"What is that?" I yelled to the pilot.

The pilot yelled something unintelligible to me.

That must be the term for a whale or a shark, I thought. But it did not have a back fin. Just slightly under the surface of the water I noticed healed scars across the animal's back. After four strong bumps, giving us a sense that our canoe would certainly capsize, this huge creature finally just disappeared. The pilot sat quietly and waited to see if it would return.

After about five minutes, he started the outboard motor and we continued down the river to the sleepy town of Livingston.

What a relief to get out of the boat and on to solid ground. We quickly walked into the fishing town where we heard the tall black people speaking a language that was foreign to us. If you listened carefully you could hear an occasional English word, a few Spanish words mixed in with some French sounds. We were intrigued by the sound of this distinct language.

It was very hot and humid and the smell of fish permeated the air. We walked up to the white, wooden building with a green tin roof and an open window that read "Public Office," in English. Flies were everywhere.

A large man sat at a table in front of an electric fan waving a hand fan in front of his face. "Yes?" he asked without moving.

I greeted him. "Buenos dias. We have come to register with the government as foreigners."

"Uh—what?" he asked in a surprised tone.

"I have come to register our family as foreigners since we live and work in your county," I explained carefully in Spanish.

"I don't know anything about this."

He seemed doubtful about my explanation, so I began again. "We received notice that we need to register as foreigners living in Izabal. And since Livingston is the county seat of Izabal, I have come here to register."

"Okay, let me see about this," he said as he slowly rose from his chair. He went into a room in the back of the rustic building.

By this time, Linda, Tad and Kenny had found a shade tree to stand under. I stayed by the window so the attendant would not forget about me.

As time passed, I entertained myself by watching the parade of people sauntering down Main Street. The large black women wore brightly colored wraps around their dresses and carried large baskets of coconut bread, bananas, green coconuts for juice, or fresh fish in baskets balanced atop their heads. They usually had two or three children with them. They happily laughed and talked as they walked.

Four men were sitting in the shade of a tree in front of a boarding house across the street. They were talking and playing cards. In the whole town there were only two cars, which would have been brought in by ferry. The four times a day when the passenger ferries arrived from and departed to Port Barrios were the important events of the town.

Finally the big man inside the office came to the window with a form. "Here. You can sign it here."

I read the paper, which was a document about agreement to buy and sell a product. "No, this isn't the one," I explained. "You have another one there that we need."

"Oh, okay," he agreed and then went back inside the office. I heard shuffling of papers and a file drawer open and close. Finally he came back and said, "I think you will have to come back another day."

My heart sank. That hard, long trip down Rio Dulce had been for nothing. Finally I said, "Do you have some legal paper?"

"Yes. I have some here," he replied.

"Good. I will write our names and our cedula numbers (identification numbers, see glossary) on the paper. I will sign it and you sign it, okay?" I tried to solve the problem.

"Well, I guess it would be all right," he answered doubtfully.

I took the empty paper and wrote our information on it and he and I signed it.

"Muchas gracias," he said.

"Muchas gracias," I responded. "Now I have one more item. We need to pay land taxes. Here is the bill and here is the check to pay the tax bill," I explained.

"Oh, okay." He happily received the check and put it in the drawer. "Gracias," he finished.

"Wait a minute," I said. "I need a receipt."

"What?" he asked and then, "Oh sure, sure. I'll get the receipt," which he wrote out. I knew if I had not asked for a receipt, he would not have remembered.

The kids had been so patient. We had to do something for fun before we got back in the canoe to go home. I also knew our canoe pilot was anxious to return as quickly as possible since the wind picked up in the afternoon and caused large waves on the El Golfete.

"Can we go down to the seashore?" Linda asked.

Tad jumped up and down with excitement.

"Okay, let's go for a quick wade in the water and then we'll have to leave," I agreed.

They ran down the steps to the beach. We waded out to about knee-deep water, which was warm and very calm. We saw colorful, large seashells larger than three adults' fists together. A lady came up to us with a basket of warm coconut bread. I purchased six rolls, some small, sweet bananas known as finger bananas and a fresh coconut for each of us. The kids quickly ate all the rolls and bananas. We drank the fresh coconut juice and returned to the canoe refreshed.

The trip back through Rio Dulce was uneventful this time. Ray was there to meet us at the crossing and take us home to El Florido. Months later I learned that a large group of manatees was living in Rio Dulce. It was a manatee that had almost capsized our boat!

21

The Killings

Virginia

On this particular afternoon many patients had come to the clinic. My clinic helper was too busy planting rice in his field to help me, so I was alone and tired.

Our village leaders, Lázaro and Vicente, came to the clinic to talk to me. Ray was gone to Guatemala City to get supplies for El Florido.

In a very quiet voice Lázaro said, "There has been a killing here on the project. Two girls are dead."

"Dead?" I asked in a louder voice. "Are you sure they're dead?" I was shocked and certain there must be some mistake.

"Yes, doña Virginia, they are dead," Lázaro responded.

"Who killed them? What happened?" I was stunned.

Vicente explained a little more excitedly than Lázaro, "We don't know who did it, but it was with a machete."

"Who are the girls?" I asked, afraid to know their answer.

"They are don Angel's granddaughter and David's wife," Lázaro quietly said.

"Oh no," I mumbled as tears came to my eyes. The pretty Indian girls were sixteen and seventeen years old.

"We are walking out to Rio Dulce to inform the police. Then we will wait for the coroner to come, which will probably be tomorrow."

"I'm sorry I don't have a vehicle to help you get there quicker," I said.

"It's okay," Lázaro assured me.

"Only God can give you wisdom and protection now," I stated since we had no idea who the killer was. "So let's pray first."

Lázaro and Vicente removed their straw hats and we prayed in front of the clinic. "Dear Lord, please be with Lázaro and Vicente as they go to report these deaths. Please protect them and give them wisdom as they talk with the officials. Please comfort the families and help us find the killer quickly," I prayed. "Thank you, Lord. Amen."

"Amen," they repeated. They quickly put their hats back on and began the walk to Rio Dulce.

I returned to the clinic, but it took a little while to calm the patients down and ease their anxiety about the partial information they had just heard. I reassured them everything was under control and would be taken care of.

After the last patient had left the clinic, I went up to our house and found Kenny playing with his erector set by himself since Tad had gone to Huehue Academy that year. Gloria was cooking supper. "I think I'll go out to the parcels and see the scene of the killings," I said to Gloria.

"Kenny, I want you to stay here with Gloria," I ordered.

"Please, Mom, I want to go with you."

"No, you have to stay here."

"Oh okay," he mumbled. I had no idea what I would find and I did not want Kenny exposed to any unnecessary trauma.

A couple of women came to our house and said, "We'll walk with you, doña Virginia."

"Good. We'll go together," I responded because I did not relish the idea of walking out there alone. It was a mile-and-a-half walk on the rustic road through the parcels of farmland, across the Branche River, and over two more small knolls to the spot where a group of our Chortí villagers were standing.

"There they are," my friend Gabriela whispered.

About one yard inside the rows of tall corn laid two young women's bodies. One girl's head was almost severed off her neck and the other's neck was deeply cut.

There was a group of about eighteen men silently standing around. It seemed as though they were watching me and my reactions to such a terrible sight.

My heart was broken because I knew that those two girls were the sole sustainers of their family. They had been raised by and were living with their grandparents who were now somewhat handicapped and dependent on them.

"Who did this?" I asked in shock.

"Ahh, we don't know," a couple of men answered.

"Doña Virginia, we will build a big fire and take turns spending the night here to keep the wild animals away," Dolores explained to me.

"The women are going to bring food and coffee to us," Benedicto added.

"Okay, it sounds like you have a good plan." I admired their faithful commitment to stand together during such times of crisis.

"Let's pray." Everyone took their hats off and bowed their heads. I cried out to the Lord, "Please help these men through the night. Lord, please help the authorities find who committed this crime. We need your protection all around us. Thank you, Lord. Amen."

As the men put their hats back on, I sadly turned to walk back to the village. As I thought about this, I realized we might have a killer lurking nearby who could strike again.

Back at the house it was twilight and Kenny was waiting for me. Gloria served us supper and went home. During supper I tried to not discuss the killing with Kenny. One of the girls was a sister to Margarito, Kenny's best friend.

Ray was helping orientate some visitors in Chiquimula and he was not sure he would accompany them to El Florido. Paul Enyart, our mission director, planned to bring the group to El Florido the very next day. Kenny and I prayed after supper that the Lord would bring only Ray to El Florido. We, who needed his help, had no telephone or other means of communication except for prayer.

Kenny prayed, "Dear Lord, please bring Daddy here tomorrow. Mommy needs his help, and the men here need his help. Please God, bring Daddy. Amen."

"Yes, Lord, please guide Ray to come tomorrow," I prayed. "And Lord, if it is Your will, please guide the visitors to not come into this very sad situation. Thank you, Lord. Amen."

Early the next morning I walked with some neighbor women who were taking tortillas and coffee to the men who had stood watch all night over the bodies out in the field.

The coroner had not arrived yet. The fifteen men were sitting together on a log. The hot, dry April sun was beating down on all of us. All the men had their straw hats on except one twenty-year-old man named Arturo.

I walked over to glance at the dead bodies and Arturo came up behind me. "Tell them I did not do this, doña Virginia," he pleaded. His words made me shudder and I turned and looked into his eyes.

"No, I can't say that, Arturo," I said sadly. "I don't know where you were yesterday morning. And we both know that you have not been attending the church services and youth services recently. So I can't say you didn't do it," I summarized.

Arturo had been active in the church services the previous year. He was a quiet leader who enjoyed playing the guitar for the church youth group. But he had backslidden. Just two days prior, Ray had hired Arturo to chop the grass in our backyard, which he completed that same day.

Slowly I walked the mile back to our house and to Kenny and Gloria, who was staying with him. Just before noon, we heard a vehicle coming into the village through the Sejá River and up the road to the house. We could hardly believe our eyes—Ray had come alone! The visitors had changed their plans. Kenny and I knew the Lord had heard our prayers and brought Ray home alone, just when we desperately needed him.

"Ray, we've had a terrible thing happen—a killing, right here in El Florido," I sadly told him.

He wanted to know all the details and of course the biggest question, "Who did it?"

"Come on, I'll show you," I instructed. Since Ray and the men had graveled the road out through the parcels of farmland, we could drive the carryall out to the killing site.

The bodies were beginning to bloat, and the horrid flies were gathering on them.

While Ray stood among the men, they explained to the two military commissioners who had come from Rio Dulce their version of what had happened. I stood with the women, who were mostly silent. It was so hot, with no trees nearby since that land had been cleared for planting corn.

Then we heard another vehicle approaching through the jungle and over the river. It was a government Jeep bringing the coroner and a helper. They jumped out with their notebooks and went to the dead bodies. They measured distances with a measuring tape. They took testimonies from the various village leaders while Ray and I stood on the periphery of the investigation. We did not try to interfere with what was going on. We had confidence in the village leaders' ability to handle the situation.

Finally the coroner said he was finished. One of the girls was pregnant, so this was considered a triple murder. The villagers brought new petates in which to wrap the bodies. The petates were held in place by rope tied around the bodies and the petates.

The village leaders loaded the two bodies into the back of the carryall, and the coroner instructed Ray to take them to the public morgue where they would do an autopsy. Ray drove the carryall to the house to pick up Kenny and the grandparents of the deceased girls and followed the coroner's Jeep to Port Barrios.

Arturo had been teasing one of the girls for some time, and everyone in the village knew it except us. On that morning when they went to get water at the Branche River, he tried to attack one of the girls sexually, and they fought him and he killed them both. The villagers had found a shirt and hat covered with blood hidden in his house. Then the coroner and the military commissioners asked Arturo if he had done this and he confessed that he had. The village leaders agreed that he had done the killing. So the military commissioners tied his hands together and took him to Port Barrios in their vehicle.

Two days later police came back to El Florido and picked up Saul, another one of our Chortí men, and took him to jail in Port Barrios. In jail, Arturo had named Saul as a witness. Saul was walking back from his parcel of land that fateful morning of the killings and came upon Arturo looking at the bodies with a bloodied machete in his hand. But Saul never told the coroner or anyone about this until Arturo told the police. So Saul was imprisoned as an accomplice.

The whole village was in shock and mourning. A son of one of the village farmers had killed two granddaughters of another village farmer. Quickly the Chortí could take sides and revert back to their old ways of settling disputes with hatred, accusations and more killings.

The pain and sadness affected all of us. Ray and I spent hours and hours listening, consoling and praying with our Chortí friends. Everyone took turns coming to talk to us about the tragedy and how it affected each of them.

For the next two weeks the church leaders and Ray and I met at the church to pray every morning between five and six o'clock. There was a silver lining to this tragedy, however. Many people found a new dependence on the Lord and more people were coming back to attend the services. I personally realized that I needed to pray more and when I did, my peace returned.

Saul, the father of six children, had been in jail for almost thirty days. His wife, along with the village leaders, came to our house asking Ray to go see if Saul could be released from jail. Ray agreed to go the next day. He had several errands to run in Port Barrios so he made the trip alone.

He went in to talk to the jailer about the release of Saul. The jailer said, "Well, you will have to pay me $15."

Ray replied, "If he is free to go with a simple payment to you, then obviously there are no formal charges against him to keep him in jail. So, you are asking for a bribe, aren't you?"

They looked each other in the eye, and the jailer shrugged and said, "I guess you could say that."

Ray responded, "Paying bribes is against our mission policy."

After a brief pause, the jailer said, "Think of it as payment for his room and board."

Ray thought for several moments about this, praying for wisdom. *What is our objective? What are we trying to get done? Saul has committed no physical crime. He unfortunately witnessed a murder and did not speak up. He has spent thirty days in jail and now his family desperately needs him.*

Ray decided to give the jailer $15. The jailer put it in his pocket, got up and left the room. Five minutes later, he returned with Saul. After shaking hands, Ray thanked the jailer, said good-bye and walked out. Saul was a free man.

Arturo was sentenced to thirty years in prison. It was calculated as ten years for every person who was killed, including the unborn infant. The advisory committee of El Florido met with Ray. Apparently after the sentencing, Arturo's father angrily threatened vengeance against other villagers. Some of the families became afraid, so this committee wanted to ask Arturo's family to leave the relocation project.

The village leader and Ray visited the family to inform them of this decision. Financial arrangements were made for this family's crops and for their land payments. And sadly, the whole family left.

It took some time for the village life to get back to normal. While El Florido banned together to support the girls' grandparents, they never did recover from their despair over their immeasurable loss.

22

God's Communication System

Virginia

This Tuesday morning in El Florido was bright and bustling with the usual sounds of roosters crowing and kids running down the path to the school. Ray, Kenny and I had finished breakfast and family worship time.

Ray looked over at me and said, "I think I'll go to Morales today." He was thinking of the weekly trip to get groceries, supplies and the mail.

"No, don't go today, wait and go on the regular day, Thursday or Friday, so you can pick up the weekly letters from Tad and Linda," I pleaded.

He hesitated and thought a minute and then said, "Yes, I feel strongly I should go today."

I felt depressed at the thought of not hearing from the kids. "Oh well, go ahead and do what you think you must do," I said. But the sad feeling did not go away.

Kenny and I had home school together that morning. After lunch I worked in the clinic taking care of many patients. Kenny went fishing with his friend Margarito at a jungle stream.

It was midafternoon when I heard the pickup come into the village and stop in front of the house. As I casually glanced out the window, I thought I saw Linda and Tad get out of the pickup. *Virginia,* I told myself, *you are thinking about the kids too much and now you think you see them getting out of the truck. You know they're in Huehuetenango.*

I blinked and took another look. "It is Linda and Tad!" I gasped and ran out of the clinic to greet them.

"What happened?" I asked. I wondered if they had been suspended from the school for some disciplinary action.

"An epidemic broke out in the school, so they had to close the school for a week and send everyone home," Ray explained.

Tad arrived home with fever and vomiting, and Linda got sick two days later. It was diagnosed as a contagious streptococcus infection, which most of the teachers and many of the students had. I immediately began their medical treatment and put them to bed.

"How did you find them, Ray?" I asked.

"I picked up the mail as I entered Morales, and there was a telegram for us saying that all the children had become sick at school and that they were being sent home today," Ray explained. "So I tried to make a telephone call to the mission headquarters in Chiquimula, but I had to wait four hours to get through. Finally I was able to talk to Winifred Enyart, who told me that Paul was driving Linda and Tad home to El Florido. When she told me the hour that they left Chiquimula, I figured he would now be close to the Morales crossing."

"And then what did you do?"

"I drove the three miles out to the Atlantic Highway and waited. In only about fifteen minutes, Paul came in the mission carryall. Paul was so surprised to see me there, because he knew there was no way he could contact us in El Florido to let us know that he was coming and bringing our kids," Ray explained. "He was relieved that he did not have to drive the last rugged hour and a half to our house."

God's communication system is pretty effective when we take time to listen. He will direct our paths when we lean on Him.

A Tragic Consequence of Superstitions

Modesta was a thirty-eight-year-old mother with nine children. She and her husband, Cirilo, moved to El Florido from the Colmenas Village.

Modesta would come to visit me in our kitchen frequently, and I enjoyed our conversations. She missed her church, family and friends in Colmenas. She told me about their difficult life in the village when they had no corn for tortillas. They stayed alive by eating *chipilin leaves* (see glossary) when there was no other food.

Now she was pregnant again. She came to visit me one day and told me that after this baby, she would like to take a pill to not have more babies. She was tired but always had a smile and a word of encouragement for me.

"Okay," I responded, "after your baby is born, we will talk about it." I wanted to encourage her faith in the Lord and commitment to be a good mother.

Three months passed, and Modesta was eight-and-a-half months pregnant when she and her son, Pablo, came to the clinic. She was walking very slowly and looked tired.

"Modesta, what's the matter?" I exclaimed. I was concerned when I saw her because she did not look well.

"I don't feel very good," she whispered.

I noticed that her feet, legs, hands and face were swollen.

I wonder what her blood pressure is? I thought as I got the blood pressure cuff and stethoscope. Her blood pressure was 210/120 and her pulse was 125.

I thought Modesta may have had eclampsia (see glossary), which was dangerous for pregnant women.

"Pablo, your mother needs to get to the hospital immediately," I explained. "She is very sick and needs to be cared for by a doctor."

"We have talked it over and have decided that we will not take her to the hospital," Pablo explained.

"Dear Lord, what can I do?" I prayed, "Help me. Please help Modesta."

Superstition and stubbornness were some of the fatal diseases we fought there. Those caught in its trap would refuse to take my advice and wanted to do things their way. It was so frustrating.

A week later, Pablo came to the house. "How is Modesta today, Pablo?" I asked as he stepped into our kitchen.

"She is not good, doña Virginia," he answered sadly. "But you don't need to come see her today." When he said this I knew they were turning to superstition. They wanted to use their traditional medicines and feared my presence would confuse the power of their treatments.

My heart was sad and I prayed for my friend. The next day, my birthday, Pablo came again. "Doña Virginia, come see my mother," Pablo stoically stated. "She can't eat."

"She can't eat?" I repeated alarmed. "This is not good."

I grabbed my blood pressure cuff and stethoscope and hurried to Modesta's house. She was lying on her bed, and the towels and blankets around her head and neck were soaked in blood.

I took her blood pressure—*nothing*. No blood pressure! I checked it several times.

"Modesta, Modesta!" I called as I tried to rouse her. She moaned but said nothing. She was almost unconscious.

"We MUST get her to the hospital immediately!" I ordered. "Go back to my house and tell don Mundo to bring Kenny and the truck quickly," I told Pablo and Cirilo, Modesta's husband.

Ray came quickly with Kenny and the truck. Pablo and Cirilo carried her to the pickup and put her in the backseat. I got in the backseat to hold her head in my lap. I held the blankets around her head as she was bleeding from her gums, her nose and from the corners of her eyes. Then she began having very irregular breathing, so I put the plastic airway in her mouth and gave her resuscitation. As long as I did that she would breathe.

Ray was driving the crew cab pickup. Kenny sat next to Ray and Cirilo was next to him. Pablo sat in the back seat, his mother in the middle with her head in my lap. We traveled an hour to Morales and to the Banana Fruit Company's private hospital. Previously the director of nurses had told me she would be glad to help treat patients from our clinic once in a while, but not too often. I decided this was the patient for that offer.

Ray pulled up to the emergency room and called for a stretcher. They came quickly to the truck. I told them, "She has to have oxygen."

I hated to let go of her but they whisked her away. I slowly walked into the emergency room, and the nurses stared at me with their mouths open. I looked down at myself. Blood covered my dress and body from my neck down to my shoes. A nurse gently led me to a nice restroom.

"Here, you wash up here," she said.

"Yes, but please, please try to save my friend and her baby," I cried.

"We'll try," she said consolingly.

After I cleaned myself up as much as possible, I waited with Ray, Kenny and Cirilo to talk with the doctor.

Finally he solemnly walked into the room where we waited. "I'm sorry, but your patient and her baby passed away," he said. "Now tell me, what was the cause of death?"

"I don't know," I sadly answered.

"Well, I have to fill out the death certificate and I don't know the cause of death," the doctor explained.

"When I found her at 10:00 a.m. today she had no blood pressure and was bleeding profusely," I explained.

"I'll put the cause of death as tuberculosis; the coroner will accept that since she had bleeding from the mouth," he said. "But you and I know it was not TB."

As we slowly walked out of the hospital I said to myself, "TB? If it was, I've just been exposed to it in a big way."

Now what do we do? How do we get a body back to El Florido and avoid being interrogated by the police?

"Let's find a casket," Cirilo directed. So he and Pablo found a casket builder near the hospital. The casket builder said he could have a simple pine casket ready in two hours.

Ray, Kenny and I waited in a park area under a shade tree.

Finally the casket was ready. We took Modesta's body from the morgue and put it into the casket and then the casket into the bed of the truck. The doctor gave us the hospital release papers and we began the very sad return to El Florido.

Our hearts were so heavy. I began crying quietly, "Lord, how are we going to tell all those little children their mommy is dead? Lord, please help us do this hard task. Where are you, Lord?"

We were silent and grief-stricken as Ray drove the two hours back to El Florido. As we pulled up to Modesta's house, there stood her eight children in a line like stairs, gazing at our truck. They looked for their mother and wondered what had happened. This sad moment was forever embedded on my memory.

When Cirilo and Ray got out of the truck and pulled out the wooden casket, they all knew what had happened. A couple of the smaller children cried, but the older girls and neighbor women hurried to make food preparations for the funeral.

Ray, Kenny and I slowly went to our home. The whole village helped with Modesta's funeral the next day.

Two months later I was visiting one of Cirilo's neighbors, Antonio, and we were discussing recent village events.

"I have no idea what caused Modesta's death," I said.

"Didn't you know, doña Virginia, they gave her a large portion of a medicinal leaf from the jungle. It causes bleeding, and they gave it to her for three days," Antonio explained.

"Really?" I asked. "Then that explains the cause of Modesta's death along with the eclampsia." The mystery was solved. But, my heart was heavy for several weeks after Modesta's death because I had lost a dear friend.

The Spider's Web

It was an early morning after a long night of rain. And now the sun was beginning to shine through the clouds. Suddenly before my eyes I saw a gigantic spider web.

The circular part of the web was four feet across. One side of it had long spun anchors to a tree eight feet away, and the opposite anchors were connected to the side of our house. The intricately woven web was placed directly in front of my kitchen window looking east.

Droplets of rain hung throughout the web. The sun that shined through the droplets reflected all the colors of the rainbow. It looked like a magnificent jeweled disk. Wow! What a stunning sight. I could not take my eyes off it.

The spider that had spun that piece of art was out of sight. Again, I thanked God for His exquisite creation. My spirit was lifted.

A Serious Case of Appendicitis

Aneliana was very sick. She walked to her sister's house in El Florido, rested and then came to the clinic. She had pain in the right lower quadrant of the abdomen and a fever of 102 degrees. I checked her other vital signs and took a careful history. Then I gave her the last exam, which was the rebound reflex of the abdominal muscle when my hand was released. She yelled in pain, and I knew she had a serious case of appendicitis with probable peritonitis. I did not doubt the diagnosis.

"Look, you must take Aneliana to the hospital immediately," I demanded. I was sorry our vehicle was not here.

The men just stood there and looked at me. I knew they heard me.

"How are we going to take her out?" one finally asked. "She can't walk."

"Let's fix a stretcher and get two other men and you can carry her out," I said, trying to get them moving. "You can do it."

They started talking among themselves, and I could tell they had formed a plan.

"We'll fix a hammock and poles," one explained.

"Good," I agreed. "I'll give her some medication for pain."

Soon we had her wrapped up and in the hammock. They positioned themselves and began the hike to Sejá to catch a vehicle that would take them the four more hours to Port Barrios. I was relieved to have her on her way to the hospital.

Then I heard it—she yelled with pain with every step they took through the jungle. Each cry was just slightly fainter than the previous cry as they walked away from the clinic.

I continued taking care of patients in the clinic and treating them. Off in the distance I heard Aneliana's yells. Then I thought I heard them louder and coming closer. Sure enough the hammock carriers were back.

"Doña Virginia, we got about halfway to Sejá, and she was in so much pain, we just couldn't do it to her anymore," one of them explained. "So we came back."

"Oh no," I groaned. "Lord, now what should I do?" I prayed. I quieted my heart before Him. "What do I have that could help her?" I asked myself. "I have several different kinds of antibiotics." I waited and listened for the Lord's direction.

Sulfa was a good antibiotic for the intestine, tetracycline was good for E. coli, ampicilllin was good for the peritoneum, and I had one other antibiotic on hand.

"Lord, she could die of peritonitis or she may have a serious reaction to the antibiotics," I prayed. "Please help me do the right thing."

I took a deep breath. "All right, we'll attack the peritonitis with all we have," I said out loud. I administered all four antibiotics at once. Then I carefully instructed her father to administer the medications during the night and bring her back to the clinic tomorrow morning. I gave them only sufficient medications for the night so they would have to bring her back the next morning. He readily agreed.

"And by the way, ask the people at church to pray for her tonight at the prayer meeting," I reminded him.

"I will," he quickly responded.

He carefully picked up his teenage daughter and they slowly left the clinic.

The next afternoon don Isidro returned with Aneliana. She was better! Her temperature was one hundred degrees and she sipped some liquids.

I was encouraged. I gave them antibiotics for the next twenty-four hours and asked them to return the next day and every day for a week. On the fifth day Aneliana was up and wanting to play ball with the kids at school. The treatment was continued for ten days until she was completely healed.

We praised the Lord with her family. God healed her. I can give the medication, but God makes the medicine do its work in the body just where the body needs it.

23

Oil Fever and a New Bridge

Ray

All the land had now been distributed. Most of the families had paid for their land and had their deeds. It was 1979 and Virginia and I were starting to branch out to other ministries throughout the Friends mission field while still living in El Florido.

The El Florido village was well established. It was functioning as we had envisioned with a church, school, stores and its own local village government structure. There was a cemetery, a road and a bridge was soon to be built over the Sejá River.

People were happy, and there had been peace throughout the land for the last few years. The last parcels were being paid for and soon everyone would have their titles. The changes we saw in these dear people of El Florido was truly remarkable. We were blessed to be part of their lives.

We were returning from being away for several days on mission business when we saw a group of men gathered by our house. As we got out of our pickup, the group walked deliberately up to us. I could tell something was bothering them.

After the normal small talk, which is never hurried, Vicente said, "A survey crew has come to the El Florido land from the Co-op farm to the north us," he said with uncharacteristic nervousness. "They staked out a line across our land on an angle and kept going into the San Humberto farm to the south."

I was dumb-founded. "This is private property, duly registered with the government," I said. Because of the boundary dispute we had had at the beginning of the relocation project, I was immediately suspicious and again concerned.

"Did you talk to any of them?" I asked. "Who are they working for?"

"Yes, we talked with them," Pedro said. "They are under contract with the Guatemalan government."

Guadalupe explained, "There is an oil pipeline being laid from the Mexican border in the department of El Petén to Port Santo Tomas at the Caribbean coast, and it is to go right through El Florido."

Oil had been discovered in the northernmost part of Guatemala, and the government had been announcing how rich the country was going to become from all the oil it would export.

"That is probably two hundred miles," I almost shouted. "Why does it have to go through El Florido?" Of course there was no answer from these men or from me.

"What else did these men tell you?" I probed.

"Tractors and other equipment are working their way down the survey line, clearing a thirty foot right-of-way," Vicente said. "They think they will be at our property within two weeks."

Two weeks! I thought. *What can be done?* The oil pipeline bisecting the El Florido land was about to become a reality. I knew in my heart we would have to deal with it. The route had been selected. El Florido was within thirty miles of Port Barrios, its final destination. That meant almost all of the right-of-way had been cleared already and it was not going to change.

"I will contact our lawyer in Guatemala City," I assured the men. "He will look into the situation and let us know what our options are and what to expect."

There was nothing more the men could do but wait. We agreed to pray that their rights be protected and that the outcome be acceptable to the eleven owners whose properties the pipeline would cross.

I contacted our lawyer, Hugo Morales, as promptly as possible. He was aware of the pipeline project but had no idea it was to go through the relocation project land. Hugo contacted the company that was going to lay the pipeline. He advised them that El Florido was deeded land, registered and protected by Guatemalan law. It could not be entered without permission.

This was going to be interesting. Virtually all of El Petén was non-deeded public land. In the department of Izabal where El Florido was located, most lands had not been registered yet, giving the oil company freedom to proceed without restrictions. El Florido posed a HUGE road-block to the accomplishment of the oil pipeline project.

An appointment was made for our lawyer and me to meet with the man supervising the project. In that meeting we objected to the pipeline going through our farmland. We were told what we already knew—there was no way to change the course of the pipeline.

Virginia and I had been gone from El Florido for several days on this matter and other mission business. When we returned, we were met by the eleven men whose properties were going to be traversed by the pipeline. Along with them was the rest of the village, all gathered around our house.

Before I could say anything, one of the men said in an excited voice, "We heard the tractors getting closer each day. Everyone in the other settlements are talking about this," he said nervously. "Yesterday they came right up to our property line and stopped. They turned off all their equipment and walked away. We don't have any idea what will happen now."

Hmm. Interesting, I thought. *The laws of personal property rights really do work.*

It took some time to explain what I had learned in our meetings with the lawyer and what would happen next.

"The oil pipeline will continue on this course," I explained to the villagers. "But they cannot clear the right-of-way on the El Florido land until you give them permission and they pay each of you for the land they will use."

Most of them just looked at me. They could not believe the land would not just be taken from them. All of their hard work and diligence in paying for their land, in this one moment, made it all worthwhile. They were being recognized and respected even though they were a group of humble Indians.

That night we were with our friends in the church service. It was always a special joy to be there. We no longer had the pressures of the early years of the relocation project, so we could be more relaxed and focus more on building stronger relationships with the people.

Mr. Solíz, the oil company representative we talked with in the capital, said he would visit El Florido as soon as possible to talk to the families and make them a financial offer for the right-of-way through their land. Since the clearing crews had stopped working, I was sure that this visit would be soon.

And it was the very next morning that he made his appearance. And what an appearance it was! About 8:00 a.m. we heard a loud racket. It was the unmistakable thump, thump, thump of a helicopter. We could not believe it. It circled once and then landed on the dirt village street just two hundred feet from our house. But more alarming was that it was only about fifty feet from the palm-thatch roof of our neighbor, Ponciano's house. Leaves, twigs and debris flew everywhere. The palm of Ponciano's roof was standing straight up at the eves with little pieces flying in all directions. Miraculously, an assessment of the house later did not find any significant damage to the frail structure or roof.

Our friend stepped out of the two-man helicopter with a big briefcase. He was wide eyed, sweating and had a nervous smile on his face. This man was visibly anguished over the pressure he was getting from the government to complete the project and it could be blocked right here in El Florido. He composed himself and then ambled toward the open shed where we were all standing, watching the spectacle. He was dressed in business attire, wearing a large Texas-style ten-gallon hat, walking with the swagger of an important man.

"I must talk with the men whose properties the pipeline will go through," Mr. Solíz quickly announced. "The work has stopped. We must come to an agreement and make a settlement today so this project can continue."

Looking around I saw that some of the men were there but others had already gone to their fields. Motioning to those men, I asked, "Could you please go find the others who have the survey line through their properties? Ask them to be here in half an hour for an important meeting."

I invited our friend into the house for coffee while we waited. He was anxious and could only talk about the importance of settling with these property owners so they could continue with the pipeline construction.

It only took about fifteen minutes for the whole group to assemble. Those who were in the fields had heard the helicopter and assumed it had landed in the village and were on their way back to see what was happening.

Mr. Solíz gave a quick overview of what was going on, which the people already knew. Then he said, "We are prepared to offer you $1.25 per linear meter for the thirty-foot right-of-way."

The men were quiet, and the looks on their faces indicated they were not sure what it all meant. So I explained what "linear foot" meant and told them, "This is an offer. You have a right to accept it or make a different offer."

I turned to the representative and said, "Let's go for a walk while the men discuss your offer and make a decision." As we turned to walk away, I caught the eye of one of the leaders and indicated that they should ask for more.

The two of us walked through the village for about twenty minutes, talking about the El Florido people and their new lives there.

When we returned, the men were ready with a response. "This whole endeavor is a big pain for us," Vicente said. "It will have a negative effect on our farming, because it goes across our land on an angle. We know we cannot stop it but we are asking that you pay us $1.35 per linear meter."

I knew Mr. Solíz was going to pay whatever these people asked, but he was making it sound like they were shrewd bargainers. "That is more than we have paid anywhere," he exclaimed. "But what can I do? I cannot leave without an agreement. We will pay what you are asking," he proclaimed as he dramatically threw one hand up in the air.

The men seemed to appreciate the power they had in their hands at that moment. But I was impressed by their lack of greed. Or was it that they were still seeing themselves as lowly Indians and were afraid the whole thing would fall apart if they asked for too much more? Regardless, they handled themselves with dignity.

Mr. Solíz reached into his briefcase and pulled out a packet of forms. He calculated the numbers and filled in the blanks. The document was read to the group for their approval, which they gave.

The company wanted to give a lump sum of money for running their line through the El Florido land, so our friend asked, "Who do I give the money to?" The men all pointed to me. Some would receive a little and some a lot depending on how much of their land was affected by the pipeline. So I agreed to accept the money and figure out the details of the distribution.

A very happy Mr. Solíz gave a quick but heartfelt thank you to the group. He immediately boarded the helicopter and gave a nervous wave good-bye as it lifted off and disappeared over the treetops.

The amount of money the men received in the settlement was quite generous considering what they had paid for their land, so we were all pleased.

The next weeks and months were challenging as the equipment and crews pushed dirt around and connected the oil pipeline through the El Florido property. The pipeline was built on low bases about eighteen inches above ground. It curved through the thirty-foot right-of-way to allow for contraction and expansion from the hot days and cool nights. Having the pipeline above ground made the repairs of ruptures and other maintenance easier for the pipeline company.

Take the Leaves out of the Table

Virginia

Kenny had joined Tad and Linda at Huehue Academy for the first time. The house was too quiet. And I kept thinking I heard them running up the path toward home. "I miss them so much, Lord, please help me," I cried. "It doesn't seem fair that all these families around us have their children with them, but our children are gone. My heart aches with emptiness, Lord. Help me."

As we sat down with our toast and coffee, I read a note that Ray wrote, putting on paper words that were too painful to be spoken out loud.

"Well, Virginia, all three of our children are at boarding school. It was hard enough to drive away from the school, but getting home last evening and not having anyone to tuck into bed hit me hard. We were probably less prepared for this than they were.

"We know that it was right for us to have our children here during their formative years. You have done a wonderful job teaching them through third and fourth grades. Now we realize that they need a better education and that they need to socialize with children of their own culture.

"We are blessed that the Huehue Academy is a Christian school that is dedicated to the highest scholastic achievement as well as strong discipline and high moral standards to which we subscribe. That satisfaction, of course, does not take away the empty feeling we now have that our children are no longer at home with us.

"As missionaries we have struggled with finding the right balance between the constant demands of the people we are serving while not neglecting our children. But as sure as we are that God called us to this work in Guatemala and that we are in His will and in His hands, we can be sure our kids are in His hands.

"You know, honey, we have so much to be thankful for! The Lord has blessed us with three great kids. He has given us and extremely rewarding ministry. We have seen people's lives transformed physically and spiritually. And there is still so much more to do. Being in God's will is such a great joy!

"Look, Virginia, let's take the leaves out of the table. You look so far away down there. I'll come around and sit next to you. We can least be close to each other.

"Whose turn is it to give thanks to the Lord?"

"Ray" was his simple sign-off of this most gut-wrenching letter.

In two weeks we would fly with MAF to Huehue to see how our kids were doing. I could hardly focus on my missionary work in the meantime.

Sejá River Bridge

Ray

Five years earlier, Gladys Ferguson, from North Holtville Friends Church in California, had visited the mission field. She stayed with us in El Florido for part of the time.

Crossing the Sejá River was the only way to get in and out of the village. During Glady's visit, the Sejá River often ran deep, and we would have to wait before we could cross. Dealing with the flooded river had become a way of life for us, but for those who visited from the States, it was nerve-racking.

Gladys saw the need for a bridge, as did most visitors to the project. "Ray, why haven't you built a bridge over the Sejá River?"

"Because, Gladys, we don't have funds in our budget for a bridge," I responded. "We are concentrating on developing the community, crop production and on the well-being of the families. We would love to have a bridge, and someday we will, but it will have to wait."

In reality, the bridge was extremely important to the long-range development of the project. The El Florido people were walking to Sejá daily to get their corn ground and shop in the stores there. Sick people from villages along the highway had to walk into El Florido for treatment. Everyone had to wade through the river coming and going. Maintenance on our pickup truck was also a continual problem. Brakes and wheel bearings had to be replaced much too frequently because of the sand and silt stirred up in the crossings. We were all longing for a bridge over the River Sejá.

Back home, Gladys began to publicize the need for a bridge in El Florido and raised money. Before long, Ed White, pastor of Denair Friends Church in northern California, and his church caught the vision and got excited about going to El Florido to build the bridge. They sent Dick and Leola Clark, Phil and Kay Short, Francis Perry and John Greer. They were joined by Ron Warrell and Dick Stearman from Brea Olinda Friends.

The bridge was designed by David Hamm. It was a reinforced concrete structure that, for cost reasons, had a low, flat profile with eight thirty-inch culverts for the water to flow through. Most of the time the river would run through the culverts, but during heavy rains the overflow would run over the bridge. Even in flooded conditions, this bridge would make crossing the river much easier. Concrete curbs would be poured on both edges, creating a visible ripple that would help the driver keep in the center of the span while crossing through the water.

When the bridge team arrived, all the materials were not yet on hand. The owner of the San Humberto property, which was now a cattle ranch, also used our road. Since he would be using the new bridge, he had promised to provide the iron and cement culverts. A quick trip to remind him paid off, and within three days all the materials were on site.

It was April, the driest month of the year, so the river was at its lowest level and could be easily diverted to both sides of the construction site. April was also the hottest month. The work was very physical and the humidity was always stifling. Keeping the crew hydrated was a primary concern.

Along with the crew from the States, there was always an equal number of Chortí men working alongside them. Their labor was part of their voluntary community service, and they would rotate shifts, making sure everyone participated.

The beautiful bridge was completed in one month thanks to the vision of Gladys Ferguson, Pastor Ed White, the work team from the States and the men of El Florido who volunteered their labor. Life now was immeasurably easier and more predictable for everyone who needed to come or go to the village.

24

Guerrilla Warfare

Virginia

Cirilo and Benito, farmers from Colmenas, had come to El Florido because they were tired and afraid of the ongoing strife and threats in the village. Colmenas was a Chortí Indian village in the mountains very close to the Honduras border. John and Joyce McNichols, along with Chon Vargas, the pastor of the Jocotán Friends Church, had taken the Good News of the Gospel to them. Almost all the villagers had accepted the Lord as their Savior.

These new Christians proudly built a small chapel with two small windows and a door out of adobe blocks made locally. They had placed a table at the front that served as a pulpit. The benches were wooden planks nailed to two short posts that were buried six inches into the packed-dirt floor. Fourteen men and their families were members of the church.

Now the El Florido people were hearing that the situation in Colmenas had become political and the anti-government guerrillas wanted to control that land. They would make threats to kill women and children and then would run across the border for safety from the Guatemalan authorities.

About once a week someone would steal chickens out of their cages. One family's pig was killed with a machete. Another family's dog was killed. And then an anonymous letter was strategically placed for everyone to read with a clear threat of murdering the villagers. Another anonymous letter was nailed to the chapel door saying if anyone dared enter, he or she would be killed. The Christians, however, wanted to continue honoring and trusting the Almighty God.

On Christmas Eve, the church members decided to ignore the threats and continue with their plans to have their Christmas program inside the chapel. Four masked men who were carrying rifles entered the chapel. They barricaded the chapel door so no one could get out. They shot and killed seven men and four older boys. They let the women and children go free.

The following morning the women dug graves for their husbands and sons. Their Christmas celebration ended in a sad village funeral.

Meanwhile in El Florido, word of the tragedy began to filter in. Cirilo and Benito were heavily burdened with concern for the surviving women and children. In seven days a group of survivors from Colmenas had arrived in Sejá and El Florido.

Cirilo and Benito's families and the El Florido Church gave loving assistance to the widows and children. Within a year, all of them had found places to settle and begin a new life around Sejá and La Libertad.

Ray

The political calm and peace that reigned in Guatemala from the mid-sixties to the mid-seventies had come to an end. The timing was right for the relocation project. The door God had opened for relocating the people from Jocotán to El Florido was now closing, but fortunately we were finished.

One of the first signs of change in El Florido was when a military officer came to the village with an order. "We know El Florido has been without the required military commissioners now for almost eight years," he said, referring to the permission that the base commander in Port Barrios had given. "We respect this village as a peaceful place of hard-working people, keeping to yourselves and not causing problems," he praised. "But the political climate is changing. It is becoming unsafe in this region. You must now name two military commissioners, like all other villages in Guatemala."

The village, of course, complied. Two leaders that they all trusted with that authority were named. The two received their orientation. They were to report to the army base regularly and keep the village informed of the guerrilla threats in the area around it as necessary.

One of the first things they were asked to do was build a guard hut in a strategic place in the village. Two men were to be on duty each night. A rotating schedule of guard duty was presented to the men of the village.

Soon we were hearing rumors of a small band of guerrillas that had formed on the nearby Co-op land that bordered El Florido. The military was responding quickly and decisively against these groups as soon as they appeared. Soon there were killings on the Co-op land.

The military now asked the commissioners of El Florido to arm themselves for protection. The men of the village thought about this, and reasoning together, concluded, "We know nothing about using guns. We are not a strong people. The guerillas want guns. If we had firearms it would be an invitation for the guerillas to attack us, kill our guards and take our guns. We are safer without them."

The El Florido military commissioners never armed themselves. The village was never attacked by the guerillas or the military. God spared these people from injustices by either side.

The Fear

Virginia

For several days there had been rumors of raids by guerrillas into neighboring villages at night. Those rumors included the possibility that the brothers of Isidro, a former member of the El Florido project, were involved in clandestine guerrilla attacks in the village of Sejá, the Co-op and La Libertad.

About every two weeks a man from one of the neighboring villages would be shot, and his body would be left along the roadside.

One afternoon while I was caring for patients in the clinic, a boy ran into El Florido and called, "doña Virginia, come help us." The boy was from the Co-op. "Please come see what they did," he begged. "They killed my six-month-old nephew and his dad."

"Where are they now?" I asked.

"The baby's body is right where he died. The family is waiting for the coroner to arrive and investigate," the boy answered. "We do not know where the baby's dad is. You see, the guerrillas came into our village at night and tied up Mario, the dad, and dragged him out of his house and out of the village. We have not seen him since," panted the boy. "As the guerrillas were leaving, they shot their gun toward the house, and the bullet went through Mercedes's arm and through the baby's head." I had known Mercedes since our Jocotán days when she was a beautiful Indian teenager and I had given her sewing lessons.

I had difficulty believing the boy's story, so I decided to visit Isidro's family to learn the truth and see how or if I could help them. Luckily the truck was available and I took Linda and Tad and drove to the Co-op.

Sure enough, the baby's body was lying on the stick bed, where he had been shot. A mosquito net had been placed over it to keep the flies out.

The bullet hole was in the center of the forehead and his eyes were open and empty. It took the coroner at least a day to arrive, so the family was waiting in the hot, humid afternoon. Mercedes had been taken to a doctor in Morales for treatment of her arm.

Where are the killers and where is Mario? I wondered. I shuddered with fear and deep sadness in this primitive home. *How unjust it is for this mother and baby.* Isidro was standing very stoically near the bed. There was no crying or wailing for the dead baby; they just kept a steady gaze on the road hoping to see the coroner coming soon.

"Who did this?" I asked.

"We don't know," they replied. "They came in before midnight and held their guns on us, and then they took Mario away."

There were other questions I wanted to ask such as, "Did Mario know his captors?" but I decided I was not the investigator. I was the nurse/missionary who tried to understand and relieve their pain and sadness.

Will the killing ever stop? I asked myself, because we had seen so much of it.

After spending some time with Isidro's family and praying with them, we returned to our house about two miles away. Mario never returned. It was rumored that the military was treating suspected guerrilla insurgents in this manner.

Ray

There was one serious incident that could have put El Florido in jeopardy. The oil pipeline that ran through El Florido had been completed. It was pumping crude oil from near the Mexican border to Port Santo Tomas on the Caribbean coast.

On a pre-dawn morning the people in El Florido were awakened by a huge explosion. Although the pipeline was about a third of a mile from the village, they were pretty sure that the explosion came from the pipeline.

Several of the men started out toward the pipeline. Before they had walked very far they encountered the pungent, acrid smell of sulfur. They knew the line had ruptured. As they crossed one of the small creeks near the pipeline, they saw it filling with crude oil. The smell was strong and their eyes began to burn and water.

Immediately they knew what had happened and knew they were in danger. The guerrillas had blown up the line on the El Florido property to make it look like there were guerrillas in the village. The guerrillas wanted the army to take action against the innocent El Florido people.

As quickly as possible, the village commissioners went to Rio Dulce, where the army had a small post. They reported the incident in detail and led the army back to the site of the explosion.

The army believed that the people of El Florido were not responsible. Nothing came of the incident because of the rapid and wise action of the El Florido officials. Also, the good reputation of the village as being people who lived peacefully and were not involved in the political struggle, saved the day and frustrated the plans of the guerillas.

A Midnight Visit by the Army Recruiters

Virginia

In the middle of the night we were awakened by the rumble of a large diesel-engine truck. *Who could that be?* we wondered. With only screens on our windows, outside sounds of the village were easily heard. After thirty minutes, the truck with the diesel engine rumbled away and we went back to sleep.

The next morning don Mario came to tell Ray that the military recruiters had entered El Florido the night before. They had gone into three houses and took three youths out of their beds to join the army. The boys were forced to go against their will. In Sejá one of those youths slipped and fell, injuring his leg. So he was sent back home.

The other two were taken by force with others from La Libertad, the Co-op and Sejá to the military base in Port Barrios. Two weeks later we took the parents to the base to visit their sons.

After two months the boys ran away from the base and hid for six months. We thought of them often and wondered what had happened to them. There were many rumors about where they were and what had happened. Whenever we asked their parents, we were told they did not know anything. We felt it was probably good that we did not know where they were or what they were doing. This way, if the military questioned us about them, we could not give any information.

Our hearts were saddened by the injustice of forcing young men to leave their families and homes against their will. A sense of distrust developed in the village because the two El Florido military commissioners were required to give the military recruiters the names and addresses of all the youth who were qualified for military service.

Six months later both young men returned to El Florido, healthy and free. They resumed their lives in the village, working in the parcels with their families. Guatemala law demands that the military police look for runaway recruits for six months. If they are not found by then, they are no longer pursued and are free.

One night after a guerrilla attack in another village, I awoke sweating and terrified from a startling nightmare. The nightmare was a scene where the guerrillas had lined up Ray, me and our three children. While they pointed their rifles at the kids, they told Ray and me if we would deny Jesus as our Lord, they would not kill our children. I was terrified about being forced to choose between protecting my children and denying my Lord. Upon waking and realizing this was only a nightmare, I asked the Lord to help me relax and go back to sleep.

That same terrifying scenario haunted my dreams for two more nights. Finally, after the third night, I got up and began talking to the Lord. "Lord what are you trying to tell me?" I prayed. "I deeply love my children, I never want to lose them. Please, Lord, I do not want to give them up."

I continued praying. "Yes, Lord, I love You with all my heart. I never want to deny You. But what would I do?"

I was afraid that in a terrified moment's notice I would succumb to the threats made to my children and deny my Lord. As I struggled with this troubling nightmare, I asked the Lord to give me a reassurance from Him.

The following morning during my devotions, I read Jesus' words in Matthew 10:19–20. He said, "But when they deliver you up, do not become anxious about how or what you will speak; For it shall be given you in that hour what you are to speak. For it is not you who speaks, but the Spirit of your Father who speaks in you." Suddenly I knew this was the Lord's answer to my fear of denying Him. A huge burden was lifted from my heart.

"Thank you, Lord, for taking away this fear!" I prayed. The nightmare never returned and I never forgot His answer.

25

The Tenth Year Landmark

Tenth Anniversary Celebration

Ray

We made it! Excitement and rejoicing filled the air. A special weekend of services was held to celebrate the blessings from the Lord. After ten years of hard work, struggles, loss, doubt, deep joy and learning we were still working together with our Chortí friends.

What a thrill to see what the Lord had accomplished in our lives and in the lives of the Chortí friends who had been helped. Homer and Evelyn Sharpless, Jim and Mary Liz Gay, Dorothy Anderson, David Hamm, Manuel Estrada, and Romolo and Melinda Hernandez were our guests. An MAF (Mission Aviation Fellowship) pilot flew Linda, Tad and Kenny home from Huehue Academy for the celebration. Several Chortí brethren from the Jocotán Friends Church also came to celebrate with us.

Romolo, who had been the pastor during the first two years of the project, spoke in the morning service and again in the evening. Homer, showed slides taken during the development of El Florido. Our Chortí friends especially enjoyed seeing pictures of themselves and their families.

As we looked back over the past ten years, we knew God had divinely appointed this relocation project to go forward. Following are the landmarks that shaped the prospering village of El Florido:

- While no financial support from the California Friends Church organization was given for the relocation project, generous donations from Quaker Men of California and from the Marshburn Brothers made it possible.
- The Sharplesses received the vision for the project, began the work and then had to return to the U.S. due to illness.

- Already having worked with the Sharplesses in a support role, the Canfields gladly stepped in and continued the work of the project development for the next ten years.
- The Kirks contributed one year of important developments.
- Many volunteers generously supported the work with their time and money.
- Various Guatemalan businessmen supplied resources.
- The Chortí people had huge difficulties adjusting to the new land, new neighbors and harsh climate, but they persevered.
- The Chortí settlers bought their own land and brought it into production.
- God blessed their hard work and faithfulness with good harvests and protected their crops from various threats.
- Turning from their former ways of feuding, the villagers learned to be a unified people and together built their church, a cooperative store, a school, roads and a water system.
- The El Florido villagers faithfully shared the Good News of the Gospel and started five new churches in surrounding villages.
- God granted good health, safety and wisdom to all of us who worked on this project.
- These impoverished and forgotten people now held their heads high with dignity, independence and a sense of personal worth.
- The Chortí people gained a new faith and hope in the Lord because they understood that God was the One who had heard their cry for help and had opened this door for a new life of unprecedented opportunities.

To Him be the glory for the great things He has done!

I Want to Be a Pastor

Lauterio was sixteen years old when he moved to El Florido with his parents. Before moving, he had served as a lay pastor in their church in Colmenas. Lauterio was of slight build and suffered chronic allergic conjunctivitis in both eyes.

One day he came to our house to talk with me. "I want to go to Berea Bible School in Chiquimula," he said.

I immediately thought about his educational deficiency. "How will you get the required sixth-grade diploma for entering the Bible School?" I asked.

"Would you teach me?" he asked.

I knew this was coming but I felt like it would be a futile goal. Then I chided myself, *Virginia, where is your faith?*

A correspondence course for sixth-grade education for adults was available. So we acquired the course and Lauterio studied reading, writing, and math with me three times a week. After a year and half he passed the sixth-grade exam and received his diploma.

Then he applied to Berea Bible School and was accepted as a new student. He struggled with the coursework and with homesickness. Upon the recommendation of the Berea Faculty, he continued his studies through the Bible School Extension Program instead of the on-campus program. He became the first Bible School graduate from El Florido.

Benefits to the Chortí Community in Jocotán

Ray

New, unforeseen help to the Chortí community began materializing. As the men cleared more and more land, they were unable to keep up with their farming on the relocation project without help. They sent word to their extended families in the villages of Jocotán, asking them to come and work for them in El Florido. The arrangement was that they would receive wages for their work and plant their own corn to take back to Jocotán when they returned. This, in turn, was an enormous boost to the families still living in Jocotán.

Secondly, families from the villages of Jocotán began to move to the coast on their own, having learned that the land was productive. And they heard that diseases, wild animals and snakes were not killing the people. Even though they knew they may never be able to own land, they would be better off working as paid laborers on one of the large coastal farms than staying where they were. These employers would almost always let their workers plant crops and have small yard animals. Once these families settled on the coast, they would never go back to their former villages.

Thirdly, as these families left the over-populated villages of Jocotán, those who stayed were better off because there was more land to farm and fewer mouths to feed, a positive influence on the quality of life in the area.

How were the relocated families responding to their newfound wealth and security of life on the coast? There was a danger that they would turn away from God and embrace a materialistic lifestyle. But for the most part the settlers remained faithful and centered their lives on the church and its outreach to the new villages springing up around them. There were those, however, who only went through the motions of being Christians or remained pretty much outside the church. Some of the boys who grew up in El Florido were going out to Sejá or Rio Dulce and drinking and being generally rebellious. This was a discouragement to the villagers and us. We entrusted them to the Lord in prayer. We understood that in all we did, we did as unto God, not man (from Colossians 3:23).

Other Ministries toward the End

Theological Education by Extension (TEE) had become an important part of leadership training for our churches which at this time were still mostly rural. TEE brought teachers to centers close to where the leaders lived so they could minister while they studied. The Chortí men asked for a center in El Florido so their leaders could more easily be trained for ministry. This blessed our hearts greatly. Pastors from Chiquimula came regularly and taught for two or three years. Another center started nearby in Buenos Aires where I was the teacher for two years. This took considerable time in preparation, traveling and teaching each week.

Lauterio served as the pastor in the El Florido Church for two years, and then he was assigned to a church in another village. He married and had three boys. I was amazed at what he could accomplish in spite of his minimal education.

Two years later Joaquin, son of Antonio, entered Berea Bible School and graduated in four years, and then his brother, Domingo, also graduated from Berea Bible School in Chiquimula. Priscilla, daughter of Lupe Perez, and Rudolfo, son of Lucio Perez, graduated from Berea Bible School.

All of these young people, except Lauterio, completed their elementary education through sixth grade in the El Florido School. Each one had committed themselves to serve the Lord wherever He called them to go.

Our Transition to Chiquimula

Virginia

In June of 1979, Ray was named field administrator of Friends Missions in Central America, and we moved from El Florido to the city of Chiquimula. The following poem explains what happened to us because we loved the people and the beautiful tropical lowlands.

"Awaiting a Miracle: Flowers or a Crown"
By George MacDonald

I said, "Let me walk in the field";
God said: "Nay, walk in the town";
I said, "There are no flowers there";
He said, "No flowers, but a crown."

I said, "But the sky is black,
There is nothing but noise and din";
But He wept as He sent me back,
"There is more," He said, "there is sin."

I said, "But the air is thick,
And fogs are veiling the sun";
He answered, "Yet souls are sick,
And your work is undone."

I said, "I will miss the light,
And friends will miss me, they say";
He answered me, "Choose tonight,
If I am to miss you, or they."

I cast one look at the fields,
Then set my face to the town;
He said, "My child, do you yield?
Will you leave the flowers for the crown?"

Then into His hand went mine,
And into my heart came He;
And I walk in a light Divine,
The path I had feared to see.

Our Kids Transition to the City

Linda was fifteen years old and in ninth grade at Huehue Academy when we moved to Chiquimula. She helped with the housework in our house in the city. She sewed two new dresses for herself. She had made several good friends among the youth in the Tabernaculo Church. She took clarinet and piano lessons. She studied tenth grade by correspondence at home.

Tad grew taller and spent a lot of time mowing lawns in Chiquimula with the power mower we bought. He fixed his bike and rode it some. He was in seventh grade and lived in the big boys' dorm at Huehue Academy and played the trumpet in the school band. He always wanted to spend more time in El Florido than was possible when we went to visit every two weeks during the summer.

Kenny was in the fifth grade, and he looked forward to getting back to school to see his teachers and friends. He did well in his course work at school and loved math. And since Huehue Academy had high academic standards, this was very good. Kenny had a winsome sense of humor and made friends easily. He also played the coronet in band at school. Building hot-air balloons with his brother was what he really enjoyed that year.

Finishing

Ray

We had to keep our minds on the goals we had set for the relocation project. We had planned to finish this ministry in about ten years. That meant that all the land was in the hands of the settlers and their deeds recorded with the government. We wanted the village to have all the amenities that other communities had: a road for access to markets, a school, a church, a store, a medical clinic, a cemetery and the appropriate elected officials.

We tried to be diligent to ensure that the Chortí people were equipped for managing their village and their lives for the future. The villagers, however, often told us they did not want us to leave. They expressed fear about managing the village alone. Since most of them had grown deep in their faith and trust in God, we were assured that they would do just fine without our presence. Toward the end of our ten-year ministry in El Florido, we served more as advisors, shifting away from the hands-on involvement of the development years.

26

The Harvest

2002

Virginia

As we prepared to attend the Centennial celebration of the Friends Mission in Guatemala, we reflected on the El Florido project that had been started thirty-three years earlier. Our reflections took us back through the twenty-three years since we had moved away from El Florido. God had used even those subsequent years to witness the growing success of our El Florido friends.

While we had been serving in the Mission Headquarters in Chiquimula, Ray and I made trips to El Florido at least once a month. We spent time with our friends offering help in whatever ways they needed. When we visited, the project committee always wanted to consult with Ray about various concerns they faced. They wanted advice on such things as what to do if a son of one of the farmers wanted to purchase his father's land, or where to survey new house lots in the village for married children. A recent census reported that 348 people lived in El Florido.

Often during our visits, Lucio consulted me about certain illnesses and how they should be treated, or he would ask me if I thought he had made a correct diagnosis. I loved to hear about how God had used him to diagnose difficult diseases correctly, treat them and ultimately bring healing. He brought me his list of needed medicines, until a drug company salesman started driving into El Florido and Lucio ordered directly from him. Then he went over his accounting of the fees he collected, and I would make sure he received the correct amount as his pay.

The last few times we talked with Lucio he was excitedly recounting his trips into the Kekchi Indian area to take the Good News of Jesus to them. He always took two or three young men from the El Florido

Church with him. This eight hour trip took up to seventeen hours one way, depending on the conditions of the road and mechanical breakdowns. On one of their trips, the bus they were on broke down, and they had to sleep in a field near the road until someone came the next day to repair the bus. But still, they enthusiastically pushed on to take the Good News to the Kekchi people who wanted to hear.

Gloria usually stopped by, and I always enjoyed her visits because she would update us on the recent village news. She also would tell us of the well-being of her family. Because she did not want to seem prideful, she never mentioned her cattle, pigs or her bread-baking business unless I specifically asked. As God had promised me, He was taking very good care of her future.

The lay pastor of the church usually stopped by to tell us the Bible lessons he had been teaching and maybe ask us to explain a Bible passage to him. We spent much time encouraging him to have patience and long-suffering with the brethren of the church. He often found that it was difficult and frustrating to lead the El Florido Church.

In 1996, Ray and I were called to serve in Cambodia, and we were only able to get back to El Florido once a year. During those visits, we were happy to see everyone and we could encourage them. The crops continued to flourish, a few older people had died, and there were many new marriages and new babies. Our visit home to the quiet jungle was always a reprieve from the bustling, noisy cities of Chiquimula and Phnom Penh, Cambodia.

*

Now on this day of the Centennial celebrations, we were walking on the sidewalk near the mission headquarters in Chiquimula, when a young man walked up behind us. "Don Mundo, don Mundo!" he called out.

He looked vaguely familiar, but we could not recognize him. He had his young wife and two small children with him.

"You don't remember me, do you?" he stated, smiling broadly.

"Well, sorry, but I just can't remember your name," Ray replied honestly. "Why don't you come into this ice cream shop and we'll buy ice cream for you and your kids."

"No, you don't have to do that," he said.

"Yes, we want to have ice cream with you and get reacquainted."

They agreed.

280

After we ordered the ice cream, Ray asked what the young man's name was.

"Mario," he answered, still smiling. "My grandfather is Apolonio from El Florido."

"Really?" we both said at once. "It is so good to see you!" We were excited to see him and his happy little family. We talked with them for a little while until we finished the ice cream. We learned he was serving as pastor in a church on the coast.

"Would you like to meet the other people who are here from El Florido for the Centennial?" he asked.

We followed him down the street to the Amigos School, where housing was given to people who came in to the city for the week of meetings at the Friends Church. We walked into the large dormitory-type building in the back. Thirty people were sitting in a circle and about fifteen small children were playing nearby.

They asked Ray and me several questions about our new ministry in Cambodia and when we were going back. They asked about our children and where they were living and how they were. I explained that all three of them had received university degrees and that Linda was married.

"Now tell us about you folks," I asked. "Please tell us your name, and who are your parents and grandparents and what you are doing."

"I am Miriam, Secundino's daughter, Inez's granddaughter, and my husband is a pastor in the Agua Largo Friends Church."

"I am Joaquin, Antonio's son, and this is my wife, and I am a pastor in the Olopa area."

"I am Rudolfo, Lucio's son, and I am a pastor at a town on the coast."

"I am Priscilla, Lupe and Berta's daughter, and I am a children's Sunday school teacher in El Florido now."

"I am Maco, Juan's son, and I am a pastor in a church in the Jocotán district."

"I am Juana, Seferino's daughter, my husband is the pastor in a church on the coast."

"I am Lucas, Apolonio's grandson, I am a pastor near Chiquimula."

"I am Domingo, Antonio's son, and I am a pastor in a church in the Kekchi Indian district."

"I am Abraham, Cirilo and Modesta's son, and I am a missionary to the Kekchi Indians."

"I am Teo, Benito's son, and I am a pastor in the Jocotán district."

"I am Maria, Seferino and Juana's daughter, and my husband is the pastor in the Port Barrios district."

"I am Secundino, son-in-law of Inéz, and I am caretaker in the Amigos Christian School."

There was a hushed silence in the room. As I looked around, I sensed the presence of the Holy Spirit. Tears came to my eyes. This was bigger than my heart could hold.

"Look! Look what God has done!" Thirteen couples were teaching the Bible and leading people to the saving knowledge of Jesus Christ. Men and women from El Florido, who heard His call, were serving the Lord full time and making an impact on their country for eternity.

He kept His promise! This is the harvest of the Lord our God. We missionaries had focused on helping our Chortí friends in farming and health. But God heard their cry, rescued them and gave them a passion to "Go and make disciples of all men." (Matthew 28: 19) They were fervently obeying.

Dear Lord, we thank you for letting us witness this. Please bless each one of these dear people who are Your Servants. We rejoice and are glad! Amen!

Epilogue

The El Florido Friends Church sent a letter to Homer and Evelyn Sharpless:

El Florido Livingston, Izabal
1994

For Mr. and Mrs. Sharpless,

Dear brothers in Christ,

By means of this letter to you we want to greet you in the name of our Lord, Jesus Christ. We are hoping that the peace of the Lord reigns in your hearts. We want you to know that the work of the Lord that you have done was not in vain. The reason we are writing to you is to remember the hard work you did for us and our village both in the spiritual and material realms. For this reason we feel very grateful to the Lord and to you folks. We have many memories of you. We hope the Lord is protecting you and He has prepared the crown of life that He will give to everyone who serves Him. Even though maybe we will not see you again in this life, we know that one day we will be reunited before the presence of the Lord.

May the Lord bless you, and following we send you some names of brethren, that maybe you will remember.

Sincerely,

Evangelical Friends Church, El Florido

Abraham Pérez	Apolonio Martínez	Nemecio Pérez
Lucio Pérez	Silverio Ramirez	Cirilo Pérez
Pedro Ramirez	Miguel Ramos	Juan Gonzales
Leandro Súchite	Santiago García	Inéz García

Note This was one more testimony of God's promise that El Florido would succeed with at least 12 faithful men.

After they left Guatemala due to health problems, Homer and Evelyn Sharpless purchased and farmed a Christmas tree farm for ten years in Strathmore, California. When they could no longer live independently, Kathleen Russell, their granddaughter and her husband, John, invited Homer and Evelyn to live with them near Porterville, California. They both went to heaven around the age of ninety years.

Glossary

Cedula: This is the official identification document that all Guatemalans over the age of eighteen are required to carry with them at all times. We had gone through the two year process of becoming legal Guatemalan residents and had been issued the cedula.

Chipilín Leaves: These leaves come from a small perennial bush that grows in the mountains of Central America. The leaves contain iron and Vitamin A and are often added to cooked beans.

Department: State.

Don or Doña: The word "Don" for the male or "Doña" for the female before the first name was a term of respect used for all adults outside the family.

Eclampsia: A major toxemia of pregnancy accompanied by high blood pressure. It affects the kidney, liver and heart.

Health Promoter: A worker in the health clinics in villages who was trained by and recognized by the government.

Ladino: A person with a mixture of Indian and Spaniard ancestry, the name is used in Central America.

Maguey: A plant with heavy fibers that are used to weave baskets and hammocks.

Municipality: County.

Parcel: A measured plot of land.

Petate: A bedroll woven from a split reed.

Tarea: Work or a job. In the context of this book, a tarea is the unit of land that a farmer is expected to complete in a day. A tarea varies in size according to conditions and location. In Jocotán, a tarea is twelve arm-lengths squared; on the coast it is fifteen arm-lengths squared.

Bibliography (Resources)

Miller, Virginia. *His Story, 1902-2002,* Friends Church in Central America, 2002.

Enyart, Paul. *Friends in Central America,* 1970, William Carey Library, South Pasadena, Calif.

Milk, G. Richard PhD. *An Evaluation of a Proposed Resettlement Project for the Chortí Indians of Department of Chiquimula, Guatemala.* Documentation by Agricultural Missions, 1966.

Passerello, John. *Chortí Agricultural Resettlement Project: From Jocotán to El Florido, Guatemala,* 1976, chairman of Social Concerns and Missions Committee of Sacramento Friends Church, Sacramento, Calif.

Girard, Rafael. *Los Mayas Eternos,* (Spanish) Libro Mex Editores, Mexico DF, 1962.

Mackie, T. Thomas MD. *A Manual of Tropical Medicine,* 2nd. edition, 1954, W. B. Saunders Company, Philadelphia and London. 346–9, 781.

Perez, Lucio. Written personal record of the El Florido Relocation Project and the organization of the church (Spanish), 1988.

Vasquez, Jose Antonio. Written personal Record of the El Florido Village and the organization of the School (Spanish), 1988.

About the Authors

Ray and Virginia Canfield were raised on farms, in Christian homes, two thousand miles apart; Ray in Whittier, California and Virginia in New Providence, Iowa. They met at East Whittier Friends Church in California and both served in youth work there. As a child, Virginia promised to serve God in missions. God spoke to Ray from Romans 10:14–15. Together on their wedding day they answered God's call to "go and make disciples of all nations" (Matthew 28:19–20).

After completing studies in agriculture and nursing at the University of Missouri, the California Friends Church Mission Board sent them to Guatemala to help the Chortí Indian people. Their small children, Linda and Tad, went with them, and Kenneth was born in Guatemala. They served a total of twenty-nine years in Guatemala.

Ray, BS, MS, is an agriculturist, and Virginia, BSN, MA, is a registered nurse. Before retirement, they began a new missionary outreach in Cambodia, Southeast Asia, for six years. They currently live in Placentia, California, where all three children and three grandchildren live near them.

CPSIA information can be obtained
at www.ICGtesting.com
Printed in the USA
FSOW01n1726060215
5074FS